Understanding
Lord of the Flies

The Greenwood Press "Literature in Context" Series
Student Casebooks to Issues, Sources, and Historical Documents

The Adventures of Huckleberry Finn
by Claudia Durst Johnson

Anne Frank's *The Diary of a Young Girl*
by Hedda Rosner Kopf

Animal Farm
by John Rodden

The Call of the Wild
by Claudia Durst Johnson

The Catcher in the Rye
by Sanford and Ann Pinsker

The Crucible
by Claudia Durst Johnson and
Vernon E. Johnson

Death of a Salesman
by Brenda Murphy and
Susan C. W. Abbotson

The Grapes of Wrath
by Claudia Durst Johnson

Great Expectations
by George Newlin

The Great Gatsby
by Dalton Gross and
MaryJean Gross

Hamlet
by Richard Corum

I Know Why the Caged Bird Sings
by Joanne Megna-Wallace

Jamaica Kincaid's *Annie John*
by Deborah Mistron

The Literature of World War II
by James H. Meredith

Macbeth
by Faith Nostbakken

Of Mice and Men, The Red Pony, and
The Pearl
by Claudia Durst Johnson

Pride and Prejudice
by Debra Teachman

A Raisin in the Sun
by Lynn Domina

The Red Badge of Courage
by Claudia Durst Johnson

Richard Wright's *Black Boy*
by Robert Felgar

Romeo and Juliet
by Alan Hager

The Scarlet Letter
by Claudia Durst Johnson

Shakespeare's *Julius Caesar*
by Thomas Derrick

A Tale of Two Cities
by George Newlin

Things Fall Apart
by Kalu Ogbaa

To Kill a Mockingbird
by Claudia Durst Johnson

Zora Neale Hurston's *Their Eyes Were
Watching God*
by Neal A. Lester

UNDERSTANDING
Lord of the Flies

A STUDENT CASEBOOK TO ISSUES, SOURCES, AND HISTORICAL DOCUMENTS

Kirstin Olsen

The Greenwood Press
"Literature in Context" Series
Claudia Durst Johnson, Series Editor

GREENWOOD PRESS
Westport, Connecticut • London

Library of Congress Cataloging-in-Publication Data

Olsen, Kirstin.
    Understanding Lord of the flies : a student casebook to issues, sources, and
historical documents / Kirstin Olsen.
        p. cm.—(The Greenwood Press "Literature in context" series, ISSN
    1074-598X)
    Includes bibliographical references and index.
    ISBN 0-313-30723-7 (alk. paper)
    1. Golding, William, 1911- Lord of the flies.   2. Survival after airplane acci-
dents, shipwrecks, etc., in literature.   3. Boys in literature.   I. Title.   II. Series.
PR6013.O35 L639   2000
823'.914—dc21   99-089787

British Library Cataloguing in Publication Data is available.

Library of Congress Catalog Card Number: 99-089787
ISBN: 0-313-30723-7
ISSN: 1074-598X

First published in 2000

Greenwood Press, 88 Post Road West, Westport, CT 06881
An imprint of Greenwood Publishing Group, Inc.
www.greenwood.com

Printed in the United States of America

The paper used in this book complies with the
Permanent Paper Standard issued by the National
Information Standards Organization (Z39.48-1984).

10 9 8 7 6 5 4

To my father, Brian Olsen,
this book is respectfully
and affectionately dedicated.

Contents

Acknowledgments

When I was a child, my family home had an entire wall of its cathedral-ceilinged kitchen devoted to books. Shelf upon shelf of books rose to a height of about fourteen feet, and a library ladder on wheels rolled along to allow access. There were other bookshelves in the house—one in the breakfast alcove, and several in my sister's room and mine—but this was the main repository of our home's printed matter. It was an astoundingly miscellaneous collection. There were cookbooks, spy novels, Victorian classics, several years' worth of *American Heritage* from the years when that magazine was still issued in hardback, encyclopedias and other reference books, and two volumes that, despite their cloth binding, had never actually been published. One was a collection of poems written by my father as a young man, and the other was his Princeton senior thesis, written in 1964 and entitled "The Novels of William Golding."

Long before I had any idea of who William Golding was and what he might have written, the thesis, with its glorious binding and my father's name on the spine, fascinated me. Its very existence proved that people I knew could write books. From that revelation it was not a very long jump to the conclusion that I could probably write a book, too. It eventually seemed so inevitable that I would do so that, in tenth grade, with characteristic hubris, I ended a report on great American authors with myself, listing my soon-to-be-immortal novels by title and future date of publication. At about that time, I began reading Golding's works, liked but did not love them, and continued on to college, where, like my father, I majored in English and took home a diploma and a hardbound thesis with my name on it.

Seven books later, I mentioned to an editor at Greenwood that I'd like to contribute a book to the "Literature in Context" series and submitted a proposed list of titles. She wrote back to say, in much nicer words than these, that no one really taught the obscure Victorian stuff to which I was passionately attached and asked whether I might not like to do something on *Lord of the Flies* instead. It did not take me long to make up my mind. I can still trace my genesis as a writer to the spot on the kitchen wall—four shelves up, twelve inches from the dining room door and about three feet from the living room—where "The Novels of William Golding," by Brian Olsen, resided. Doing this book was a chance to repay, in part, the debt of inspiration that every happily employed person owes to someone. Serendipitously, in the process of writing the book, I discovered that I like Golding infinitely better as a thirty-three-year-old than I did as a sixteeen-year-old. I sincerely hope that I have succeeded in conveying some of my augmented enthusiasm and comprehension to readers of every age.

I am grateful, as always, to my husband Eric Voelkel, who makes it possible for me to write in a country where, to paraphrase Michener, a writer can make a fortune but not a living. He is that rarest of all treasures, a person of both enormous intellect and great kindness, and his companionship and love have made me a calmer and more rational creature. I am fortunate also in having two wonderful children, Emily and Devon, who are smart and compassionate and who love to see their names in print. They, as well as my mother Nancy and sister Erica, have often made it possible for me to take time to shut my office door and get a few more paragraphs typed. Thanks especially to Erica, whose contributions to the religion chapter were invaluable.

To editors Barbara Rader, Lynn Malloy, and Claudia Durst Johnson, thanks for suggestions, advice, and support.

Introduction

Few novels as brief as William Golding's *Lord of the Flies* raise as many fascinating questions. Are human beings evil? How does evil arise? What is the nature of isolation? What is the origin of superstition and religion? Why and how do we choose our leaders? What are a leader's responsibilities? The list could continue for several pages and still barely scratch the surface, yet each is a significant question worthy of consideration. How, then, does a teacher "cover" such a work in the practical confines of class time, and why should we venture outside the text to investigate its historical background, when the text itself is so rich?

In answer to the first question, I can relate an anecdote that one of my professors, Dr. Sid Lester, told in class when I was studying for my own teaching certificate. He said that a teacher of his acquaintance addressed his American history class on the first day of school and said, "I have been told by the district that we have to cover this entire text by the end of the year." He laid the book, a social studies text, on his desk, and put another book on top of it. "There," he said. "I've covered it." He then proceeded to teach a year of brilliant, in-depth lessons on a selection of subjects.

The moral of the story is that no one can adequately cover *Lord of the Flies*. I read the book twice in high school, once in college, and so many times during the preparation of this text that I have lost track. At every reading, I found something new. Sometimes, the questions and ideas arose so fast that some of them slipped away before I could get them down on paper. The text employs such simple, ancient symbols—meat, fruit, an island, snakes, pigs, the hunt, a mountain, fire—that thousands of years of cultural history can be read into them. A reader could spend an entire year tracking down allusions, interpretations, and sources.

It is my hope that this book will make that task somewhat easier. I hope it also enables readers, like the American history teacher above, to cover the basics and then dive headfirst into the really juicy stuff. One person may choose to emphasize the political aspects of the book, while another may be more fascinated by the way it parodies, subverts, and draws on certain popular genres. Teachers may decide to focus all their attention on one aspect of the novel using one of the chapters in this text as a guide, to assign different chapters to different students or groups, or to touch briefly on each chapter. I have tried to include documents and questions adapted to all three strategies.

The first chapter of this text provides a basic critical overview of the novel, and some theories about its broad appeal. The main characters and themes, and their relevance to everyday life and experience, are discussed here. The second chapter explores the concepts of civilization and savagery and their connection to British imperialism. The third chapter is concerned with the British school system, which was very different in Golding's day than today, and which was vastly different from present-day schools in other countries. The hierarchy and atmosphere of violence in such schools are strongly reflected in *Lord of the Flies*. Chapter 3 also investigates literature set in British public schools and compares aspects of this genre to aspects of Golding's novel. Chapter 4 explores a different but equally relevant literary genre: the adventure novel. *Lord of the Flies* was intended in part as a subversion of outlandish tales for boys, and Chapter 4 analyzes such tales and gives examples of their major characteristics. The religious background of the novel is the subject of Chapter 5. Here readers will find information on Anglican and Calvinist approaches to sin, Simon's role as a Christ figure, and Biblical allusions within the text. Chapter 6 takes on the nature of man from a biological perspective, helping the reader to determine how genetics and evolution might affect the boys' behavior and whether their behavior constitutes a sound evolutionary strategy. Finally, in Chapter 7, the horrors of World War II and the dismal deprivation and tedium of its aftermath shed light on the novel's essential pessimism.

Each chapter includes discussion and essay questions Some might be best adapted to a brief oral discussion, while others could form the basis of a major research paper or creative project. Suggestions for further reading, and in some cases for complementary movie viewing, can be found throughout the text. It may be impossible to "cover" *Lord of the Flies* completely, but this material should help stimulate some thinking and provide ideas for further study.

As to the second question, why bother to study the novel's historical background at all, it seems to me to slight Golding's achievement to ignore these influences. He wrote the book, in part, to stimulate contemplation about human nature. To discuss a book laden with religious symbolism without a knowledge of the texts to which it alludes is to neglect an important part of the great centuries-old discussion to which it contributes. To discuss its plot and setting without a knowledge of adventure literature, for example, is to be oblivious of the skill with which Golding exposes the genre's flaws. To explore the novel's pessimism without understanding the political events and environment of its time may lead, in more optimistic eras, to an underestimation of Golding's insight. The fact that you are using this book means that I am no doubt preaching to the choir on this subject, but it is my belief that every novel benefits from its readers' comprehension of the world that produced it. One may read *The Canterbury Tales* without knowing much about the monastic system or pilgrimages; one may read *Pride and Prejudice* without knowing how to dance a minuet or how to distinguish between a phaeton and a barouche. However, the reader who knows these things will, all other things being equal, derive more pleasure and edification than the one who comes to Chaucer or Austen in ignorance.

The same is true of *Lord of the Flies*. Some of Golding's influences, one finds, are quite immediate, such as wartime atrocities and rationing, which occurred within a decade or so of his first novel's publication. However, there is also relevant source material that is much older. The scientific debate about the origins and nature of man (as opposed to the philosophical and religious debates) arguably began in earnest with Darwin in the mid-nineteenth century. Evolution and its implications for religion and morality have been a subject of lively discussion ever since. The public-school novel also had its roots in the nineteenth century, though it remained a popular art form well into the twentieth. The adventure genre is even older, tracing its history to the early eighteenth century and *Robinson Crusoe*. Since the main subject of *Lord of the Flies* is human nature, readers would find it worthwhile to trace some of the major contributions to the study of human nature, delving into eighteenth-century Enlightenment philosophy, sixteenth-century Reformation theology, and ancient religious texts. For such an apparently timeless novel, *Lord of the Flies* has its roots in thousands of years of thought and writing.

All page references to *Lord of the Flies* are from the Perigee paperback edition, published by Penguin Putnam in 1954.

1

Literary Analysis

> Absurd and uninteresting fantasy about the explosion of an
> atomic bomb on the colonies and a group of children who
> land in jungle country near New Guinea. Rubbish and dull.
> Pointless.
> —Verdict of a manuscript reader on the first version of
> *Lord of the Flies*, then titled *Strangers from Within*

The very idea of putting *Lord of the Flies* into a social and historical
context seems, at first, absurd. After all, it is a deliberately mythic
novel, almost as abstract as it is possible for a work of fiction to
be. The setting is never identified. It could be almost any small
island in the tropics. The characters, except for Jack (and Percival
Wemys Madison, whose last name exists solely as a symbol of lost
civilization) have no surnames; many of them, including most of
the littluns and choirboys, do not even merit first names. The war
that brings them to the island in the first place is mentioned only
briefly. An early draft of the novel contained additional chapters
outlining the course of the nuclear war that occasions the boys'
evacuation, but Golding's editor felt that the novel was stronger
without this material,[1] and the chapters in question were cut. Thus

stripped of unnecessary detail, the central conflicts come into sharper focus, and the story seems more nearly universal.

Yet *Lord of the Flies*, like all novels, comes from its author's experiences and interests. It is shaped by Western ideas about civilization and savagery and by the British colonial past. It reacts to the pervasive belief in the superiority of British culture and to the belief that to be British was in some sense the direct opposite of being a savage. It evolves from Christian, perhaps even Calvinist, theories about human nature and sin. It is influenced by debates about biological determinism, by the English school system that both produced and employed Golding, by the adventure stories that boys of Golding's time read, and by the events and aftermath of World War II. The remarkable thing is that, despite being very much a product of its place and time, full of dated schoolboy slang and cold war anxiety, *Lord of the Flies* remains an influential and powerful commentary on human evil.

In part this is because it explores some of the most intense urges and emotions in our repertoire: the desire for power, the fear of the unknown, fear of other people, anger, and jealousy. In short, this novel asks hard questions about what Golding, taking a cue from Conrad, calls "the darkness of man's heart" (202).

THE UNIVERSAL FASCINATION WITH POWER

Anyone who has watched children at play for a significant length of time observes, over and over, the exercise of power. Children, powerless in so much of their daily lives, act out roles that they believe come accessorized with power: mother, father, teacher, police officer, king, queen, and hero. Even their animal play, once they become aware of the predator-prey relationship, is informed by a desire for power. Few children choose to be the brachiosaurus or zebra if they can be the *T. rex* or the lion. Similarly, when they play with dolls, blocks, and other toys, they see themselves as little gods, determining what happens to their tiny creatures much as their own fates are dictated by parents and others.

Golding recognizes this tendency in children and even includes an example of it in *Lord of the Flies*. One of the younger children, Henry, amuses himself on the beach by trapping, herding, collecting, and thereby controlling, small sea creatures (61). Significantly, Golding describes Henry's experience not as actual power but as an "illusion of mastery," a phrase that could describe many of the power relationships in the novel. Is Piggy master of himself or his fate? Clearly not. When put to the test, he cannot even retain control over his own eyeglasses. Is Ralph master of anything? He appears to be, but his political power proves, too, to be an illusion, as evanescent and as incapable of containing living beings as Henry's tiny footprints in the sand. Even Jack's power is illusory or at least temporary, vanishing the moment an adult authority arrives on the island.

Golding thus simultaneously taps into one of our greatest desires and one of our greatest fears: the desire to control ourselves and others and the fear that any sense of control we possess is ultimately false. He shows us the means by which power is ordinarily seized: physical force, knowledge, size, beauty, insight, currency (in the case of the island, the currency is pork), and friendship. Every reader has tried to gain the upper hand in some situation by at least one of these means. Yet, in the novel, every one of them proves to be a trap or a mirage. Small wonder that most readers feel a sense of horror at the disintegration of the island's small society. It is not only the fictional community that is dissolving, but also the readers' own sense of personal control.

THE UNIVERSALITY OF FEAR

Another strength of *Lord of the Flies* is its attempt to explain one of our most fundamental emotions: fear. Fear is, in Darwinian terms, a good thing. It urges creatures in danger to flee, fight, or hide and thus allows them to live longer and to pass on their wariness to their offspring. Like power struggles, it can result in a stronger, fitter community and a more successful species.

However, like power struggles, fear can exceed useful limits and become a destructive force. A diurnal animal in the wild needs to be alert even at night, sleeping lightly and in a relatively safe place, and exercising special caution at times when its vision is impaired. Even so, it may fall prey to nocturnal predators better adapted to the dark. Fear, in this context, is rational and directed at a specific threat.

A child safe at home in bed may fear the dark for the same reasons but without the threat. Its ancient evolutionary instincts tell it that danger lurks in the unseen. It is primarily a visual creature, with faint powers of smell and hearing, and it relies on its eyes. When light is removed, it must assume, according to its evolutionary programming, that danger is eminently possible. The parents, with the benefit of years of experience of safe sleeping, know that there is no danger. The child, however, has only the instinctive alertness and fear that kept its ancestors alive. With no namable threat close by, it creates something to fill the place left empty by jaguars and lions and bears. Therefore, there are monsters under the bed, in the closet, outside the window, down the hall—in short, in all the unseen places that a wild creature would be reasonable to fear.

Early human societies had plenty to fear. Besides wild beasts and natural disasters, there were diseases, infections, accidents, enemy tribes, false allies, and food shortages. Their inventions, like the monster in the closet, gave tangibility and limits to intangible or uncontrollable fears. They named gods and demons, told stories about them, and gave them faces and attributes. A nine-headed hydra, a goat-footed devil, a many-breasted goddess, and a jackal-headed god were mysterious, yet easier to understand than bacteria, viruses, electromagnetic charges, cold fronts, and betrayal. If a child falls ill and dies without apparent cause, what does it mean? Whom does it help? Who might fall ill and die next? In the absence of the answers, humans make a demon. Something unseen ate the child, wanted it, hated it, or wanted something it possessed. Appease the demon, hunt it, drive it out of the village, oppose it, find it, trick it, destroy it, or bribe it, and the problem will be solved. Sometimes it actually worked. A frightened village might isolate itself, hoping to ward off evil spirits, and by quarantining itself escape a plague. A violent member of the community might do less damage if presumed to be possessed by evil spirits and driven away or subjected to public scrutiny or punishment. A fortunate coincidence might lead to the natural disappearance of a threat at about the time a purifying ritual was performed. Even when such tactics did not work, appeasing unseen dangers made the community feel that it had taken action.

But what if, as in the child's bedroom, there is no threat? The alertness and wariness do not vanish simply because no rational threat is present. This is the situation on the island, where there are no predatory animals, no enemy tribes, and no purely natural disasters. Still, the boys have two basic problems. The first, as Golding recognizes, is that the tendency to find and name enemies does not evaporate. In the absence of real danger, people—especially children, accustomed to sudden and apparently inexplicable changes imposed from above, and lacking the experience to judge the rationality of their fears—often create an imaginary danger to take its place.

The second problem is that there is one genuine cause for fear on the island, but it is the one thing that must remain unspoken. Despite their initial joy at being away from all adult authority, the boys are terrified that they will never be rescued. The importance of the fire to rescue is often stressed, but the natural consequences of failure are voiced only by Piggy, who states his fear that they could stay there until they die. Ralph, confronted with this horrible fate, pushes it away. He asserts that his father will come for them, and when Piggy asks how he will know the boys are there, Ralph cannot even give voice to his fear or to his denial of fear (14). These children come from a British schoolboy culture that valued stoicism and often separated boys from their parents at quite a young age. Boarding-school boys would see pining for parents and home as babyish, and the boys—the "biguns," at least—are old enough to want to seem like men. Unable to gaze into the dark corners of their worst fear, the boys are left with an empty closet and a willingness to put a monster into it.

Into this void steps the birthmarked boy with his tale of a "beas-tie," a "snake-thing, ever so big" (35). Just as he denied his fear of abandonment, Ralph denies the existence of the beast. As if to reinforce his point, he follows his last denial with a renewed statement of faith in rescue (37). However, this merely delays the hunt for a beast. It is an ineradicable part of human nature, Golding seems to be saying, to make a beast where none exists or to put a beast in the place of a more abstract threat. Soon the boys are enacting all the universal responses to demons—searching for the beast, opposing it, appeasing it. By this time, however, the fear of dying on the island has been joined by a new fear, a fear of each other. One could also argue, given that the actual "beast" is the decaying body of a paratrooper, that the beast also represents the boys' generalized fears of and about the war in which their country is engaged. The attempt to make their vague and terrifying fears concrete is mocked by the beast itself: "Fancy thinking the Beast was something you could hunt and kill!" (143) says the pig's head to Simon. The real horror, Golding seems to imply, is that our worst fears have no names—or the wrong names.

THE UNIVERSALITY OF THE CHARACTERS

Much of the novel's strength also lies in its characters, who, despite all the "waccos" and "wizards," remain recognizable as the sort of people everyone has known in school, work, and society. Almost everyone has known a Piggy—a person set aside by some defect or difference who becomes the target of all sorts of teasing and torment. Plenty of people have known, or been, the littluns, the people on the fringe of the real action, motivated only by fear and hunger, victimized at random (60), seemingly unable to direct the course of events themselves, led by whomever promises the fastest end to fear and hunger.

Piggy

Of all the characters, the one who often makes the most lasting impression is Piggy. Partly it is his nickname that makes him memorable; partly it is the distinctiveness of his physical incapacities. Fat, asthmatic, nearsighted, unable to swim (13), and a whimpering mama's (or auntie's) boy, he is by no means suited to an adventure in the wild. Yet it is he who has most of the best ideas. He tries to make a sundial (64–65), names and organizes the boys, and insists on the rights of the littluns. He even, on one occasion, serves as the littluns' literal voice, repeating the words of the birthmarked boy so that the full group can hear (35). It is he who identifies the conch shell that becomes the symbol of parliamentary order on the island, and it is he who first gives it a purpose, changing it from a purely natural object into a tool of civilization (16). Furthermore, it is Piggy who provides, albeit somewhat unwillingly, the tool that bestows the power to create fire—his spectacles (40–41). It makes sense that he tries to re-create civilization in the wilderness, because he must know, at some level, that in civilization lies his best protection. Civilization protects the weak and different; the wilderness does not.

The wilderness, in fact, as symbolized by Jack, Roger, and their adherents, chooses the weak and different as its first prey. From this simple and brutal fact of predation comes Piggy's concern with fairness and his defense of the littluns. It is no coincidence that, in the wake of the fire, the boy who is called "Fatty" and told by Jack to "shut up" should be the first to notice the absence of "[t]hat little 'un . . . him with the mark on his face" (45–46). Piggy, a marked man in his own way, is good at spotting his own kind, and it does not take very long for the boys to identify the relationship between the boy Piggy and the animal piggies. In the debate over the existence of the beast, the subject of the predator-prey relationship is enlisted on the side of reason by Piggy, but the other boys ignore the logic and make a leap that the astute reader has already made, from the actual pigs on the island to the one boy named after a pig (83). In the wild, zebras survive by forming herds, confusing their enemies with numbers and movement. In politics, the disenfranchised, the weak, and the poor survive by forming parties or staging riots and demonstrations. Piggy, if he were able to form the littluns and other marginal boys into some kind of coalition, might be able to survive, but he is a poor leader. The minute he is left in charge, the littluns scatter (46). The herd is doomed.

In a happy version of the story, Piggy's good ideas and spectacles would compensate for his physical differences, his bad grammar, and his nagging insistence on behaving like grownups. It is possible that this could happen in real life as well. But it is equally plausible, perhaps more plausible, that things would work out as Golding envisions, with Piggy made into a favorite victim and someone, sooner or later, realizing that the spectacles can be possessed without the wearer. His good ideas, in the end, count for nothing. It is sad but true that a good idea can be torpedoed simply by being espoused by the wrong person. Piggy is not beautiful, popular, strong, or charismatic, and his only advantage is that he is, for the most part, right. It is not enough.

It is, in fact, in Piggy's hands, something of a disadvantage. No one likes Piggy, with the halfhearted exception of Ralph, and so no one really wants him to be right. When he is, they resent him for it. He sounds perpetually like Cassandra foretelling the fall of Troy, cursed with foreknowledge and bad timing. Over and over, he thrusts himself forward, strong in his convictions, but weak in presentation. He is too shrill, too repetitive, too disdainful of fun. He is too much like a parent, and few of the boys on the island seem to want their parents back in any form. He in fact chides them for acting like children, virtually guaranteeing that he will become an outcast. And, like Cassandra, he can see his own fate (14). He knows he is saying the right things in the wrong way and he knows how Jack feels about him. (93). Yet he cannot stop himself. He remains the voice of civilization, of parents and nannies and policemen and teachers, to the last: "Which is better—to have rules and agree, or to hunt and kill?" (180) As always, he misjudges the mood of his audience, or perhaps does not care enough about their mood. To mention hunting and killing at this juncture is no hollow piece of rhetoric, but practically an invitation.

Ralph

If Piggy is civilization's voice, Ralph is its public face. He is a profoundly average boy, better-looking than some, but of average capacities. He shares the average boy's desires, for rescue and fun, in that order or not as the whim takes him, and he has good, but not brilliant, oratorical skills. In a moment of stress, for example, he discovers that "his voice tend[s] either to disappear or to come out too loud" (104). Sometimes he finds the right words, but often he fails, as when Jack apologizes for letting the fire go out (72).

Ralph follows this misstep with another, an "ingracious mutter" (72) to relight the fire. He is, after all, a frightened and angry boy, not a master statesman. His initial election as the boys' chief is haphazard and nearly instinctive, and he is chosen for much the same reasons that many people select their leaders: "The most obvious leader was Jack. But there was a stillness about Ralph . . . there was his size, and attractive appearance, and most obscurely, yet most powerfully, there was the conch" (22). At first, Ralph is delighted to play leader. Like the conch or the vote, power itself is a toy. Later, like most elected officials, he worries both about his responsibilities and about maintaining power.

His responsibilities are few enough, and they constitute the basic set of duties of any leader, whether parent or president: feed his charges, shelter them, protect them from harm, work for their greater security or salvation. The boys constantly measure Ralph's success as a leader by his ability to perform these tasks, yet every one of these responsibilities is twisted by circumstances into a symbol of failure or futility. Feeding the boys is no trouble, since there are crabs and fruit on the island, but food, in the form of roast pork, becomes the boys' sole focus. Meat becomes the island's money. It is hard to obtain but can be gotten with hard work and skill, and the getting of meat interrupts all other work. Shelters go unbuilt, and Ralph is powerless to force the boys to build. The hunt plays havoc with the schedule for keeping the fire lit, making salvation difficult to obtain. Most of all, the idea of protection from danger is warped by the conditions on the island. There are no natural enemies on this small scrap of land, yet danger is such a part of the boys' notion of adventure that danger must be invented if it does not exist. Thus the beast is conjured from dreams and glimpses, while the real danger, the all-consuming desire for power and acceptance among the boys, goes unheeded by almost all. Ralph recognizes his essential failure to lead, even while the outward forms of leadership remain intact. Nevertheless, every time he loses power to Jack, he seems surprised by this latest turn of events and newly shocked by his incapacity to perform his duties.

He has options, of course, but fails to make use of them. He could yield power to Jack and ask to be placed in charge of a fire detail, sacrificing his own vanity and ambition to the greater good of rescue. He could challenge Jack physically and defeat him once and for all. He could lend Piggy more assistance in forming a coalition. Yet he lacks something—vision, urgency, a willingness to be unembarrassed by Piggy's friendship, or something else altogether—that would give him the courage to force the issue. Instead, he embarks on a campaign of appeasement and diplomacy.

Golding, of course, was writing within recent memory of one of history's great diplomatic failures: the policy of appeasement that preceded Britain's entry into World War II. The British prime minister, Neville Chamberlain, averted his eyes while Hitler's Germany armed for war and began invading its neighbors, and it was not until Chamberlain's replacement by Winston Churchill and Hitler's invasion of Poland that Germany's aggression was met with a significantly aggressive response. The world was fortunate to have a Churchill at the time and a Roosevelt who urged support for Britain despite an isolationist climate in the United States. However, there is not always a Churchill or a Roosevelt in the right place at the right time, a failure of political systems made all too clear in the 1990s by worldwide dithering over genocide in Rwanda and the Balkans. Political and moral cowardice, after all, are nothing new. Martin Luther King, Jr., derided it when he declared that evil triumphs in the absence of action by good people, and Susan Sontag, referring to the violence in Bosnia and to the defiant post-Holocaust slogan "Never again," reflected, "Never again doesn't . . . mean anything, does it. I mean, never again will Germans be allowed to kill Jews in the 1940s. That's . . . true. But do we have the will and the interest to prevent a genocide in Europe now?"[2]

Ralph is Chamberlain, and Clinton, and every other leader who fails to act at the perfect time, in the perfect way, to avoid a monumental tragedy. In other words, he is a good many of the world's leaders throughout history—flawed, uncertain, trapped by a multiplicity of possibilities in a web of inaction or wrong action, too tangled to find the way out.

All he knows for certain is that he is bound to be a better leader than Jack, whose desires are for pleasure and power and self-glorification, with no room left for the good of the community. Ralph at least has some sense of responsibility. So he blunders on, unwilling to yield to the bad boy. To retain his power, he even resorts to hunting, attempting to become more like Jack in order to steal back some of Jack's growing glory. Unfortunately, his attempt is all too successful. Flushed with a small success, he adopts, for the moment at least, Jack's value system: " 'I hit him, all right. The spear stuck in. I wounded him!' He sunned himself in their new respect and felt that hunting was good after all" (113). The rest of this chapter details Ralph's descent into Jack's world. Instead of returning to Piggy and the island's small civilization, he remains with Jack, leaving Simon to carry out his responsibilities. He and Jack spar verbally, with Ralph mostly on the defensive. His one attempt to cut through the posturing to the "darkness of man's heart," his query to Jack on the reason for his hatred is an embarrassing failure (118). The chapter ends, significantly, with Ralph's direct encounter with the beast, the novel's supreme symbol of fear and evil. In the end, Ralph can only co-opt Jack's leadership qualities by living in the wilderness of predation, aggression, and fear, and he cannot tame Jack and absorb him into the civilized world.

Therefore, Ralph fails as a leader. He neither preserves his people nor retains his position as chief, mostly because he never understands the fragility of his power. Like most politicians, he has (or at least develops) a sense of the people's mood, and he has a talent for shifting responsibility (37). Eventually, he also learns a few basic principles of government, for example, that important things have to be repeated to be understood (78). In this sense, he understands that he is addressing an audience of children, but he never quite manages to be the leader, the parent, that they and Piggy want him to be. For, despite their resentment of control, the children simultaneously miss the safe boundaries and the freedom from decision making that their parents and teachers provided them. Ralph never gains real control of the household, or the state, since he has no rewards to offer for good behavior and no punishments to threaten for disobedience. Unlike a parent, he cannot offer food or playthings as rewards. Food is abundant on the island and can be taken at will, while playthings like sticks and crabs are everywhere and "civilized" playthings are entirely absent. Similarly, he cannot send the boys to their rooms or rescind their privileges. Unlike the state, he cannot offer tax breaks or incentive programs as rewards, nor can he jail the boys or impose corporal punishment for their laziness or mutiny. Just as the conch appears to be a symbol of power, but in fact is subverted whenever it suits the purpose of the moment, Ralph appears to be the chief but has no actual power, only a slight influence that ultimately dissipates. He cannot force the boys to build shelters (80) or to keep the fire lit, and even the eventual rescue is only indirectly caused by him.

Ralph is not a fool. He knows that everything is going wrong, and his responsibilities begin, literally, to devour him. He begins biting his nails beyond the quick, almost entirely unconsciously (131). Eating is never simple in *Lord of the Flies*; it always carries heavy symbolism. Eating fruit is synonymous with laziness, and eating meat is synonymous with violence. Ralph is doing neither. As the symbol of the civilized community that almost was, he is slowly consuming himself. It is the group's sin of self-cannibalism, a literally gnawing awareness of his failure, that torments him.

Jack

Ralph's most significant failure is his inability to control Jack. If he could make Jack his faithful servant or ally, as successful politicians make servants or allies of the military, he might actually have some leverage over the rest of the boys, because Jack has the one real reward on the island under his control. This reward is the knowledge of the hunt. Unlike the task of keeping the fire lit, which is tedious and apparently unending, Jack's hunt offers camaraderie, hard work, esoteric knowledge, a clear end to the task, and a tangible reward at its end. The hunt is also something that the boys cannot easily duplicate on their own. In Jack's case, it takes a great deal of study to learn to track and kill the wild pigs on the island; a good example of his efforts can be found at the beginning of Chapter 3. For the littluns, acquiring this knowledge on their own is impossible. Even for the older boys, it would be tiresome and difficult to repeat Jack's experience. Therefore, Jack has the only currency on the island, and he knows it.

It is Jack, not Ralph, who is the clear choice as leader on the island. Unlike Ralph, Jack is a grand master of manipulation and public image. Almost everything he does, whether by instinct or calculation, increases his power over the boys. He grants or withholds meat, grants or withholds the right to hunt, stages public recreations of the hunt to demonstrate his hunters' prowess (115), makes use of uniforms—first the choirboys' uniforms and then the hunting paint—to create a sense of belonging, and, cleverest of all, hints at the exclusivity of his band while intending to absorb the entire island population under his control: "If you want to join my tribe come and see us. Perhaps I'll let you join. Perhaps not. . . . He was safe from shame or self-consciousness behind the mask of his paint" (140). It is the mention of "shame or self-consciousness" that makes Jack one of Golding's most ingenious creations. Jack is the Freudian id, the wild man, Hitler, the school bully, a smug and devious co-worker, a savage, a killer. Yet he is also a boy, frightened of the other boys' disapproval, frantic to be popular, and jealous of Ralph's friendship with Piggy (91). All of his evil, all of his machinations and displays, come from such basic human insecurities that it is possible, in our most honest moments, to see ourselves in Jack as well as in Ralph or Piggy.

It is thus possible to detest Jack's use of power and to admire the skill with which he obtains it. In the beginning of the novel, he has nothing but the leadership of his choir, a leadership that the elected leader, Ralph, bestows upon him. The conch, symbol of parliamentary discourse, is in Ralph's control. Jack cannot even manage to wound a pig, let alone kill it (31). Yet, with sheer political genius, he elevates the hunt while denigrating the conch until the former becomes the whole focus of the island and the latter is destroyed. He begins by speaking out of turn, without the conch (87), later shouting down those who hold the conch. Each encroachment on the conch's power as a symbol is either tolerated or ineffectively opposed. By the time Piggy asks to carry the conch (171), the conch is the one thing that Jack no longer needs.

Even as he undermines the conch's significance, Jack magnifies that of the hunt. From the time of his first kill in Chapter 4, he surrounds the hunt with the kind of ritual that humans seem to crave. There are processions, chants of "*Kill the pig. Cut her throat*" (69), and re-enactments of the kill, complete with sound effects and vivid narrative. Finally, there is the tangible reward of the hunt—roast pork—which exceeds anything offered by the fire or the shelters for sheer physical pleasure. Even the fact that the hunters neglect the fire, obtaining their first kill at the expense of a chance of rescue, becomes less important in the rapture of the feast.

From that point, the hunt becomes not only a hobby and a source of sustenance but a determinant of manhood and worth. After the first kill, Jack justifies withholding pork from Piggy because he did not hunt (74). Ralph, afraid of pursuing the beast, tries to get Jack to go after it by saying, "You're a hunter," and then hunts it himself because he realizes that it is his job as chief to hunt a threat to his tribe (104). Jack then follows him and joins this hunt (106). Is he unable to let Ralph hunt the beast alone because of their friendship, because of duty, or because of the personal glory attached to a perilous hunt? Given what we know about Jack at this point in the novel, the last explanation seems most likely. Then, when Jack is knocked down during a hunt, and it is Ralph who wounds the boar, Jack manages to turn events to his advantage once again, displaying his own wound to general admiration (114). Almost immediately, there is another hunt re-enactment, with Robert unwillingly playing the role of the pig, and a new element is added to the ritual—a human stand-in for the prey, who will be subjected to increasing tortures and even murder as the novel progresses.

Eventually, Jack tries to make hunting a prerequisite for leadership. He calls Ralph a coward and attacks him for his failure to hunt, using this as a basis to challenge him for the chieftainship (126–27). Though the tactic fails in the short term and results in Jack becoming an outcast, he turns the situation to his advantage, withholding meat from those who will not support him and offering knowledge of the hunt to those who will. In Jack's society, meetings are not run according to the principles of equality and free discourse symbolized by the conch, but according to the fierce rituals of the hunt, with chants, violence, and displays of personal power dictating the outcome. By breaking the old rules and making his own, Jack comes to leadership at last, but he lacks Piggy's insight, and in the end, he has nowhere to lead the boys but into hell.

Roger

The logical product of Jack's society is Roger, a boy who is far harder to understand or appreciate than his nominal leader. If Ralph is Chamberlain and Jack Hitler, Roger is the Gestapo, an instrument of torture and terror released from conventional morality and thus capable of unspeakable cruelty. He and Simon are the two most inscrutable major characters and serve as foils for each other. Both seem to understand that the lack of real authority on the island creates a potential for great evil, but for Simon this represents a threat to be contested, while for Roger it represents an opportunity to be embraced. Little by little, Roger tests his lack of limits. At first he explores cruelty in secret, lobbing stones at an unwitting Henry. Then he throws himself wholeheartedly into the half-serious torment of the pig-Robert (114), a public and socially acceptable outlet for his violence. The hunt is his element, a glorified excuse for madness and killing, and he is particularly savage in this activity, spitting a live sow on the point of his spear by stabbing her in her rectum (135). Yet even the slaughter of animals cannot contain his mounting capacity for cruelty, and Jack's bid for power gives him the chance to display its full range. Robert informs Roger that Jack intends to beat the bound Wilfred for no stated reason; he has finally found the society that will impose no humane limits on behavior.

Now his aggression is directed at humans, publicly and with increasing viciousness. He feels powerful flinging stones at Sam and Eric (175). He dehumanizes Ralph and Piggy in his mind and murders Piggy "with a sense of delirious abandonment" (180). Jack imposes no penalties for this act, giving it his tacit approval, and Roger becomes imbued with "a nameless authority" (182). It is he, it seems, who hurts Samneric, and it is he, even more than Jack, whom they fear (188–89). The last specific reference to him in *Lord of the Flies* is a hint that he is torturing the twins during the hunt for Ralph (192), and the penultimate reference to Roger is the most chilling of all, an implication that he means not only to kill Ralph but to behead him and display the severed head (190). Roger's behavior is horrifying and seemingly incomprehensible, but not, unfortunately, unusual. Human sacrifice, medieval tortures, genocide, purges, and a host of other atrocities testify to the capacity of *Homo sapiens*, "wise man," for murder and terror and a host of unwise acts when authority approves or fails to resist.

Simon

If we find it hard to see anything of ourselves in Roger because identifying with him is distasteful, we find it equally hard to see ourselves in Simon, though for different reasons. Simon is so decent, so selflessly brave, so opaquely meditative, so unjustly executed, that it is as desirable yet difficult to identify with him as it is to identify with Christ, after whom he is modeled. In fact, in the first draft of *Lord of the Flies*, Simon was so obviously a Christ figure that Golding's editor suggested that the analogy be toned down a bit.[3] Simon is thus made less completely Christlike, but no less obscure and mysterious than before, as Golding explained. "Simon," he said in an interview, "is understood by nobody, naturally enough."[4] The other boys certainly do not understand him. They call him "queer," "funny" (55), and "batty" (157). Piggy, as the voice of science and reason, is especially unsympathetic to Simon's spiritual approach. Asked if Simon could be climbing the mountain in search of the beast, he replies, "He might be. . . . He's cracked" (132).

Simon, in the finished version of *Lord of the Flies*, has characteristics that are not pointedly Christlike. He faints (20, 22), he is shy (25) and uncomfortable speaking before groups (103), traits not shared by the Bible's carpenter-rabbi who always seemed to have a parable ready. Simon happily enters into the business of the world, symbolized by his willingness to accompany an exploratory expedition and his excitement about making a map of the island (24–30). His ascetic appearance, barefoot, barely clad, long-haired, and dark-skinned (55–56) is subverted by "eyes so bright they had deceived Ralph into thinking him delightfully gay and wicked" (55). Simon is thus no point-by-point counterpart to Christ.

Yet he is the most spiritual of the boys. Unlike Piggy, who follows the rules because it is in his own interest to enforce them, Simon is no automatic outcast. He appears to respect the rights of the disenfranchised not because he is, by extension, defending his own rights, but because he really believes in the virtue of the rules. Ralph and Piggy often insist on the rule of the conch, usually when they are trying to make themselves heard, but Simon actually follows the rule without self-interest, stifling his own comments deliberately on at least two occasions (34, 86) because someone else has the conch. Alone among the boys, he thinks about the welfare of others, not because he believes it is his duty or because he believes it will help him, but because it is his inescapable nature to do so.

Incident after incident demonstrates Simon's essential generosity and empathy. He defends Piggy's role in starting the fire to Jack by pointing out that Piggy's glasses were of help (42). He helps build shelters long after the others have yielded to the temptations of swimming and hunting (50). Like Christ, who fed the masses with loaves and fishes, Simon feeds those incapable of feeding themselves. He gives his own meat to Piggy when Jack refuses to give Piggy any (74) and picks fruit for the littluns (56). He also, in order to ease a littlun's fear of a beast, confesses that he has been going off by himself at night. He is, as perhaps he suspected he would be, rewarded with ridicule. All of these acts are humble, self-abnegating, and as anonymous as it is possible for any act to be in such a small community. Most people would probably like to have Simon's gift for quiet charity, but most people would probably also end up swimming, hunting, and trying to stay on Jack's good side. Nonetheless, Simon resembles a rare type of person who does exist. There are people who give of themselves because it is their nature or their sole ambition. They do consider their own needs from time to time, but they are principally concerned with the needs of others.

Therefore, it is likely that Golding's readers have known someone at least somewhat like Simon. The reader may have known someone poorly understood, someone who really believed in society's rules, or someone who was innately generous. It is even possible that the reader knows someone who shares all three of these characteristics. What makes Simon unique, and thus harder to comprehend than any of the other boys, is that to these three personality traits Golding adds a fourth, rarer than the other three: a yearning and an aptitude for seeing the truth. In the midst of the dark jungle, Simon finds a private pocket "of heat and light" (56), light here serving as a metaphor for knowledge in the midst of ignorance and superstition. Unfortunately for Simon, he lacks the words to express what he perceives. Like Piggy, he sees to the heart of the boys' animosities, but, unlike Piggy, he does not attempt to name the hatred he observes (68). He understands the essence of the beast even before his conversation with it, but he cannot communicate his vision (89). Undermined, ridiculed, belittled, Simon persists in his quest, even if he no longer attempts to explain it to his companions. He remains silent, with an awareness still more visual than verbal (103). Not until his direct conflict with the Lord of the Flies does Simon find adequate words, and then it is unclear whether the words are a true description or a weapon in a verbal battle. Succinctly, he calls the Lord of the Flies what, in the physical world at least, it really is: "Pig's head on a stick" (143). However, this is not a complete identification of the beast. The pig's head, beginning to rot and preyed on by scavenging flies, is only a symbol of the beast, not the beast itself, and Simon cannot fully express in words the nature of what he sees.

Small wonder, then, that the boys think him a little crazy. He prophesies. He speaks to visionary demons. He sees things and understands great issues but cannot explain well what he knows. He may indeed be ill, either physically or mentally. During his conversation with the pig's head, Simon's own head wobbles as he feels "one of his times" coming on (143). The phrase "one of his times," combined with Simon's fainting spell at his first appearance with the choirboys, implies epilepsy or a similar disease. Clearly, Simon has episodes of some kind with some frequency. He recognizes the state he is entering. Golding never explains what Simon's "times" are or whether they are to be perceived as a state of illness, madness, or awareness, but these distinctions are hardly relevant. Whether Simon is ill or not, he sees the truth, and to dismiss the truth because its messenger may be ill is itself a little crazy.

Simon behaves like a person with a mental illness, yet he is the only one on the island who fully comprehends what is going wrong and why. Is Golding saying that crazy people are crazy because they see more truth than the rest of us, or that seeing truth resembles insanity so closely that the one is bound to be mistaken for the other? The novel is lean enough not to give away the answer to that question, but it is true that in the modern world, a Simon, a Jesus, a Buddha, or a Mohammed is more likely to be institutionalized than revered. Who is really crazy, after all: The boy who talks to a pig's head, or the boys who murder him? The man who talks to the Devil in the desert, or the society that nails him to two boards and outlaws his teachings? These are among the provocative questions that *Lord of the Flies* raises.

Simon's perception is clearer than that of the other boys, and he is willing, despite his own fears and the probability of unpleasant consequences for himself, to stare unblinkingly into the face of ugly realities. He sees past superstition, past loyalty, even past the power of words to convey what he sees. To find this extraordinarily uncommon characteristic in harness with the previous three is beyond the personal experience of most readers. If they have known such a person, they have probably, like the boys on the island, misunderstood him or her. Simon is thus the least universal of the novel's characters.

Sam and Eric

It is hard to imagine oneself as Simon, but all too easy to imagine oneself as Samneric, the twins so lacking in individual identity that they have one voice, one work shift, and one merged name. In fact, Golding's readers are, in the act of reading, very much like Samneric, passive observers of events, swept along and approving or objecting as events dictate, but unable to alter the unfolding of the disaster. Samneric are the ordinary person's surrogates. They do not rule, or make rules, or have the best ideas, or stage coups, or invent horrible tortures, or see the essence of evil for its true self, or really change anything at all. Basically decent but ineffective, they act when acted upon. They react.

Samneric cannot act independently (96). This is true from quite early in the novel, when they find a log for the fire but can "do nothing" without the others (39). The fire will test them again and again, and they fail each time. They fall asleep tending it. They question the good of keeping it alive, lacking the innate will to seek rescue (163). They are the least perceptive of the big boys, the least original thinkers, less imaginative even than some of the littluns. In Chapter 6, they are the first to spot the downed parachutist, but instead of investigating, they flee from it. The idea of a beast has been planted in their minds, and like the great mass of humans everywhere, they perceive things according to their preconceptions. They do not, like Simon, question what they have witnessed or attempt to formulate an alternative explanation.

In fact, their encounter with the parachutist is emblematic of · their approach to everything. They run from conflict at every turn, sometimes aware of the right course of action but seldom strong enough to take it. When Jack hosts a feast, they yield, with most of the other boys, to the lure of meat. The twins are swayed by the proximity of an influence. When Jack is near, they drift toward him; when Ralph returns, they sidle his way and pretend that nothing has happened. In a similar vein, they willingly enter into the selective memory of Simon's murder (158), a revisionist-history scene that, coming as it does not quite ten years after the end of World War II, begs to be likened to the convenient forgetfulness of war criminals.

Samneric stay with Ralph longer than any of the biguns except Piggy, but to no avail. They simply lack enough moral strength and determination to do him much good as allies. Captured and tortured by Jack's tribe, they yield quickly (182). They make a feeble attempt to provide him with inside information, but what they offer is of little use. Jack means to hunt him; Ralph could probably have figured that out on his own, though it shows some good will on Sam's part to overthrow his "new and shameful loyalty" (187) for long enough to reveal Jack's plan. Still, they have not the brains or the imagination to figure out why Roger is sharpening a stick at both ends, and instead of trying to rebel against Jack, they can offer Ralph no better option than to run. Even this plan is ruined by their cowardice. Tortured again, they reveal Ralph's hiding place, betraying him once again (192). One wonders about the boys' lives after they are rescued from Golding's island. One suspects that many of them would be tormented by nightmares, guilt, and self-loathing. Samneric, however, might very well be able to convince themselves that they had behaved as well as humanly possible, and exonerate themselves in all but the deepest recesses of their consciences. It is, after all, how many people rationalize their own bad behavior or inertia. Golding's application of everyday cowardice to an extraordinary situation is one of the reasons that *Lord of the Flies* is so disturbing.

CONCLUSION

This analysis has frequently mentioned the behavior of children for the same reason that Golding chooses children as his subjects in *Lord of the Flies*. Children have spent fewer years absorbing the particular cultural quirks of their societies. Their behavior is, therefore, closer to "nature"—to the genetic programming with which each of us is born. In this novel, Golding explores some of the universal traits that define humanity: power hunger, fear, faith, betrayal, jealousy, curiosity, logic, cowardice, and violence, among others. His conclusions about people are deeply saddening. In at least one kind of situation, the novel says, politics (Ralph) fails, science (Piggy) and spirituality (Simon) are murdered, power (Jack) and cruelty (Roger) prevail, and the ordinary decent fellow (Samneric) cannot do anything to change the course of events. The use of children to illustrate these concepts strips away layers of social conditioning that would be found in adults and increases the novel's atmosphere of abstraction.

However, the use of children practically requires that Golding mention play, since children spend a good deal of their time playing. Play, in all species where it occurs, serves as training for adult activities. Baby wolves play at hunting, while baby humans play at talking on the phone and driving cars. In Golding's day, boys played sports, board games, and make-believe adventure games, and though games are never extraordinarily prominent in this novel, they are mentioned, subtly, throughout. There are references to rugby (115), chess (117), and other games from time to time. The boys play at controlling sea creatures and each other, and the naval officer who lands on the island to rescue the boys at first interprets their hunt for Ralph as an ordinary children's game. This introduces an entirely new level of complexity into an already many-layered novel. Is the whole thing a game or not, the natural behavior of humankind (including children) or an imitation of the adult world?

At first glance, it seems deadly serious. Even the officer is taken aback when the answer to his joking question, "Nobody killed, I hope? Any dead bodies?" is "Only two" (201). Furthermore, the presence of the very real warship off the island's coast is an ample reminder that war is no game. Yet the whole saga of these stranded schoolboys seems to be game and reality at once. The conch is not a symbol of authority but a boy's toy version of a symbol of authority, serving the same purpose as a toy telephone. Until the arrival of the navy, there is no voice at the other end of the line. By the same token, the voting for chief, Ralph's authority, the hunt, the kill, and the feast each follow the pattern of child's play, as the boys imitate what their elders might do in similar circumstances. Each chapter reveals a new game or a new stage of the game.

How many people get married, or take certain jobs, or have children, or join certain organizations simply because it seems to be the next step in the game? Perhaps the boys hunt Ralph simply because it seems to be the next step in the game and because there is no outside authority to call them in for dinner. There is a long, shaded continuum between the toddler with a toy soldier and a water pistol, the older boy hunting animals with a real gun or blasting aliens into bloody body parts on a computer screen, and the adult general moving markers on a map to represent real bodies dying somewhere in battle. We can all put ourselves somewhere on that continuum between play and earnest, between what we naturally wish and the patterns set by our predecessors. Golding thus touches another universal aspect of humanity. *Lord of the Flies* is a novel that encourages questions about the human condition, not the least of which is this: At what point do you put down your toys and decide not to play anymore?

TOPICS FOR WRITTEN OR ORAL EXPLORATION

1. Do you know someone like Piggy? Ralph? Jack? Any of the other boys? Why do these people remind you of the characters in the book?

2. What are some ways that people exert power over each other in school or in the wider world?

3. Describe a time when you were afraid of something mysterious.

4. When you were little, how did your games, toys, and activities mimic the adult world?

5. Golding says that Henry, on the beach, has the "illusion of mastery." Is power always an illusion?

6. Do you find the boys' slang hard to understand at times? Make a list of the slang terms they use and what you think they mean. Listen to yourself and your friends for a day, catalogue all the slang terms you hear, and define them. Do you think your children or grandchildren will still be using the same words when they are in school?

7. The littluns on the island are, for the most part, ignored or mistreated. How do you treat younger children? How do your friends treat them?

8. On the island, the littluns are the most powerless people. Who would you say are the most powerless people in the real world? Are they treated like littluns?

9. The conch shell serves as a symbol of governmental power in the novel. What are our society's symbols of governmental power? What gives these symbols meaning and force? Do they all have something in common? What are some real-world symbols for chaos or violence? What are the symbols of chaos and violence in the novel?

10. If Piggy kept a diary, what do you think his last entry might look like? Write a diary for Piggy, Ralph, or one of the other boys.

11. Pretend you are one of the officers who comes to the rescue at the end. Write a report to your superiors on what you have found on the island.

12. Why is it important that the boys are on an island, rather than, say, in the Arctic, or in the Amazon rain forest? Why do you think Golding chose an island?

13. Write a newscast that demonstrates how a TV station or network would cover the events on the island. Videotape your coverage. Does the television "coverage" distort the story? How?

14. Stage a mock trial of the boys who killed Piggy.

15. Golding could tell us a lot more about the boys' previous home life, background, country of origin, method of arriving at the island, and parents. Why doesn't he? Do you think he made the right choice?

16. Would this be a different story if the stranded people on the island were grown-ups? If so, how? Is it important that the castaways are children, and, if so, why?

17. Look up a definition of "foreshadowing." How is Piggy's death foreshadowed?

18. When do you first realize that this story is not going to have a happy ending? What makes you realize this?

19. Some people argue that allowing children to play war games, or to play with toy guns, encourages them to be violent. Is there evidence of this in *Lord of the Flies*? Do you agree?

20. Who is the smartest character in the novel? Why do you think so?

21. In the absence of authority and institutions, the boys set up an authority structure of their own. Draw a diagram that shows who is in command and who is commanded. Explain what each boy's role is in this structure.

22. If the boys were to manage to get along peacefully, what sorts of institutions would they need to create? How do these institutions compare to those in the real world?

23. Before they physically hurt him, the boys dehumanize Piggy. They separate him from themselves in a number of ways and make his feelings seem unimportant. Describe how they do this.

24. Is there special significance to Golding's choice of the name "Piggy"?

25. Are there groups in our society that get treated like Piggy? How?

26. Look up the words *dictatorship, monarchy, oligarchy, anarchy, republic, theocracy,* and *democracy*. Which most resembles the power structure on the island?

27. Write a short story in which Piggy's ghost visits Ralph.

28. Write a memoir of the island experience from the perspective of one of the boys twenty years later. What might a man with such a past want to tell his own son?

29 What is more important on the island—the rights of the individual or the rights of the group?

30. Why does Golding end the novel where he does? Why not before Piggy's death, or just after? Why does he show the rescuers arriving?

31. Write a dialogue between a police interrogator and one of the boys after the boys are rescued.

32. Watch the movie *Lifeboat*, directed by Alfred Hitchcock. How is the behavior aboard the lifeboat similar to that on the island? How is the ending similar?

33. Make a map of the island. List the ten events that you consider most important in the novel and indicate their locations on the map.

34. Watch a movie version of *Lord of the Flies*. What parts of it do you feel capture the spirit of the book? What parts of it do not? Why?

35. Who is the "Lord of the Flies"?

36. On page 139, Ralph asks, "What makes things break up like they do?" This is the central question of *Lord of the Flies*, and various answers are offered, including Ralph and Piggy's theory that it is Jack who makes "things break up." What do you think it is? Try to come up with an answer that applies to the novel and to the real world as well.

37. Disney movies are famous for glossing over the unpleasant parts of the works that they take as their inspiration. For example, Disney omits the tragic ending of *The Hunchback of Notre Dame* and the unintentional murders committed by both Hercules and his wife in *Hercules*. Write or outline a script for a Disney version of *Lord of the Flies*. Is there any way of giving this story a happy ending without making it seem ludicrous?

38. What is the "crude expressive syllable" that Jack considers "the dirtiest thing there is" (89)? What do you think Simon really meant?

39. Being brutally honest with yourself, which character do you think you most resemble?

NOTES

1. Charles Monteith, "Strangers from Within," in *William Golding: The Man and His Books*, ed. John Carey (London: Faber and Faber, 1986), 58.

2. Susan Sontag, on *Charlie Rose*, August 2, 1995.

3. Monteith, "Strangers from Within," 59.

4. Jack I. Biles, *Talk: Conversations with William Golding* (New York: Harcourt Brace Jovanovich 1970), 14.

SUGGESTIONS FOR FURTHER READING

Babb, S. Howard *The Novels of William Golding*. Columbus: Ohio State University Press, 1970.

Baker, James R. *Critical Essays on William Golding*. Boston: G. K. Hall & Co., 1988.

Boyd, S. J. *The Novels of William Golding*. 2nd ed. New York: Harvester, 1988.

Dickson, L. L. *The Modern Allegories of William Golding*. Tampa, FL: University of South Florida Press, 1990.

Friedman, Lawrence S. *William Golding*. New York: Continuum, 1993.

Hodson, Leighton. *William Golding*. Edinburgh, UK: Oliver and Boyd, 1969.

Kinkead-Weekes, Mark, and Ian Gregor. *William Golding: A Critical Study*. New York: Harcourt, Brace & World, 1967.

Page, Norman, ed. *William Golding: Novels, 1954–67*. London: Macmillan, 1985.

Reilly, Patrick. *Lord of the Flies: Fathers and Sons*. New York: Twayne, 1992.

Whitley, John S. *Golding: Lord of the Flies*. London: Edward Arnold, 1970.

2 _____

The Ignoble Savage

Man is born to sin. Set him free, and he will be a sinner, not Rousseau's "noble savage."

—William Golding

An Imperial Timeline

1922   Britain ends its Egyptian protectorate and recognizes Fuad I as King of an independent Egypt.

1946   Transjordan (later Jordan) is granted independence from Great Britain.

1947   India achieves independence from Britain on August 15 and splits immediately into two countries, India and Pakistan. Within the first month of independence, hostilities break out between Hindu-dominated India and Muslim-dominated Pakistan, with perhaps 150,000 dead in the Punjab alone by early September.

1948   After violence and lobbying by Zionists, Britain's colony of Palestine is partitioned into Arab and Jewish territories, with the nation of Israel scheduled to come into being on May 15. Jewish immigration increases, as does violence by both Arabs and Jews. Bomb attacks in various places and rifle fire in the border town of Haifa are prelude to the outbreak of war on the fifteenth, as Syria, Transjordan, Lebanon, and Egypt attack Israel. The United States and U.S.S.R. quickly recognize Israel, but Britain hesitates, appearing in many quarters to side with the Arabs.

Burma gains independence from Britain. "Burma's period of tutelage is over," announces the new premier as he lowers the Union Jack and raises the new nation's flag.

1949   All of Ireland except six northern counties declare independence from Great Britain. In May, Britain recognizes the new government.

1950   Britain still has thirty-nine colonies.

Britain formally recognizes the state of Israel.

1951   Egypt moves to force the British from the Suez. Fighting between the two sides continues into 1952.

1952   In Kenya's Mau Mau Rebellion, Europeans, Africans sympathetic to the British presence in Kenya, and others are attacked. By 1956, more than 10,000 Mau Mau rebels will have been killed by British forces.

Anti-British riots erupt in Egypt. A series of coups and appointments result in six different Egyptian governments in six months.

1953   Jomo Kenyatta and five others are convicted of leading the Mau Mau.

1953   British colonies in the Caribbean form a federation with the goal of eventual self-government.

Elizabeth II, who became queen in 1952 when her father died, is crowned.

1954   *Lord of the Flies* is published.

A coup is staged in Egypt by Colonel Gamal Nasser.

Hundreds of Kikuyus are arrested in Kenya for suspected Mau Mau involvement.

1970   Tonga declares independence from Great Britain.

EUROPEAN VIEWS OF THE SAVAGE

In 1755, the French philosopher Jean-Jacques Rousseau, in an attempt to define how certain aspects of society had evolved, envisioned what humans might be like in the absence of culture. He knew that such a case was purely hypothetical, "a state which no longer exists, perhaps never did exist, and probably will never exist," but he thought it a valuable exercise anyway "in order to form a proper judgment of our present state."[1] If one could determine which part of humanity's behavior was natural and which part of it artificial, one might be able to alter the artificial parts for the greater good. The idea was not new. People have been wondering about what they share and how they differ since the first strangers from different tribes met each other. It is a debate that has still not been adequately resolved, even with advances in neurology, genetics, and psychology, and it is a debate that resonates throughout *Lord of the Flies*. Why *do* things go wrong? Is it culture that makes fascists, murderers, and sadists, or is it a natural capacity for cruelty?

Rousseau addressed the question by postulating a natural man, a savage in the purest state. His savages are strong and nimble: "Accustomed from their infancy to the inclemencies of the weather and the rigour of the seasons, inured to fatigue, and forced, naked and unarmed, to defend themselves and their prey from other ferocious animals, or to escape them by flight, men would acquire a robust and almost unalterable constitution."[2] They need no doctors. They sleep lightly. They are indelicate, with "extremely coarse" senses of taste and touch but "exceedingly fine and subtle" senses of sight, hearing, and smell.[3] Savages are not immoral but amoral; they "are not bad merely because they do not know what it is to be good: for it is neither the development of the understanding nor the restraint of law that hinders them from doing ill; but the peacefulness of their passions, and their ignorance of vice."[4] They are compassionate, because even animals, according to Rousseau, possess innate compassion. They have "no true conception of justice,"[5] having no quarrels great enough to require a formal system of detection and punishment. They choose mates without regard to beauty, merit, love, or admiration, and thus engage in no quarrels for the sake of jealousy or desire. They need nothing from their fellow humans and bear them no ill will. Rousseau dismisses as "absurd" the picture of "savages . . . continually cutting one another's throats to indulge their brutality,"[6] and to illustrate his various surmises about the pre-civilization human condition, he makes frequent reference to existing "savage" cultures, especially in the Caribbean and North America.

Civilized humanity, in comparison, is decadent, indolent, dissatisfied, passionate, and generally evil. "We hardly see anyone around us," he writes, "except people who are complaining of their existence; many even deprive themselves of it if they can and all divine and human laws put together can hardly put a stop to this disorder. I would like to know if anyone has heard of a savage who took it into his head, when he was free, to complain of life and to kill himself. Let us be less arrogant, then, when we judge on which side real misery is found."[7] The civilized man, like a domesticated animal, "grows weak, timid, and servile; his effeminate way of life totally enervates his strength and courage."[8]

Rousseau's ideas became well known among intellectuals and entered the main stream of Western thought. In time, despite the philosopher's disclaimers that he was speaking of a purely theoretical humanity, predating the development of speech, law, or even the ability to recognize other individual humans, Western discourse often came to refer to almost any isolated, unindustrialized culture as being composed of "noble savages." A certain segment of the industrialized world still lauds any undeveloped culture as purer and more wholesome than its own while decrying the miseries imposed on the world by technology and pollution. This view seems to have become more prevalent since the 1960s, and words such as *primitive, backward*, and *savage* have become politically incorrect as a result.

However, prior to the 1960s, the idea that unindustrialized societies were pure and noble was a minority viewpoint. Far more prevalent were two other perspectives, one a leftover of Victorian imperialism, the other the result of postwar realism. The Victorian perspective was that "savages" were inferior to industrialized peoples and that civilization must be imposed on them for their own good, whether they liked it or not. Thus societies in Africa, Australia, North America, and elsewhere were subjugated and offered or force-fed European-style commerce, government, clothing, medicine, religion, education, and languages. Some believed that savagery was the product of culture and could be educated away. Others favored the idea that savages were born that way and suited only for servitude in the homes or businesses of their conquerors. The latter view tied in nicely with the evolutionary theories of Charles Darwin, which held that the fittest creatures survived longest to reproduce and to carry their genetic material to the next generation. Social Darwinists held that the victors in imperialist or capitalist battles were, by definition, the fittest and that science stood on the side of conquest. If European hegemony seemed to be everywhere, why, that was because Europeans had had the foresight to employ (check all that apply, depending on the colony in question) guns, horses, cannon, smallpox, superior numbers, religion, or treachery.

If this way of looking at the world seems irrelevant to Golding's era, keep in mind that he was born and raised well before Britain's worst colonial setbacks, when it could still be claimed with some justice that "the sun never set on the British Empire." Boys of Golding's generation and even later read stories thick with adventurous conquest, threats of torture or execution by "savages," and the worshipful admiration and servitude of "good" people of color for the stalwart white heroes. Hollywood in 1954 was still portraying the battle for the American West as one of good, white, God-fearing settlers against bad, dark-skinned, whooping, ignorant Indians. Not until much later would popular culture begin to question the demonization of aboriginal peoples.

However, by the 1950s, Britain had lost a great deal of its empire and much of its smugness. Around the globe, the sun was indeed setting as colony after colony declared itself ready for self-rule. Faced with a rising tide of resistance from without and self-doubt from within, many Britons adopted a tone of liberal rationalism in talking about their colonies. For instance, during Kenya's Mau Mau Rebellion in 1952, correspondents to London's *Times* and officials on the scene in Africa spoke of tolerance and compromise, proclaiming that they understood the Kenyans' very real and laudable desire for independence or at least an airing of grievances, denouncing overt acts of violence by Kikuyu tribesmen, praising the "great devotion to duty"[9] of whites and some Africans, and reaffirming a belief in the essential good will and good behavior of the majority of Kenyans. A typical speech was that made to several hundred Kikuyus by district commissioner N. F. Kennaway. It combines a liberal belief in political cooperation with an imperialist condescension.

> I have no doubt many of you here have taken the disgusting Mau Mau oath. If you wish to progress, go and cleanse yourselves and return to sanity. The path of Mau Mau must lead to destruction. . . . The Government is perfectly ready to forgive and wishes nothing

more than to build peace, order, and real progress. I hope the steps taken by the Government are sufficient to turn you into the right path. The Government is determined you shall return to a state of peace and sanity and be cured of the disease that has been going through the tribe.[10]

It sounds a bit like a parental lecture after some act of household mayhem, and the Kenyans were unconvinced. Kenya gained its independence in 1963 and elected as its first prime minister Mau Mau leader Jomo Kenyatta.

When even the best-intentioned and most strongly motivated speakers had trouble thinking of dark-skinned people as equals, it may well be imagined that more casual or hostile commentators had little praise for non-Europeans, or even for foreigners of any kind. George Orwell, in an essay about weekly magazines targeted at boys, noted that characters of particular races or nationalities in such periodicals could always be expected to display certain traits:

> In papers of this kind it occasionally happens that when the setting of a story is in a foreign country some attempt is made to describe the natives as individual human beings, but as a rule it is assumed that foreigners of any one race are all alike and will conform more or less exactly to the following patterns:
>
> FRENCHMAN: Excitable. Wears beard, gesticulates wildly.
>
> SPANIARD, MEXICAN, etc.: Sinister, treacherous.
>
> ARAB, AFGHAN, etc.: Sinister, treacherous.
>
> CHINESE: Sinister, treacherous. Wears pigtail.
>
> ITALIAN: Excitable. Grinds barrel-organ or carries stiletto.
>
> SWEDE, DANE, etc.: Kindhearted, stupid.
>
> NEGRO: Comic, very faithful.[11]

Thousands of examples of early- and mid-twentieth-century stereotyping could be listed, and not only in Britain. Tintin comics, Charlie Chan and Tarzan movies, minstrel shows, books, and songs displayed the willingness of many nations to reduce whole cultures to a simple formula.

When unindustrialized cultures were represented in popular media, the formula seldom developed along noble-savage lines. The stereotypical savage was cruel. He ("he" because gender stereotypes came in the same package) was a cannibal, a scalper, or a taker of prisoners. He possessed natural physical abilities such as extraordinary strength or endurance, insusceptibility to great heat or cold, silence, swiftness, or skill in tracking. His cruelty and strength were like the cruelty and strength of nature itself, with which the savage was closely associated. He was immoral or amoral. He was a fearsome enemy and a loyal slave or servant when conquered and shown kindness; he responded best to a controlled display of European strength and superiority. He wore outlandish clothes or no clothes at all. It is this stereotype that Golding invokes whenever he uses the word *savage* in *Lord of the Flies*, not the imagined noble savage of Rousseau's philosophy or the trainable, Anglicizable savage of liberal imperial policy, but the dark, Victorian savage, the savage barely recognizable as *Homo sapiens*.

Clothing

It seems silly even to mention the question of clothing. Surely we are more concerned with behavioral stereotypes and with the behavior of Golding's characters than with attire. Yet it turns out that clothing, or at the very least, appearance, is perhaps the most important part of the stereotype. Examine any industrialized nation in Darwin's time, or Golding's, or our own, and you will see cruelty, strength, swiftness, inimical behavior, and loyal service. As naturalist Charles Darwin noted in one of the following reprinted passages, cruelty can be found in any group of people who are given the opportunity to be cruel; the Europeans he describes are no more laudable than the so-called savages of South America. Yet even Darwin, sometimes subtly, sometimes even in his attempts to be evenhanded, divides the people he encounters into civilized people and savages. He cannot see past different manners, appearance, and clothing to judge everyone's behavior equally. He judges people as examples of their races.

To be fair to Darwin, he was describing Tierra del Fuego and other parts of South America for British readers who had never seen, and probably would never see, those parts of the world. It was logical for him to describe the appearance of people and places different from those in Britain. However, Darwin is hardly alone in allowing appearance to affect his conclusions. Every day,

we make judgments about people's wealth, age, attitude, and life-
style based solely on their appearance, even before we consider
their behavior. Golding, knowing this, dresses the boys in ways
that will trigger a visceral response in his readers. In the beginning,
when the boys are still in possession of their civilized veneer, they
are dressed in school uniforms, clothes that make readers think of
lessons, rules, and authority. Almost immediately, however, these
symbols of order come under attack. The boys strip to swim or for
the sheer anarchic fun of being naked. They allow their neatly
trimmed hair and nails to grow unchecked. They forget hygiene.
Their clothes, their teeth, and their bodies become dirty (109).
True, the boys do plenty of swimming, but anyone who has swum
routinely in salt water knows that one does not, once dry, feel
precisely clean. "Sticky" is perhaps a better word. It is intriguing
that by this point in the novel, a boy who once thought of adventure as an island with no parents now thinks of "adventure" as
doing laundry. One wonders if Ralph might not have maintained
better control over the boys if he had made an effort to stay clean
and crisp. Perhaps he could, through clothing and grooming alone,
have evoked the forgotten world of rules and authority. He senses
this opportunity, too late, when he tries to get Piggy's glasses back
(172). He and Piggy clean up as best they can, but by this point,
there is too much momentum toward Jack's side of the island for
such minimal efforts to succeed.

For the most part, Ralph does not maintain his civilized dress,
and in allowing it to become tattered and dirty, he begins to resemble the savage stereotype. He is long-haired, ragged, filthy, and
probably browned by the sun. Instead of evoking order and discipline, his appearance recalls all the traits associated with the savage of literature, movies, and imperialism. The resemblance is
strengthened by Jack, who makes himself appear even more outlandish by adding face paint to his costume. Even Jack hardly recognizes himself after donning the paint; he becomes "an awesome
stranger" (63). Like a shy actor, he is given courage by adopting
his role and finds it easier to speak behind this savage mask. Unfortunately, he begins to play the part too well, as do the boys who
follow him. During the hunt for Ralph at the end, behavior and
dress have merged so smoothly into the savage caricature that
Ralph can hardly remember the civilized incarnations of his former
companions. He spots one of the hunters and thinks, "This was

not Bill. This was a savage whose image refused to blend with that ancient picture of a boy in shorts and shirt" (183). The boy wants to play at being his idea of a savage, so he dons a costume he thinks appropriate to the game, which liberates him to act like his idea of a savage, which makes the costume seem more natural, which makes the behavior seem more natural as well. Savage behavior and savage appearance, in play and in earnest, escalate each other until no one, not even Ralph, can tell where image and reality meet.

The horror of the hunt, and of all the other violent episodes in the novel, is that the capacity for savagery—in the sense of brutal, wanton cruelty—lurks in every society. The problem is that, to recognize evil and not excuse it, people usually need to dress it in a stranger's clothes. It needs to look like a comic-book savage or a war-movie Nazi. When it comes in the guise of little English boys, boys in shorts and shirts and caps, boys who don savage attire and then revert to their shamefaced civilized selves the minute an adult appears, it is hard to excuse and explain away. In this sense, Golding's use of clothing is anything but trivial. The boys' clothes change (and presumably, after the return to civilization, change back), but their moral equipment has been the same all along. The difference between civilization and savagery is simply a matter of costume.

Cruelty

As evidence for the trival differences between savage and civilized people, readers could cite the cruelty—supposedly the natural characteristic of the savage—detailed in *Lord of the Flies*. Instances of such cruelty are too numerous to list exhaustively here, but at least two are notable for their ironic mention of civilization. In the first, Roger throws stones near Henry purely for the evil pleasure it brings him, yet he cannot yet bring himself to throw stones directly *at* another person (62). In the second episode, Jack's hunters, who now include nearly every boy on the island, restrain and torture Samneric (178–79). Both passages explicitly equate civilization with the protections of law and morality. Here is the strict Victorian sense of the word *civilization*, used at times when supposedly civilized boys are committing, or thinking of committing, extremely uncivilized acts. The passages call into question the strength and resilience of civilization; if it can be so easily stripped away, then surely it is an artificial construct worn over humanity's natural skin of beastly, vicious propensities.

These two instances are also significant in the ways they indirectly mention savagery. The torture of Samneric is the blunter and more characteristic of the two. In this passage, Golding uses, yet again, the "black-and-green mask" of "the painted group" to clothe the boys in archetypal savage dress. Their descent into evil is measured by their resemblance to the Indians of American western films, the cannibals of old cartoons, and all the other stock savage characters.

However, in the Roger-Henry episode, Golding uses another word, perhaps intentionally, perhaps not, that seems to undermine the "savage = evil" equation that permeates the rest of the novel. He refers to civilization's dicta against harming others as "the taboo of the old life." *Taboo*, meaning "prohibited" or "prohibition," is a Tongan word, by Victorian standards a word of savage origins. It came into the language through European exploration, the sort of exploration that preceded conquest and empire, and originally it described things forbidden, or permitted only to privileged people, in Polynesian culture. The systems of taboos observed on various islands were considered by most Europeans to be primitive, superstitious, and irrational, yet the word *taboo* was, by the mid-nineteenth century, in general use in England as a term for anything prohibited or restricted. Golding's use of the word to denote the behavioral restrictions of British culture carries, therefore, a lot of imperial baggage. Here is a word that, all by itself, calls to mind the fact that every culture has a moral structure, even cultures defined by past centuries of explorers, administrators, and armchair imperialists as savage. On the one hand, the use of *taboo* seems to destroy Golding's carefully constructed symbolism by suggesting that savagery is not always evil. On the other hand, it goes beyond mere symbolism to illustrate his theme that everyone, Tongan, British, German, Indian, Kenyan, French, and American, is potentially civilized but essentially savage.

Amorality

The difference between the civilized person and the savage one, in *Lord of the Flies*, is not simply one of costume, though costume helps the reader recognize the difference, or of cruelty, though cruelty, in the novel, is savagery's natural outcome. The difference is that civilization has many rules and savagery only one: might makes right. Again and again, Englishness is equated with civilization, with rational behavior and with rules. Even Jack, initially, espouses this view, stating the need for rules after the boys adopt a parliamentary structure for their meetings. "After all, we're not savages. We're English,. . . . So we've got to do the right things" (42). Yet within hours of the making of the rules, Jack is breaking them and making exceptions, and the reinforcement of the rules by Ralph does not manage to make Piggy an equal member of the society. Repeatedly, the rules are broken. Rights are stripped away from the more helpless boys. As the island society collapses, many of the boys find themselves expressing, in one way or another, Ralph's plaintive cry, "Are we savages or what?"

Golding's answer, of course, is yes. We are savages, all of us, kept in check by the fragile safeguards of rules, customs, and the belief in something better than ourselves. Without these things, the boys revert to an older, darker way of life. They do not measure time as did the classic English literary castaway, Robinson Crusoe, by making a visible mark for each passing day, but by changes in weather (58). They choose their leader, in the end, according to physical prowess in the hunt. Eventually, they stop comparing themselves to savages and asking if they're savages. They become savages; on page 176, Golding mentions "the sniggering of the savages," the first time in the novel that this word is a flat description, not part of a question or a comparison.

In the epigraph to this chapter, taken from a newspaper interview, Golding seems to disagree with Rousseau's conclusions about the native character of *Homo sapiens*. Yet Golding is asking the same questions as Rousseau: In the absence of civilization, what are we, and what has civilization made of us?

CANNIBALS AND SLAVES: AN EARLY DEPICTION OF SAVAGERY IN BRITISH FICTION

Defoe's Robinson Crusoe, based in part on an actual marooned sailor named Alexander Selkirk, is arguably the most famous castaway in all of literature. He was so successful a character in his own time that Defoe, after writing *Robinson Crusoe* in April 1719, followed up with a second, less frequently reprinted volume in August and a sequel, *Serious Reflections*, in 1720. In the second volume of adventures, a party of Spaniards and Englishmen, together with the hero Crusoe, Crusoe's native servant Friday, and Friday's father, are hiding from a band of cannibals. Greatly outnumbered and anxious to protect themselves and their flock of goats, the party agrees on a little espionage. The resulting discoveries make for a nearly textbook example of the British view of savagery. The savage is brave, bloodthirsty, naked, brutal, strong, and in some way—in this case, by eating the enemy—beyond the pale of moral, civilized conduct.

FROM DANIEL DEFOE, *THE LIFE AND STRANGE ADVENTURES OF ROBINSON CRUSOE*, VOL. 2 (1719)

After having mused a great while on the course they should take, and beaten their brains in considering their present circumstances, they resolved at last, while it was dark, to send the old savage, Friday's father, out as a spy, to learn if possible something conserning them, what they came for, and what they intended to do. The old man readily undertook it, and stripping himself quite naked, as most of the savages were, away he went. After he had been gone an hour or two, he brings word that he had been among them undiscovered, that he found they were two parties, and of two several nations, who had war with one another, and had had a great battle in their own country, and that both sides having had several prisoners taken in the fight, they were by mere chance landed all in the same island for the devouring their prisoners, and making merry, but their coming so by chance to the same place had spoiled all their mirth; that they were in a great rage at one another, and that they were so near, that he believed they would fight again as soon as daylight began to appear; but he did not perceive that they had any notion of anybody's being on the island but themselves. He had hardly made an end of telling his story, when they could perceive, by the unusual noise they made, that the two little armies were engaged in a bloody fight.

Friday's father used all the arguments he could to persuade our people to lie close, and not be seen. He told them their safety consisted in it, and that they had nothing to do but lie still, and the savages would kill one another to their hands, and then the rest would go away; and so it was to a tittle. But it was impossible to prevail, especially upon the Englishmen, their curiosity was so importunate upon their prudentials, that they must run out and see the battle. However, they used some caution too, viz., they did not go openly just by their own dwelling, but went farther into the woods, and placed themselves to advantage, where they might securely see them manage the fight, and, as they thought, not to be seen by them; but it seems the savages did see them, as we shall find hereafter.

The battle was very fierce, and if I might believe the Englishmen, one of them said he could perceive that some of them were men of great bravery, of invincible spirit, and of great policy in guiding the fight. The battle, they said, held two hours before they could guess which party would be beaten; but then that party that was nearest our people's habilitation began to appear weakest. . . . The residue of the conquered people fled to their canoes, and got off to sea; the victors retired, and made no pursuit, or very little, but drawing themselves into a body together gave two great screaming shouts, which they supposed was by way of triumph, and so the fight ended; and the same day, about three o'clock in the afternoon, they also marched to their canoes. And thus the Spaniards had their island again free to themselves, their fright was over, and they saw no savages in several years after.

After they were all gone, the Spaniards came out of their den, and viewing the field of battle, they found about two and thirty dead men upon the spot. Some were killed with great long arrows, some of which were found sticking in their bodies; but most of them were killed with their great wooden swords, sixteen or seventeen of which they found in the field of battle, and as many bows, with a great many arrows. These swords were strange great unwieldy things, and they must be very strong men that used them. Most of those men that were killed with them had their heads mashed to pieces, as we may say, or, as we call it in English, their brains knocked out, and several their arms and legs broken; so that 't is evident they fight with inexpressible rage and fury. We found not one wounded man that was not stone dead; for either they stay by their enemy till they have quite killed him, or they carry all the wounded men, that are not quite dead, away with them.

This deliverance tamed our Englishmen for a great while. The sight had filled them with horror, and the consequences appeared terrible to the last degree, even to them, if ever they should fall into the hands of those creatures, who would not only kill them as enemies, but kill them for food, as we kill our cattle. And they professed to me that the thoughts of being eaten up like beef or mutton, though it was supposed it was not to be till they were dead, had something in it so horrible, that it nauseated their very stomachs, made them sick when they thought of it, and filled their minds with such unusual terror, that they were not themselves for some weeks after. (Part II, 56–60)

New York: The Jenson Society, 1907.

In the first volume of *Robinson Crusoe*, Defoe makes his viewpoint equally clear. Savagery—exemplified by foreign speech, nakedness, and cannibalism—is to be despised. Crusoe acquires his native servant, the first person to whom he has spoken in twenty-five years, by saving him from a rival band of cannibals. As soon as his new friend has pledged undying loyalty as repayment for his rescue, Crusoe begins civilizing him.

It never occurs to either of them to live as equals. Both of them assume that Crusoe is the master and that the native, whom Crusoe christens Friday, is the slave, and both of them feel perfectly happy in this arrangement. In fact, when Crusoe attempts to liberate Friday and send him home to his own people, Friday indicates that he would rather die than leave Crusoe. In fact, Friday would prefer that his entire people subject themselves to Crusoe's tutelage: "You teach wild mans to be good, sober, tame mans; you tell them know God, pray God, and live new life."[12] Such willing submission to the superior virtue of Christianity and tameness must have been gratifying to Defoe's English readers. Indeed, any other relationship would likely have deeply offended them.

Immediately after Friday's rescue, the two men bury their fallen enemies. Crusoe gives Friday food and a place to sleep. Friday naps for half an hour or so, and then begins his lessons in being "good, sober, [and] tame."

When he espied me, he came running to me, laying himself down again upon the ground, with all the possible signs of an humble, thankful disposition, making a many antic gestures to show it. At last he lays his head flat upon the ground, close to my foot, and sets my other foot upon his head, as he had done before, and after this made all the signs to me of subjection, servitude, and submission imaginable, to let me know he would serve me as long as he lived. I understood him in many things, and let him know I was very well pleased with him. In a little time I began to speak to him, and teach him to speak to me; and, first, I made him know his name should be Friday, which was the day I saved his life. I called him so for the memory of the time. I likewise taught him to say master, and then let him know that was to be my name. I likewise taught him to say Yes and No, and to know the meaning of them. I gave him some milk in an earthen pot, and let him see me drink it before him, and sop my bread in it; and I gave him a cake of bread to do the like, which he quickly complied with, and made signs that it was very good for him.

I kept there with him all that night; but as soon as it was day, I beckoned to him to come with me, and let him know I would give him some clothes; at which he seemed very glad, for he was stark naked. As we went by the place where he had buried the two men, he pointed exactly to the place, and showed me the marks that he had made to find them again, making signs to me that we should dig them up again, and eat them. At this I appeared very angry, expressed my abhorrence of it, made as if I would vomit at the thoughts of it, and beckoned with my hand to him to come away; which he did immediately, with great submission. (Part I, 231–32)

New York: The Jenson Society, 1907.

THE VICTORIAN PERSPECTIVE: THE BURDENS OF EMPIRE

At the end of the nineteenth century, the United States, which had already expanded its territories across the breadth of the North American continent, became, somewhat unexpectedly, an empire. Its victory in the Spanish-American War left it with several new possessions, among them the Philippines. Author Rudyard Kipling, already a well-known voice of British imperialism, welcomed the United States to its new position with the following poem. While *The White Man's Burden* was controversial, it had its enthusiastic admirers, among them the wildly expansionist Theodore Roosevelt, who approved of the sentiment if not of the poetry itself. There are few better expressions of the lofty, condescending attitude of the "civilized" imperialists toward the "savage" colonies.

RUDYARD KIPLING, *THE WHITE MAN'S BURDEN* (1899)

Take up the White Man's burden—
  Send forth the best ye breed—
Go, bind your sons to exile
  To serve your captives' need;
To wait, in heavy harness
  On fluttered folk and wild—
Your new-caught, sullen peoples,
  Half devil and half child.

Take up the White Man's burden—
  In patience to abide,
To veil the threat of terror
  And check the show of pride;
By open speech and simple,
  An hundred times made plain.
To seek another's profit,
  And work another's gain.

Take up the White Man's burden—
  The savage wars of peace—
Fill full the mouth of Famine
  And bid the sickness cease;

And when your goal is nearest
  (The end for others sought)
Watch sloth and heathen folly
  Bring all your hopes to nought!

Take up the White Man's burden—
  No iron rule of kings,
But toil of serf and sweeper—
  The tale of common things.
The ports ye shall not enter,
  The roads ye shall not tread,
Go, make them with your living,
  And mark them with your dead!

Take up the White Man's burden—
  And reap his old reward—
The blame of those ye better
  The hate of those ye guard—
The cry of hosts ye humour
  (Ah, slowly!) toward the light:—
"Why brought ye us from bondage,
  "Our loved Egyptian night?"

Take up the White Man's burden—
  Ye dare not stoop to less—
Nor call too loud on Freedom
  To cloak your weariness.
By all ye will or whisper,
  By all ye leave or do,
The silent, sullen peoples
  Shall weigh your God and you.

Take up the White Man's burden!
  Have done with childish days—
The lightly-proffered laurel,
  The easy ungrudged praise:
Comes now, to search your manhood
  Through all the thankless years,
Cold, edged with dear-bought wisdom,
  The judgment of your peers.

The Times (London), February 4, 1899, 14.

THE VICTORIAN PERSPECTIVE: EVOLUTION AND CIVILIZATION

When Darwin set sail aboard "Her Majesty's ship Beagle, a ten-gun brig, under the command of Captain Fitz Roy," in December 1831, the world was a very different place from that which exists today. Technology, obviously, was considerably more basic. Significant sections of the globe, especially in Africa and at the poles, remained uncharted and unknown to Europeans such as Darwin and his companions; indeed, the purpose of the *Beagle*'s journey "was to complete the survey of Patagonia and Tierra del Fuego."[13] Slavery was still permitted in many places, including the United States and Brazil. Though illegal in Britain, slavery would not be abolished in British colonies until 1833. The justification for slavery was usually a barely modified version of Defoe's attitude toward savages: Their behavior was unacceptable, even shocking, yet they seemed to have some human emotions and responses; by forcing them to labor on one's own behalf, one could benefit while congratulating oneself on the inevitable betterment of the savage through contact with civilization.

Even a cursory examination of nineteenth-century literature, anthropology, and political discourse reveals that non-European people were considered by European to be, at best, benighted, and, at worst, members of an entirely different species or set of species. Some clearly felt that it was no worse to enslave a dark-skinned human than to require labor and obedience from a cart horse or a hunting dog, and they felt that as long as the human was fed and sheltered and seldom beaten, it had no more right to complain of its lot than did a beast. Darwin did not fall into this camp. He was a scientist, a good scientist, and was probably willing to entertain almost any theory about humanity that accorded with the known facts, but his opposition to slavery appears to be less a matter of carefully reasoned theory than of simple empathy. After leaving Brazil aboard the *Beagle*, he wrote,

> I thank God, I shall never again visit a slave-country. To this day, if
> I hear a distant scream, it recalls with painful vividness my feelings,
> when passing a house near Pernambuco, I heard the most pitiable

moans, and could not but suspect that some poor slave was being tortured, yet knew that I was as powerless as a child to remonstrate. . . . Near Rio de Janeiro I lived opposite to an old lady, who kept screws to crush the fingers of her female slaves. . . . I have seen a little boy, six or seven years old, struck thrice with a horse-whip (before I could interfere) on his naked head, for having handed me a glass of water not quite clean; I saw his father tremble at a mere glance from his master's eye. . . . I was present when a kind-hearted man was on the point of separating for ever the men, women, and little children of a large number of families who had long lived together. . . . And these deeds are done and palliated by men, who profess to love their neighbours as themselves, who believe in God, and pray that his Will be done on earth! It makes one's blood boil, yet heart tremble, to think that we Englishmen and our American descendants, with their boastful cry of liberty, have been and are so guilty.[14]

Clearly, Darwin is no friend to the slave trade, and earlier in his voyage he meets an African-born "negro lieutenant" whom he describes as the most "civil and obliging" person he met on his trip.[15]

Yet even he cannot entirely escape the tendency to see his own society as civilized and those he visits as barbarous. He views slavery and genocide as aberrations, uncivilized conduct by civilized people. When he encounters common ground with the people of Tierra del Fuego, it is treated as a similar aberration, a surprisingly civilized characteristic of a savage people. It never really occurs to him to think of the Fuegians as civilized or himself as savage. He perpetuates stereotypes like that of "the constitutional gaiety of the negro"[16] and continually interprets the behavior of Indians in terms of his own society's morality. Of villagers near the Rio Negro, he says, "These Indians are considered civilized; but what their character may have gained by a lesser degree of ferocity, is almost counterbalanced by their entire immorality. Some of the younger men are, however, improving; they are willing to labour, and a short time since a party went on a sealing-voyage, and behaved very well. They were now enjoying the fruits of their labour, by being dressed in very gay, clean clothes, and by being very idle."[17] Here, as in the following excerpts, Darwin's notions of civilization and savagery are evident. Civilized people work hard and dress well, among other things. Savages are fierce, immoral, and lazy. Again and again in his works, violence, indolence, and drunkenness are the traits of the savage. As a great scientist, he feels compelled to note instances of these characteristics among Europeans as well as among Indians, but when he finds them among natives, he is unsurprised. When he finds these qualities among his own people, he is truly shocked and disgusted. His reaction, in other words, is the reaction of Golding's naval officer upon finding the British schoolboys gone savage (201–2).

In this first passage, Darwin describes the behavior of Spaniards and Indians at Bahia Blanca. In the second passage, he describes his first encounter with the inhabitants of Tierra del Fuego.

FROM CHARLES DARWIN, *THE VOYAGE OF H.M.S. BEAGLE* (2nd ed., 1845)

During my stay at Bahia Blanca, while waiting for the Beagle, the place was in a constant state of excitement, from rumours of wars and victories, between the troops of Rosas [the local general] and the wild Indians. One day an account came that a small party forming one of the postas [post-houses] on the line to Buenos Ayres, had been found all murdered. The next day three hundred men arrived from the Colorado, under the command of Commandant Miranda. A large portion of these men were Indians (*mansos*, or tame), belonging to the tribe of the Cacique Bernantio. They passed the night here; and it was impossible to conceive anything more wild and savage than the scene of their bivouac. Some drank till they were intoxicated; others swallowed the steaming blood of the cattle slaughtered for their suppers, and then, being sick from drunkenness, they cast it up again, and were besmeared with filth and gore. . . .

In the morning they started for the scene of the murder, with orders to follow the 'rastro,' or track, even if it led them to Chile. . . . One glance at the rastro tells these people a whole history. Supposing they examine the track of a thousand horses, they will soon guess the number of mounted ones by seeing how many have cantered; by the depth of the other impressions, whether any horses were loaded with cargoes; by the irregularity of the footsteps, how far tired; by the manner in which the food has been cooked, whether the pursued travelled in haste; by the general appearance, how long it has been since they passed. They consider a rastro of ten days or a fortnight, quite recent enough to be hunted out. . . . What other troops in the world are so independent? With the sun for their guide, mare's flesh for food, their saddle-cloths for beds,—as long as there is a little water, these men would penetrate to the end of the world.

A few days afterwards I saw another troop of these banditti-like soldiers start on an expedition against a tribe of Indians at the small Salinas, who had been betrayed by a prisoner cacique. The Spaniard who brought the orders for this expedition was a very intelligent man. He gave me an account of the last engagement at which he was present. Some Indians, who had been taken prisoners, gave information of a tribe living north of the Colorado. Two hundred soldiers were sent; and they first discovered the Indians by a cloud of dust from their horses' feet, as they chanced to be travelling. . . . The Indians, men, women, and children, were about one hundred and ten in number, and they were nearly all taken or killed, for the soldiers sabre every man. The Indians are now so terrified that they offer no resistance in a body, but each flies, neglecting even his wife and children; but when overtaken, like wild animals, they fight against any number to the last moment. One dying Indian seized with his teeth the thumb of his adversary, and allowed his own eye to be forced out sooner than relinquish his hold. Another, who was wounded, feigned death, keeping a knife ready to strike one more fatal blow. My informer said, when he was pursuing an Indian, the man cried out for mercy, at the same time that he was covertly loosing the bolas from his waist, meaning to whirl it round his head and so strike his pursuer. 'I however struck him with my sabre to the ground, and then got off my horse, and cut his throat with my knife.' This is a dark picture; but how much more shocking is the unquestionable fact, that all the women who appear above twenty years old are massacred in cold blood! When I exclaimed that this appeared rather inhuman, he answered, 'Why, what can be done? they breed so!' Every one here is fully convinced that this is the most just war, because it is against barbarians. Who would believe in this age that such atrocities could be committed in a Christian civilized country? The children of the Indians are saved, to be sold or given away as servants, or rather slaves for as long a time as the owners can make them believe themselves slaves; but I believe in their treatment there is little to complain of. . . .

. . . The warfare is too bloody to last; the Christians killing every Indian, and the Indians doing the same by the Christians. It is melancholy to trace how the Indians have given way before the Spanish invaders. . . . Not only have whole tribes been exterminated, but the remaining Indians have become more barbarous: instead of living in large villages, and being employed in the arts of fishing, as well as of the chase, they now wander about the open plains, without home or fixed occupation. (98–102)

• • •

When we came within hail, one of the four natives who were present advanced to receive us, and began to shout most vehemently, wishing to direct us where to land. When we were on shore the party looked rather alarmed, but continued talking and making gestures with great rapidity. It was without exception the most curious and interesting spectacle I ever beheld: I could not have believed how wide was the difference between savage and civilized man: it is much greater than between a wild and domesticated animal, inasmuch as in man there is a greater power of improvement. . . .

Their very attitudes were abject, and the expression of their countenances distrustful, surprised, and startled. After we had presented them with some scarlet cloth, which they immediately tied round their necks, they became good friends. This was shown by the old man patting our breasts, and making a kind of chuckling noise, as people do when feeding chickens. I walked with the old man, and this demonstration of friendship was repeated several times; it was concluded by three hard slaps, which were given me on the breast and back at the same time. He then bared his bosom for me to return the compliment, which being done, he seemed highly pleased. The language of these people, according to our notions, scarcely deserves to be called articulate. Captain Cook has compared it to a man clearing his throat, but certainly no European ever cleared his throat with so many hoarse, guttural, and clicking sounds.

They are excellent mimics: as often as we coughed or yawned, or made any odd motion, they immediately imitated us. (200–201)

New York: D. Appleton and Company, 1915.

TOPICS FOR WRITTEN OR ORAL EXPLORATION

1. To what extent do the boys in *Lord of the Flies* embody the English stereotype of savages? In what way(s) do they differ from the stereotype? What does it mean that Golding merges the savage and the civilized in the very same boys? What behavior would you define as civilized? What behavior would you define as savage?

2. The first passage from Darwin demonstrates that both the Europeans and the Indians are making use of violence, though Darwin treats the European use of it as evil (because he thinks they should know better) and the Indian use of it as savage (because it seems to him to be their natural state). Find some other accounts of early encounters between natives and explorers, in any part of the world. How do the two sides behave? How is their behavior interpreted?

3. Think about Rousseau's attempt to separate natural from artificial characteristics. What characteristics do you think are natural, or inborn, in the human species? What characteristics are added on by our cultures? Do you think that people in so-called primitive societies are any better or worse than people in industrialized societies?

4. Though Kipling's *White Man's Burden* seems dated and offensive today, it was intended as a serious commentary on race relations and, specifically, on the responsibilities of industrialized nations toward less-developed ones. Try writing a poem about relations today between races or nations. Use Kipling's rhyme scheme and meter if you like.

5. Is Golding's view of savagery abstract and philosophical (like Rousseau's), idealistic (like the popular perception of Rousseau's), imperialist, liberal, or something else? Give examples to support your conclusion.

6. When we discuss the interaction of cultures and nations today, do we still speak or think in terms of "civilized" and "savage" behavior, even if we don't use those specific words? Think of a recent conflict between cultures or nations. Did the debate about it, or the news coverage of it, assume that one side was more civilized than the other?

7. Read some other works by Kipling, such as *Kim, The Jungle Book*, or *Just So Stories*. What is his view of "savage" and/or colonial peoples in these works?

8. In 1609, Inca author Garcilaso de la Vega's *Comentarios reales* told a similar story to that of Robinson Crusoe. De la Vega recounted the ordeal of Pedro Serrano, a stranded sailor who barely survived for

three years on a miserable island and then discovered another
stranded European. They shared the chores of searching for food and
keeping their fire alight, quarreled over their respective duties, and
eventually were reconciled. How does the following passage about
their fight remind you of *Lord of the Flies?*

> Thus they lived for some time, but scarcely a day passed without their
> quarrelling, and so they came to eat apart, and all but came to blows
> (so may it be seen how great is the baseness of our passions). The
> cause of the dissension was that one said to the other that he was
> not taking good care of what was necessary to do; and this anger and
> the words that accompanied it put them out with each other and set
> them apart.[18]

9. Mary Shelley's novel *Frankenstein* can be seen as a Rousseauist fable
    in which a pure and noble savage, the monster, is perverted and
    made violent and cruel by the civilized world. Can you think of other
    stories that feature a "noble savage"? What usually happens to such
    characters?

10. Why do you think people are fascinated with the idea of wild men—
    Bigfoot, Sasquatch, the Yeti?

11. Golding uses the decay of the boys' clothing as a symbol of the decay
    of their civilization. He makes them seem more savage by making
    them appear more like stereotypical savages. How do clothes affect
    your judgment of people? Watch people for a fixed period of time—a
    day or a week—and keep a record of what they are wearing. What
    do their clothes tell you about them? Are there certain kinds of
    clothes that send stronger messages than others? Are your judgments
    based on appearance likely to be accurate?

12. In addition to describing the so-called noble savage, Rousseau also
    described what he called the social contract. Simply put, the social
    contract is the agreement (often unspoken) between people to accept
    certain rules or authorities because of the mutual benefit that results:
    I will agree to have a police force that prevents me from stealing your
    stuff, because the same police force will keep *you* from stealing *my*
    stuff. Do you think that *Lord of the Flies* is a novel about the social
    contract? Why or why not?

13. Look at how some European and American artists, such as Remington
    and Gauguin, have portrayed people considered to be "savages." Are
    the artists representing their subjects as "noble savages" or Victorian-
    style savages (demonized or caricatured)? How can you tell? What
    details or techniques reveal the artist's attitude?

NOTES

1. Jean-Jacques Rousseau, *Discourse on the Origin of Inequality* (1755; reprint, New York: Alfred A. Knopf, 1993), 44.

2. Ibid., 53.

3. Ibid., 58–59.

4. Ibid., 72–73.

5. Ibid., 76.

6. Ibid., 78.

7. Ibid., 70–71.

8. Ibid., 57.

9. *The Times* (London), Oct. 21, 1952, 6.

10. *The Times* (London), Oct. 25, 1952, 6.

11. George Orwell, "Boys' Weeklies," *A Collection of Essays* (Garden City, NY: Doubleday, 1954), 297.

12. Daniel Defoe, *The Life and Strange Adventure of Robinson Crusoe*, Part 1 (1719; reprint, New York: The Jenson Society, 1907), 255.

13. Charles Darwin, *Journal of Researches into the Natural History and Geology of the Countries Visited During the Voyage of H.M.S. Beagle Round the World*, 2nd. ed. (1854); reprint, New York, D. Appleton and Company, 1915, 1.

14. Ibid., 492–94.

15. Ibid., 73.

16. Ibid., 493.

17. Ibid., 63.

18. Roger Bartra, *The Artificial Savage: Modern Myths of the Wild Man*, trans. Christopher Follett (Ann Arbor, MI: University of Michigan Press, 1997), 124.

SUGGESTIONS FOR FURTHER READING

Bartra, Roger. *The Artificial Savage: Modern Myths of the Wild Man.* Translated by Christopher Follett. Ann Arbor, MI: University of Michigan Press, 1997.

Conrad, James. *Heart of Darkness.* 1902. Reprint. New York: Penguin, 1986.

Hergé. *Tintin: Prisoners of the Sun.* 1949. Reprint. Boston: Atlantic Monthly/ Little, Brown, 1975.

Hobbes, Thomas. *The Leviathan.* Ed. Richard Tuck. 1651. Reprint. Cambridge: Cambridge University Press, 1991.

Huxley, Aldous. *Brave New World.* 1932. Reprint. New York: Bantam, 1960.

Mead, Margaret. *Sex and Temperament in Three Primitive Societies.* 1935. Reprint. New York: Morrow Quill Paperbacks, 1980.

Rousseau, Jean-Jacques. *The Social Contract and the Discourses.* New York: Alfred A. Knopf, 1993.

3

Education

School was the unhappiest time of my life, and the worst trick it ever played on me was to pretend it was the world in miniature. For it hindered me from discovering how lovely and delightful and kind the world can be.

—E. M. Forster

If schools are what they were in my time, you'll see a great many cruel blackguard things done, and hear a deal of foul bad talk.

—Tom Brown's father, in Tom Hughes's
Tom Brown's Schooldays

An Education Timeline

1857   Thomas Hughes publishes *Tom Brown's Schooldays*. Immediately popular, it runs through 52 editions by 1892 and acquires many fans, including Alfred, Lord Tennyson and his wife, Dr. David Livingstone, Sir Alexander Arbuthnot (vice-chancellor of Calcutta University and a former Rugby boy), and Leslie Stephen.[1]

1858   Frederic William Farrar publishes *Eric, or, Little by Little*. By 1894, this sentimental novel, which features a dismal end for a boy who breaks school rules, has sold 60,000 copies.[2]

1862   Frederic William Farrar publishes *St. Winifred's, or, the World of School*. This novel, essentially a repeat of *Eric* but with a happy ending, sells 43,000 copies by 1894.[3]

1905   Horace Annesley Vachell publishes *The Hill: A Romance of Friendship*, a best-selling exploration of the intense spiritual (though not physical) love between two public school boys. Hailed as true-to-life by most readers, it goes through twenty-one editions by 1914.

1911   William Golding is born on September 19, son of a suffragist and a senior master of Marlborough Grammar School.

1917   Seventeen-year-old Alec Waugh, still smarting from the humiliation of a near-expulsion from Sherborne, writes *The Loom of Youth* in seven and a half weeks. A best-seller, it addresses the conflict between scholarship and athletics, each of which is represented by a different master. The hero is initially enamored of games but later realizes that "Games don't win battles, but brains do, and brains aren't trained on the footer field."[4]

1922   Ernest Raymond, a prep school master and World War I army chaplain educated at St. Paul's, publishes *Tell England*, a novel about the connection between public schools and World War I combat.

1930   Golding attends Oxford, starting by studying science but switching to English literature and taking his degree in 1935.

1939   Golding becomes a teacher of English and classics at Bishop Wordsworth's School in Salisbury. He will leave in 1940 to serve in the Navy during World War II.

1945   Golding returns from the war to Bishop Salisbury's school. He will be remembered by one of his pupils as untidy, an uninspired teacher, an enthusiastic sailor who taught seamanship to the school's Combined Cadet Force, a natural performer who loved acting and music, and "an observant, reflective, thoughtful man apparently brooding on problems which he did not seem to share with anyone else."[5]

1954   *Lord of the Flies*, Golding's first novel, is published on September 17.

1947   The incredibly prolific Frank Richards, whose career produced about 60 to 70 million published words, writes *Billy Bunter of Greyfriars School*. Bunter was the most memorable of a host of schoolboy characters created by Richards, who did per-

haps more than any other twentieth-century author to idealize
public school life for a non–public school audience.

1993   Golding dies on June 19.

Lord of the Flies is not usually thought of as a genre novel, and in
fact, it is difficult to pigeonhole. Despite its setting in the future,
it is not precisely science fiction. Despite the fact that murder is
committed in its pages, it is no murder mystery. Yet it is the child
of two distinct genres, each with its own forms and traditions, but
both marketed to the same audience: boys. One of the genres, the
adventure story, will be discussed in the next chapter. The other
genre is the school story, not a popular form in America, but one
with a long and sturdy history in Britain.

Stories about public schools—the British equivalent of American
private schools—abound from the mid-nineteenth century on, remaining well read for well over a century. Through novels like *Tom
Brown's Schooldays, Stalky and Co., The Longest Journey*, and
Mike, public-school graduates (known as "old boys") disseminated
the culture of Eton, Harrow, and the like, spreading an awareness
of public-school slang, manners, punishments, recreations, and
morality throughout Britain's class system. School stories were
read not only by the 3 percent of students who might actually
attend a public school, but also by middle and working-class children. An 1888 survey of boys' favorite books listed the thirty-year-
old *Tom Brown's Schooldays* in sixth place, tied with the Bible. A
similar survey in 1908 put *Tom Brown* first, with four other school
stories—*The Fifth Form at St. Dominic's, Eric, Stalky and Co.*, and
St. Winifred's—in the top twenty-four. A 1940 survey of 1,570 boys
ranked *Tom Brown* fourth among twelve-year-olds and second
among thirteen-year-olds.[6] By the time these polls were conducted,
boys could absorb public-school culture not only through novels
but through magazines as well. From the late nineteenth century,
several periodicals, including *The Boy's Own Paper, The Magnet,
The Gem, Chums*, and *The Captain*, serialized school stories in
their pages. The most popular magazines around 1940 were the
Gem, Magnet, and *Wizard*, while *The Boy's Own Paper* and *The
Captain* peaked earlier.[7] Even after World War II, the genre remained marketable, with public-school stories comprising 60 to 65
percent of boys' comics.[8]

By the early twentieth century, school stories had become largely formulaic. The classic plot, according to E. C. Mack, was as follows: "A boy enters school in some fear and trepidation, but usually with ambitions or schemes; suffers mildly or seriously at first from loneliness, the exactions of fag-masters, the discipline of masters and the regimentation of games; then makes a few friends and leads for a year or so a joyful irresponsible and sometimes rebellious life, eventually learns duty, self-reliance, responsibility and loyalty as a prefect, qualities used to put down bullying or overemphasis on athletic prowess; and finally leaves school with regret for a wider world."[9] There were variations on the theme, some books emphasizing cricket, others football, others intense attachments (sometimes sexual, sometimes platonic) between boys, others religion and morality, others academics and the humiliations meted out to small, sensitive, unathletic boys. As in American movies about high schools, where the Cheerleader, the Jock, and the Geek are instantly recognizable archetypes, the British public school novel had a cast of stock characters who could be called into service. P. G. Wodehouse mentions a few of them quite directly in *Mike* when Psmith asks Mike, "Are you the Bully, the Pride of the School, or the Boy who is Led Astray and takes to Drink in Chapter Sixteen?"[10] To Golding, and to his British audience, the traditional schoolboy characters and plots were eminently familiar, and *Lord of the Flies* can be seen as an extreme variation on the school-story theme—a school story in which the school has been removed.

This is not to say that school life is entirely absent from *Lord of the Flies*. Indeed, if any aspect of the outer world is present on the island, it is the school. The all-boy, insular community bears a strong resemblance to the populations of Britain's single-sex, endowed boarding schools. At least some of the boys have come from such schools, to judge from their infrequent references to the outside world. Ralph mentions getting hurt playing rugby (115), and rugby football is strongly associated with the public schools. He also remembers the house he lived in before being sent away to a boarding school (112). Jack, too, seems to be from such a school, since he objects to Ralph's chieftainship on the grounds that Ralph "isn't a prefect" (126). Sam and Eric discuss one of their old schoolmasters, whom they call by the nickname "Waxy" (97), and when the Lord of the Flies finally speaks to Simon, it speaks with a schoolmaster's voice (143). The recreations, prohibitions, and hierarchy of school life are very much a part of these boys' personalities. In fact, the characters mention school life more often than they mention their families. Furthermore, even when they do not specifically speak of school, their reactions to each other are conditioned by its structure and morals. Accordingly, some discussion of the nature and traditions of public school life seems appropriate.

Public schools have existed in one form or another since the Middle Ages, but until about the mid-nineteenth century, they were chaotic, brutal places indeed. Pupils tortured each other in ways that would have seemed quite familiar to Golding's characters. They gambled, drank, engaged in all sorts of sexual practices, and ran roughshod over their teachers, who had little practical authority. During the Victorian Age, however, the general moral conservatism of the nation trickled into the public schools. The prefect system was introduced to enlist the older boys in maintaining order. Religion became a stronger presence, and "games"—sports like cricket and rugby—increased in importance, eventually surpassing academic life altogether and seeming, by the turn of the century, to be almost the entire purpose of the public school. The goal was to produce not scholars but administrators, inscrutable and fearsome to their subordinates, well respected, able to lead, decent, honorable, Christian, physically courageous, and emotionally subdued. Though there were reforms, changes in emphasis, and an expansion in the number of such schools between the 1850s and the 1950s, there is a remarkable consistency in the tenor of the reflections of "old boys" through the decades.

THE TRADITION OF VIOLENCE

One of the most universal aspects of the public school experience was the giving and receiving of beatings. Corporal punishment was the chief method of enforcing discipline, and masters beat boys for a variety of offenses. The school genre is full of beating episodes: a flogging in *Eric*, canings in *Tell England*, canings over the hand in *Tom Brown*, and on and on at sickening length. Sometimes the beatings were administered on the spot, in class; sometimes they took place in private, after a lecture on one's misdeeds. George Orwell, author of *Animal Farm* and *1984*, recalled being lectured and beaten at the same time, so that the words "you dir-ty lit-tle boy" kept time with the riding crop. Afterward, he adopted the preferred attitude of all public school boys in such circumstances—cheerful nonchalance—for which he was beaten, on the spot, again, with such force that the riding crop broke.[11] Not all schools beat children frequently, but there are isolated cases of mass floggings, particularly in the nineteenth century, that make one's head reel. The worst culprits, in some cases, doled out as many as 700 blows to groups of boys in a single day, even injuring their own arms in the process.[12] Even in the twentieth century, canings created an atmosphere in which might made right and in which authority granted extreme physical powers over those ruled.

Boys needed no help transferring this moral order to their own community. Bertrand Russell, at age ten, reasoned, "The bigs hit me, so I hit the smalls; that's fair."[13] However, even if the boys needed no assistance in learning to beat each other, they were given plenty of help in the form of the prefect system. Masters, except those who really enjoyed it, seldom beat boys for minor offenses. They left this to prefects, sixth-form boys empowered to assist with discipline and to demand errand-running and custodial services from younger boys known as "fags." (Unlike the American slang term for a homosexual, the word *fag* does not, in this usage, have a sexual connotation, though romances between boys were hardly unknown in the public schools.) In its ideal form, the prefect system brought the older boys into line at the peak of their physical and rebellious powers, by investing them in the smooth running of the school; prevented boys from terrorizing their juniors without authority; and gave younger boys something to which they might aspire if they survived their early school years. This was certainly the view of Dean Frederic William Farrar, author of *Eric*, who wrote, "Any who have had personal and intimate experience of how schools work with it and without it, know what a Palladium it is of happiness and morality; how it prevents bullying, upholds manliness, is the bulwark of discipline, and makes boys more earnest and thoughtful, often at the most critical periods of their lives, by enlisting all their sympathies and interests on the side of the honourable and just."[14]

If the new prefect system was "a Palladium . . . of happiness and morality," one wonders how bad schools were beforehand. For, in practice, prefects were often no better than the bullies they were supposed to restrain. Official beatings could be doled out for the most trivial infractions of the most arcane rules. L. P. Hartley, who attended Harrow in the early twentieth century, recalled that boys could be "whopped" for "leaning too far out of the window on Sunday, letting a sixth former's fire go out when 'On Boy,' [or] walking in the middle of the High Street when not a 'blood' or with a 'blood.' "[15] Cyril Connolly recalled similarly flimsy excuses at Eton in about 1917:

> The captain of the school, Marjoribanks, . . . was a passionate beater . . . in one satisfactory evening Marjoribanks had beaten all the lower half of college. Thirty-five of us suffered. Another time we were all flogged because a boy dropped a sponge out of a window which hit a master, or we would be beaten for 'generality' which meant no specific charge except that of being 'generally uppish'. . . . We knelt on the chair, bottoms outwards, and gripped the bottom bar with our hands, stretching towards it over the back. Looking round under the chair we could see a monster rushing towards us with a cane in his hand, his face upside down and distorted. . . . The pain was acute. When it was over some other member of sixth form would say 'Good night'—it was wiser to answer.[16]

This is a system in which *Lord of the Flies'* Jack and Roger would be quite at home.

Yet these were only the official, or semi-official, beatings, the ones that came from prefects or the equivalent. It does not include the hosts of powerful boys who imposed their will on younger ones and got away with it. The attitude toward such behavior seems to have depended on whether one was a victim or perpetrator. P. G. Wodehouse, one suspects, was not bullied a great deal, to judge from his blasé description of Stone and Robinson in *Mike:*

> There was, as a matter of fact, nothing much wrong with Stone and Robinson. They were just ordinary raggers of the type found at every public school, small and large. . . . The Stones and Robinsons are the swashbucklers of the school world. They go about, loud and boisterous, with a wholehearted and cheerful indifference to other people's feelings, treading on the toes of their neighbour and shoving him off the pavement, and always with an eye wide open for any adventure. . . . Sometimes they go through their whole school career without accident. More often they run up against a snag in

the shape of some serious-minded and muscular person who objects to having his toes trodden on and being shoved off the pavement, and then they usually sober down, to the mutual advantage of themselves and the rest of the community.

. . . Small boys whom they had occasion to kick, either from pure high spirits or as a punishment for some slip from the narrow path which the ideal small boy should tread, regarded Stone and Robinson as bullies of the genuine "Eric" and "St. Winifred's" brand. Masters were rather afraid of them.[17]

Kicking small boys, shoving people off the sidewalk, and frightening teachers are apparently not enough, in Wodehouse's eyes, to constitute "much wrong." A similar boys-will-be-boys perspective is displayed in the popular school stories of the extraordinarily prolific Frank Richards, whose hundreds of tales filled the pages of such periodicals as *The Gem* and *The Magnet*. One of his serial characters is Billy Bunter, an overweight, bespectacled, food-pilfering, cowardly boy known as "The Fat Owl of the Remove." Bunter is, in appearance though not in personality, a dead ringer for Piggy, and his typical fate in Richards's stories is to serve as a satisfying whipping-boy. As one critic puts it, Bunter is "a larger-than-life embodiment of human failings, weaknesses and prejudices. His regular chastisement by beating, booting, bouncing, detention, suspension and exclusion confirms the need to check these weaknesses."[18] In other words, the symbol of restored order in one of Britain's most popular series for boys was the physical abuse of a fat kid with glasses.

The original school story, *Tom Brown's Schooldays*, actually lauds violence between boys as a means of keeping order and promoting self-discovery. East's and Tom's battle against the bully Flashman is presented as the only possible means of ending the conflict, and Hughes gives his approval to the use of regular boxing matches to let off steam. He justifies fist fights at least twice, once before Tom fights Slogger Williams, when he asks,

After all, what would life be without fighting, I should like to know? From the cradle to the grave, fighting, rightly understood, is the business, the real, highest, honestest business of every son of man. Every one who is worth his salt has his enemies, who must be beaten, be they evil thoughts and habits in himself, or spiritual wickedness in high places, or Russians, or border-ruffians, or Bill, Tom, or Harry, who will not let him live his life in quiet till he has thrashed them.

It is no good for Quakers, or any other body of men, to uplift their voices against fighting. Human nature is too strong for them, and they don't follow their own precepts. Every soul of them is doing his own piece of fighting, somehow and somewhere. The world might be a better world without fighting, for anything I know, but it wouldn't be our world; and therefore I am dead against crying peace when there is no peace, and isn't meant to be. I am as sorry as any man to see folk fighting the wrong people and the wrong things, but I'd a deal sooner see them doing that than that they should have no fight in them.[19]

After the fight, Hughes again justifies fighting and admonishes his readers to learn to box.

Boys will quarrel, and when they quarrel will sometimes fight. Fighting with fists is the natural and English way for English boys to settle their quarrels. What substitute for it is there, or ever was there, amongst any nation under the sun? What would you like to see take its place?

Learn to box, then, as you learn to play cricket and football.

Not one of you will be the worse, but very much the better, for learning to box well. Should you never have to use it in earnest, there's no exercise in the world so good for the temper, and for the muscles of the back and legs.

As to fighting, keep out of it if you can, by all means. When the time comes, if it ever should, that you have to say "Yes" or "No" to a challenge to fight, say "No" if you can—only take care you make it clear to yourselves why you say "No." . . . And if you do fight, fight it out; and don't give in while you can stand and see.[20]

Hughes, though he denounces bullying, falls solidly into the Wodehouse and Richards camp. Boys, in his view, should be tough enough to take it, whatever "it" might be. His Tom not only tolerates fagging for the older boys and being tossed in a blanket, he volunteers for it. Another of Hughes's protagonists, the budding scientist Martin, administers electric shocks to younger boys who come into his study uninvited, a premeditated and apparently habitual activity that is presented as no more than an amusing quirk. This was, in fact, the majority's mantra, both in and out of public schools, for the century preceding the publication of *Lord of the*

Flies: Boys will be boys; boys need toughening up; take it like a man; stand up for yourself; fight if you must.

Yet even Thomas Hughes recognized that not every fight was a fair one. Though he maintains that the younger boys need to learn to defend themselves, he does not condone the behavior of Flashman, an older boy (but not a prefect) who demands, against custom, that the new boys fag for him. Tom and some other boys stage a strike against Flashman and his cohorts, with violent results, and their war is seen by the narrator as a just uprising against a tyrannical oppressor.

Other "old boys" were far harsher in their condemnation of bullying. They were often the sorts of boys, like Piggy or Simon, who attracted ridicule and harassment. At times, there hardly seems to be a male British intellectual in the past century and a half who was not the victim of bullying at school. Kipling suffered it,[21] as did Frederic Farrar, author of the school novel *Eric*. James Maurice Wilson, one of Farrar's contemporaries at King William's College, recalled,

> The bullying and cruelty which we both suffered in the first two years was almost incredible. . . . I doubt whether any school could have been . . . worse. . . . The day boys only suffered from bad teaching—teaching I imagine almost as bad as it could be. But we [boarders] suffered from dirt and slovenliness, from insufficient food, from horrible bullying and indecencies indescribable. We took it all as a matter of course and never complained at home. . . . It was a lawless, dirty, degraded life, and few survived it without real damage.[22]

Robert Graves was bullied at Charterhouse, and one of E. M. Forster's schoolmates, reminiscing in the 1950s, said, "Forster? The writer? Yes, I remember him. A little cissy. We took it out of him, I can tell you."[23]

The tortures devised by boys for their schoolmates were no less creative and chilling, in their way, than those on Golding's imaginary island. Winchester boys in the 1840s used the "tin glove" treatment, in which new boys were burned on the hands with hot sticks until a grid or "glove" of blisters was raised. At Marlborough, in the 1920s, "you had to crawl along a red hot radiator singing 'clementine' and at the end 'take a face', that is have your face slapped."[24] In the 1950s, on the eve of the expulsion of a sixteen-year-old for homosexuality, "some boys made a solution of treacle and water and gave him an enema of this with a bicycle pump. The next day he had to carry his suitcase on foot from the school to the station. The route was lined with boys hurling eggs, tomatoes and filth at him."[25] Sometimes there seemed to be no end to the physical abuse.

POWER AND HUMILIATION

Yet the physical abuse did not exist in isolation. It flourished in an atmosphere of constantly exerted or threatened power that proved ideal for emotional abuse as well. Masters singled out boys for punishment and lectured them on their faults, exertions of power that were often quite justifiable but that nonetheless humiliated and embarrassed the boys. The boys, in turn, considered the masters their universal enemy and found ways of exerting their own power. They collaborated to cheat, pulled pranks, smoked, drank, swore, stole, absented themselves from campus without leave, and engaged in illicit sexual behavior. While, in the school stories, such behavior often has bitter consequences, including expulsion, ostracism, or even death, there is a certain admiration, both in fact and fiction, for the boy who breaks the rules and gets away with it. Cheating, for example, is sanctioned by the student community in Alec Waugh's *The Loom of Youth*, and Horace Vachell, author of the public school novel *The Hill*, later wrote that he and his classmates "believed that scamping of work which escaped detection and punishment was a feather in our caps."[26]

The boys also savaged each other. The fictional teacher Rickie Elliott of Forster's *Longest Journey* recalls that, during his own school days, "There was simply an atmosphere of unkindness, which no discipline can dispel. . . . Physical pain doesn't hurt—at least not what I call hurt—if a man hits you by accident or in play. But just a little tap, when you know it comes from hatred, is too terrible."[27] There were all kinds of ways and reasons that students wounded each other. A physical difference, an unpopular hobby, or homesickness could single out a boy as a likely victim. In *Tom Brown's Schooldays*, Tom teaches his young protégé, George Arthur, what to avoid:

". . . look here now, you must answer straight up when the fellows speak to you, and don't be afraid. If you're afraid, you'll get bullied. And don't you say you can sing; and don't you ever talk about home, or your mother and sisters."

Poor little Arthur looked ready to cry.
"But please," said he, "mayn't I talk about—about home to you?"
"Oh, yes, I like it. But don't talk to boys you don't know, or they'll call you home-sick, or mamma's darling, or some such stuff."[28]

Penalties for seeming weak, or for any other violation of the unspoken schoolboy code, could include anything from insults to "Coventry," a kind of peer shunning imposed by the prefects.[29] The cruelties of the system were well known to old boys and masters alike, perhaps less so to parents, since boys were supposed to keep quiet about their torments when they were at home on holidays.

GAMES

For some boys, the only consolation of the public school existence was the opportunity it afforded to play sports, chiefly cricket and rugby football. For other boys, the hegemony of games was merely another source of humiliation and discomfort, something to be endured, like the bad food and miserable hygiene that were standard elements of public school life. Regardless of a boy's attitude toward them, however, games were nearly inescapable. In the second half of the nineteenth century, they became increasingly important, surpassing academic achievement as a measure of school virtue and prowess, and eventually creating an anti-intellectual environment within the schools. The Reverend Frederick Brooke Westcott, a rugby coach at Sherborne in about the 1890s, felt that "[i]f a boy could speak at the end of a match, it was a sign of inadequate effort and he was beaten. A senior could seize, was expected to seize, a new boy's umbrella and beat a scrum of juniors till the umbrella broke."[30]

Some observers, even at the frenzied peak of games worship, could see the oddness of the emphasis on sports. J.E.C. Weldon, who attended Eton and served as headmaster of Harrow from 1885 to 1898, noted, among other oddities of schoolboy behavior, their disdain of academics, their admiration of vice or at least the appearance of vice, and their obsession with games. In his school-genre novel, *Gerald Eversley's Friendship* (1895), he wrote, "Nobody can be intimate with a community of schoolboys and not feel that a morality so absolute, yet so narrow, and in some ways so perverted, bears a certain resemblance to the morality of a savage tribe. . . . Of the achievements of the intellect, if they stand alone, public school opinion is still, as it has always been, slightly contemptuous. But strength, speed, athletic skill, quickness of eye and hand, still command universal applause among schoolboys as among savages."[31] There was no question, in Weldon's day, of whether boys would rather succeed at classwork or sports.

Games were lauded as ritual combat, as preparation for imperial service, and as tests of gentility and courage, and shirking at them was equated with both moral and physical cowardice. Physical ineptitude was considered despicable and shameful, and though this belief came to be less strongly held after World War I, and even less strongly held after World War II, its echoes can be found in the treatment of Piggy in *Lord of the Flies* and in Jack's desperation to redeem his social standing through the hunt.

ATTITUDES TOWARD THE PUBLIC SCHOOLS

The reason that the old-fashioned public school was tolerated, the reason that fathers sent their sons to schools where they themselves had been mistreated, the reason that mothers gave their sons into the keeping of strangers, was that the schools were believed to confer advantages on those who attended them. In the first place, it was believed that public schools offered boys a chance to make contact with those of their own class, or the class directly above them, giving them useful connections in business or the military after school. Secondly, it was believed by many that boys were simply, basically, bad to begin with, a "fact" that was taken for granted and used, depending on the perspective of the author, to justify the existence of public schools (to beat some sense into them before they grew up bad) or to condemn public schools (as being likely to worsen a bad situation).

Sometimes, authors painted a relatively balanced portrait of the British boy. *The Atheneum*, in a review of Rudyard Kipling's school novel *Stalky and Co.*, described the British boy's "infinite capacity for fun, his finite capacity for subordination, his coarseness in word and act, modified by an ultra-sensitive delicacy of feeling in certain directions."[32] Yet other writers were less flattering. H. G. Wells called Stalky and his fictional friends "mucky little sadists." E. M. Forster, through the character Rickie Elliott in *Longest Journey*, declares that "boys do hate one another: I remember it and see it again. They can make strong isolated friendships, but of general good fellowship they haven't a notion." Frederic William Farrar speculated "that there must be in boyhood a pseudo-instinctive cruelty . . . which no amount of civilization can entirely repress," and Farrar's son Reginald wrote in 1904 that "the clever modern public-school boy is too often an amateur of cynicism, [who] . . . detests emotion, sneers at it in others, and stoically suppresses it in himself." Horace Vachell called "the ordinary boy" "amoral." Cyril Connolly, brutally honest, describes himself at Eton from 1918 to 1922 as "dirty, inky, miserable, untidy, a bad fag, a coward at games, lazy at work, unpopular with my masters and superiors, anxious to curry favour and bully when I dared."[33] Even Thomas Hughes, whose descriptions of boyish shouting, pea-shooting, and bodily risk-taking have the tone of a knowing chuckle, sees most boys as fundamentally mindless. "Boys follow one another in herds like sheep," he writes in *Tom Brown*, "for good or evil; they hate thinking, and have rarely any settled principles. Every school, indeed, has its own traditionary standard of right and wrong, which cannot be transgressed with impunity. . . . This standard is ever varying, though it changes only slowly, and little by little; and . . . it is the leading boys for the time being who give the tone to all the rest."[34] In this, Hughes was very much like his mentor and hero, Dr. Arnold, headmaster of Rugby, who loathed "the evil of boy nature" and felt that boys needed a great deal of active help to overcome their natural inclinations. "My object will be," wrote Arnold, "if possible, to form Christian men, for Christian boys I can scarcely hope to make. I mean that, from the naturally imperfect state of boyhood, they are not susceptible of Christian principles." If boys were evil, mean, lazy, cowardly, and unchristian, went some people's arguments, then any lawful means must be used to form them into civilized men.

In the popular mind, the public schools succeeded in turning out civilized men, unintellectual perhaps, but decent and presentable. Those boys who had been reasonably well liked and successful at school certainly agreed with this view. Alec Waugh, brother of Evelyn Waugh, adored his public school for all of the most obvious reasons: "I was the kind of boy who gets most out of a public school. I loved cricket and football and was reasonably good at them. I was in the first XV and my last summer headed the batting averages. My father had lit in me a love of poetry and an interest in history and the classics. More often than not I went into the class-room looking forward to the hour that lay ahead. I enjoyed the whole competitive drama of school life—the cups and caps and form promotions."[35] In his classic public school novel *The Loom of Youth*, Waugh praised the system, though he mentions, as so many authors do, the instinctive, mindless nature of the schoolboy:

> The average person comes through all right. He is selfish, easy-going, pleasure-loving, absolutely without conscience, for the simple reason that he never thinks. . . . Very few Public School men ever do a mean thing to their friends. And for a system that produces such a spirit there is something to be said after all.

He qualifies this judgment immediately afterward, however, by warning that "for a boy with a personality school is very dangerous."[36] J.E.C. Weldon came to a similar conclusion in *Gerald Eversley's Friendship*, attributing to schoolboys a "lack of sympathy—nay the positive indignation and contempt—with which they regard anything like eccentricity or individualism. . . . Far stricter, and enforced by far more terrible penalties than the rules which masters make for boys, are the rules which boys make for themselves and for each other. . . . There is no reason to deny that the public school system is good for the majority of boys. But it has its victims."[37] This is one view of the public schools that crops up repeatedly: They are very good for the majority and terrible for a small minority of boys.

Another view, held by many old boys and to a large extent by the general British public, was less qualified in its enthusiasm. The Reverend T. L. Papillon considered the public school graduate barely literate but possessed of "something beyond all price, a manly, straightforward character, a scorn of lying and meanness, habits of obedience and command, and a fearless courage. Thus equipped, he goes into the world, and bears a man's part in subduing the earth, ruling its wild folk and building up the Empire."[38] There was a near-universal consensus that the public schools produced leaders, men who could administer colonies around the world or serve in government at home. G.W.E. Russell, a Liberal Member of Parliament and a Harrow "old boy" wrote of his alma mater that "[i]t was there that one first realized one's own capacities, great or small; first felt the promptings of honourable ambition; first dreamed of unselfish efforts for the service of others; first learned to take pride in membership of a body."[39] That particularly successful old boys should attribute their eminence to their schooling is not surprising; what is surprising is the degree to which this rosy view of the public schools was held by people who had never attended one and whose children and grandchildren would likely never attend one. For these people, it was school stories in print and in the movies, depicting the comic adventures of Billy Bunter and Tom Brown, sentimentalizing Mr. Chips and frail George Arthur, and praising the cleverness of Stalky and Psmith, that perpetuated the haloed image of public school life.

In contrast to the popular view, there was a minority intellectual view of the public schools, fueled chiefly by the sensitive, creative boys who were the system's preferred victims, and who often tended to grow up and write books about how miserable they had been in school. Critics of the system blamed the schools for promoting bullying, ignorance, snobbery, conformity, homosexuality, and an outdated classical curriculum. W. H. Auden compared his school to "a Fascist state,"[40] and the high culture, especially after World War I, tended to agree with him, even though popular culture did not.

A widely held belief in the ideal of the public school boy persisted for decades. There is no better evidence for this phenomenon than the continued popularity of Frank Richards's school stories well into the 1940s. The stories perpetuated an inaccurate and dated view of public schools, but it was a view that the public liked. Preteen and teenage boys gobbled up stories in which adolescent aristocrats excelled on pristine cricket fields, the sun never set on the empire, littluns did the dirty work, prefects ruled wisely, the school won all the important matches, only rotters got beaten up unrevenged, and brave little boys rose through the ranks to maturity as England's future leaders. A public school eulogy for an old boy, a Boer War hero, in Vachell's novel *The Hill*, sums up what impossible perfection was expected of public school boys in the common mind:

> To die young, clean, and ardent; to die swiftly, in perfect health; to
> die saving others from death, or—worse—disgrace; to die scaling

heights; to die and to carry with you into the fuller, ampler life beyond, untainted hopes and aspirations, unembittered memories, all the freshness and gladness of May—is not that cause for joy rather than sorrow. I say—yes. . . . Better death, a thousand times, than gradual decay of mind and spirit; better death than faithlessness, indifference and uncleanness.[41]

Such are the beliefs, perhaps, of the naval officer who lands on a tropical island to find a host of dirty, half-naked English boys who have spent their time killing each other and defecating on the beach. Would he agree with the judgment that death is better far than "faithlessness, indifference and uncleanness"?

Against this literary background, the behavior of the boys in *Lord of the Flies* is doubly horrific. The "prefects," Ralph and Jack, battle each other to the death, permit the most extreme forms of bullying, and scrabble for top rank only to realize that there is no empire left to rule. *Lord of the Flies* is, in fact, less closely related to *Tom Brown* and *The Gem* than to the high-culture tradition of novels that sided with the weak, studious, artistic "cissy" and emphasized the shadowy, brutal aspects of public school life. Forster's characters would probably have been far less shocked and surprised than those of Hughes or Wodehouse by the pig's head buzzing with flies on a lonely island mountaintop. Nonetheless, in its atmosphere of sanctioned violence, its contempt for the intellectual, its worship of physical prowess, its widespread moral cowardice, its inertia, its laziness, and its avoidance of displays of emotion, Golding's island community is perfectly consistent with fictional public school populations from *Tom Brown* on.

Over the decades, the British public schools have been blamed or credited for numerous events and trends, including the cult of the amateur, the maintenance of the empire, the loss of the empire, the outcomes of World Wars I and II, and the decline of Britain's industrial base. However, given that only a small percentage of children ever attended these schools, it is important to remember that it was not simply the schools that affected the national character, but the idea of the schools and their product. The myth of the public school and its boys was at least as powerful as the reality.

A Public School Glossary

Bloods	The fashionable, popular boys in a school
Dormitory	Sleeping quarters shared by several boys
Fag	Young boy required to run errands for older boys
Form	A class or academic grouping according to ability. Typically, the sixth form is the highest; when further distinctions of ability are necessary, the forms are broken into upper and lower levels, e.g., "upper fourth" or "lower fifth."
House	A residential division within a school, supervised by a house master and often competing with other houses in sports and academics
Master	A teacher
Prefect	An older student, usually a sixth-former, empowered with certain disciplinary and supervisory powers
Ragging	Playing practical jokes or otherwise annoying one's peers and masters
Rotter	A mean, unlikeable boy
Study	A special room, usually shared by at least two boys, for schoolwork and recreation, distinct from the living quarters in the dormitories

THE SCHOOLBOY ARCHETYPE: TOM BROWN

First published in 1857, *Tom Brown's Schooldays* is the grandfather of the public school genre. Relying heavily on the author's years at the Britain's Rugby school (1833–1842), the novel painted a nostalgic portrait of the school under the hand of reforming headmaster Dr. Thomas Arnold. *Tom Brown* remained a schoolboy favorite for decades, shaping children's expectations of school life long after the conditions it described were out of date. For many boys too poor to attend a school like Rugby, *Tom Brown* and books like it shaped their ideas about public schools for life.

The novel's hero, Tom, is typical of the genre's protagonists: brave, good at sports, willing to fight to preserve his privileges or honor, not brilliant academically, rather more lazy than not, loyal, outdoorsy, and, for most of the book, irresponsible. The novel charts his entire career at Rugby and, though it includes many small episodes of mischief and many characters of relatively minor importance, spends most of its time describing two relationships: Tom's quarrels with Flashman (an arrogant older boy who, though not in the sixth form, claims the sixth form privilege of having younger boys fag for him) and Tom's friendship with a younger boy, George Arthur, a frail, pious, bookish fellow placed in Tom's care in the belief that looking out for such a boy will make Tom more mature and responsible. The pairing has the desired effect, and the final outcome of the friendship, Arthur's death during an epidemic, makes Tom even more thoughtful and religious.

Tom, like Adair in *Mike*, is a nearly ideal public school boy, embodying the national impression of what such a boy ought to be like. As such, he makes a good window into the basics of public school life, such as fagging, fighting, bullying, cheating, and the like. It is worth comparing the likable, reasonably popular, but not too bright Tom to Golding's Ralph, for Tom succeeds at leadership where Ralph fails. Similarly, the aggressive Flashman, whose worst faults stem from a sense of injured pride, corresponds closely to Jack.

The first excerpt illustrates the principle of fagging.

The second excerpt details the war between Flashman and the younger boys, led by Tom. This occurs at a point when the sixth-formers are all incapable of maintaining order, and Flashman and his friends impose their own tyrannical rule. Particular attention should be paid to the parallels between Flashman and Jack and between Flashman and Roger. Note not only the similarity of their behavior and motivation but also the narrator's casual attitude toward the episode. There is none of the ominous tone of *Lord of the Flies*. Whereas Golding draws attention to boys' behavior and commands the reader to shudder at human nature, Hughes describes bullying, fighting, and intimidation as part of a glorious adventure.

FROM THOMAS HUGHES, *TOM BROWN'S SCHOOLDAYS* (1857)

In the house . . . all went well. The end of the half-year was drawing near, which kept everybody in a good humour, and the house was ruled well and strongly by [the praepostors, or prefects] Warner and Brooke. True, the general system was rough and hard, and there was bullying in nooks and corners,—bad signs for the future; but it never got farther, or dared show itself openly, stalking about the passages and hall and bedrooms, and making the life of the small boys a continual fear.

Tom, as a new boy, was of right excused fagging for the first month, but in his enthusiasm for his new life this privilege hardly pleased him; and East and others of his young friends discovering this, kindly allowed him to indulge his fancy, and take their turns at night fagging and cleaning studies. These were the principal duties of the fags in the house. From supper until nine o'clock, three fags taken in order stood in the passages, and answered any praepostor who called "Fag," racing to the door, the last comer having to do the work. This consisted generally of going to the buttery for beer and bread and cheese (for the great men did not sup with the rest, but had each his own allowance in his study or the fifth-form room), cleaning candlesticks and putting in new candles, toasting cheese, bottling beer, and carrying messages about the house; and Tom, in the first blush of his hero-worship, felt it a high privilege to receive orders from and be the bearer of the supper of old Brooke. And besides this night-work, each praepostor had three or four fags specially allotted to him, of whom he was supposed to be the guide, philosopher, and friend, and who in return for these good offices had to clean out his study every morning by turns, directly after first lesson and before he returned from breakfast. (140–41)

• • •

"Down with the tyrants!" cried East; "I'm all for law and order, and hurra for a revolution."

"I shouldn't mind if it were only for young Brooke, now," said Tom, "he's such a good-hearted, gentlemanly fellow, and ought to be in the sixth; I'd do anything for him. But that blackguard Flashman, who never speaks to one without a kick or an oath—"

"The cowardly brute," broke in East, "how I hate him! And he knows it too; he knows that you and I think him a coward. What a bore that he's got a study in this passage! Don't you hear them now at supper in his den? Brandy punch going, I'll bet. I wish the Doctor would come out and catch him. We must change our study as soon as we can."

"Change or no change, I'll never fag for him again," said Tom, thumping the table.

"Fa-a-a-ag," sounded along the passage from Flashman's study. The two boys looked at one another in silence. It had struck nine, so the regular night-fags had left duty, and they were the nearest to the supper-party. . . .

"Fa-a-a-ag," again. No answer.

"Here, Brown! East! you cursed young skulks," roared out Flashman, coming to his open door; "I know you're in. No shirking!"

Tom stole to their door and drew the bolts as noiselessly as he could; East blew out the candle. . . .

In another minute they heard the supper-party turn out and come down the passage to their door. They held their breaths and heard whispering, of which they only made out Flashman's words, "I know the young brutes are in."

Then came summonses to open, which being unanswered, the assault commenced. Luckily the door was a good, strong oak one, and resisted the united weight of Flashman's party. . . .

Then came attacks on particular panels, one of which at last gave way to the repeated kicks. But it broke inwards, and the broken piece got jammed across (the door being lined with green-baize), and couldn't easily be removed from outside; and the besieged, scorning further concealment, strengthened their defences by pressing the end of their sofa against the door. So, after one or two more ineffectual efforts, Flashman and Co. retired, vowing vengeance in no mild terms.

The first danger over, it only remained for the besieged to effect a safe retreat, as it was now near bedtime. They listened intently, and heard the supper-party resettle themselves, and then gently drew back first one bolt and then the other. Presently the convivial noises began again steadily. "Now, then, stand by for a run," said East, throwing the door wide open and rushing into the passage, closely followed by Tom. They were too quick to be caught; but Flashman was on the look-out, and sent an empty pickle-jar whizzing after them, which narrowly missed Tom's head, and broke into twenty pieces at the end of the passage. "He wouldn't mind killing one if he wasn't caught," said East, as they turned the corner.(164–66)

• • •

. . . [T]he morning after the siege the storm burst upon the rebels in all its violence. Flashman laid wait, and caught Tom before second lesson, and receiving a point blank "No" when told to fetch his hat, seized him and twisted his arm, and went through the other methods of torture in use. "He couldn't make me cry, though," as Tom said triumphantly to the rest of the rebels, "and I kicked his shins well, I know." And soon it crept out that a lot of the fags were in league, and Flashman excited his associates to join him in bringing the young vagabonds to their senses; and the house was filled with constant chasings and sieges and lickings of all sorts; and in return the bullies' beds were pulled to pieces and drenched with water, and their names written up on the walls with every insulting epithet which the fag invention could furnish. The war in short raged fiercely; but soon, as Diggs had told them, all the better fellows in the fifth gave up trying to fag them, and public feeling began to set against Flashman and his two or three intimates, and they were obliged to keep their doings secret, but being thorough bad fellows, missed no opportunity of torturing in private. Flashman was an adept in all ways, but above all in the power of saying cutting and cruel things, and could often bring tears to the eyes of boys in this way, which all the thrashings in the world wouldn't have wrung from them. . . .

The storm had cleared the air for the rest of the house, . . . but an angry dark spot of thunder-cloud still hung over the end of the passage where Flashman's study and that of East and Tom lay.

He felt that they had been the first rebels, and that the rebellion had been to a great extent successful; but what above all stirred the hatred and bitterness of his heart against them was, that in the frequent collisions which there had been of late, they had openly called him coward and sneak,—the taunts were too true to be forgiven. While he was in the act of thrashing them, they would roar out instances of his funking at football or shirking some encounter with a lout of half his own size. These things were all well enough known in the house, but to have his disgrace shouted out by small boys, to feel that they despised him, to be unable to silence them by any amount of torture, and to see the open laugh and sneer of his own associates . . . made him beside himself. Come what might, he would make those boys' lives miserable. (170–71)

New York: Thomas Y. Crowell, 1890.

FIGHTING FOR RESPECT

In P. G. Wodehouse's classic school story *Mike*, boys have three chief ways of settling problems: wit, sports, and violence. Since only one of the boys, Psmith, is witty enough to make words his weapon of choice, and since not every boy can shine at cricket or football, fists are called into play quite often. Wodehouse's boys consider it perfectly logical and acceptable to bully those younger and smaller than themselves. In moments of crisis, boys who stand up for themselves prevail. Boys who employ a little trickery or strategy to gain an advantage over their opponents also do well and are respected by their comrades for their ingenuity. Refusal to fight would be disastrous in this community, resulting in a loss of both privileges and the esteem of one's peers; the kind of restraint (or hesitation) shown by Ralph in *Lord of the Flies* would win him no points with Wodehouse. Little wonder that the boys on the island, coming from this sort of culture, gradually lose respect for Ralph as he fails, repeatedly, to demonstrate his dominance over Jack.

In the second half of *Mike*, Wodehouse's heroes, Mike Jackson and Psmith (pronounced "Smith"), meet at a public school, Sedleigh, to which each has been banished in the equivalent of his senior year. They have been assigned to the same "house"—that is, to a particular unit within the school where boys sleep and study, governed by a house master. On their first day, still getting their bearings, they must stake out territory: a dormitory for sleeping and a separate study for doing schoolwork. Psmith in particular is unwilling to settle for what would normally fall to new boys, so he picks out one of the best studies in his new house and determines to make it his by a combination of guile and force. First he overwhelms the rightful proprietor, whom he calls "an insignificant-looking little weed," with a barrage of double-talk. Then he insinuates himself into a teacher's good graces and gets official sanction for his theft. Finally he defends his conquest, with Mike's help, in a battle against the rightful owner and some cohorts, who stage a nighttime ambush. Psmith's escapades are always dealt with in a jolly manner that indicates approval for his superior intellect and strength and the attitude that he deserves whatever he can wrest away from others. Wodehouse thus, in a comic tone, deals with the same sort of jockeying for status that Golding treats with deadly seriousness.

In the following excerpt, the captain of the cricket team, Adair, deals with a rebellion in his ranks. Two of his players, Stone and Robinson, have failed to appear at a special early morning practice. An important match is due to take place soon, and Adair feels that the team needs some extra preparation. Stone and Robinson would rather sleep in. If Adair yields the point, he knows that other boys will stop coming to the practices as well. The stakes in this case are much lower than in *Lord of the Flies*, but the issue is as much a test of Adair's leadership abilities as the questions of fire and hunting are of Ralph's. Adair, unlike Ralph, settles the matter with a fight.

FROM P. G. WODEHOUSE, *MIKE* (1909)

Many captains might have passed the thing over. To take it for granted that the missing pair had overslept themselves would have been a safe and convenient way out of the difficulty. But Adair was not the sort of person who seeks for safe and convenient ways out of difficulties. He never shirked anything, physical or moral.

He resolved to interview the absentees.

It was not until after school that an opportunity offered itself. He went across to Outwood's and found the two non-starters in the senior day-room, engaged in the intellectual pursuit of kicking the wall and marking the height of each kick with chalk. Adair's entrance coincided with a record effort by Stone, which caused the kicker to overbalance and stagger backwards against the captain.

"Sorry," said Stone. "Hullo, Adair!"

"Don't mention it. Why weren't you two at fielding-practice this morning?"

Robinson, who left the lead to Stone in all matters, said nothing. Stone spoke.

"We didn't turn up," he said.

"I know you didn't. Why not?"

Stone had rehearsed this scene in his mind, and he spoke with the coolness which comes from rehearsal.

"We decided not to."

"Oh?"

"Yes. We came to the conclusion that we hadn't any use for early-morning fielding."

Adair's manner became ominously calm.

"You were rather fed-up, I suppose?"

"That's just the word."

"Sorry it bored you."

"It didn't. We didn't give it the chance to."

Robinson laughed appreciatively. . . .

"It's no good making a row about it, Adair. You must see that you can't do anything. Of course, you can kick us out of the team, if you like, but we don't care if you do. . . ."

. . . "What are you going to do? Kick us out?"

"No."

"Good. I thought you'd see it was no good making a beastly row. We'll play for the school all right. There's no earthly need for us to turn out for fielding-practice before breakfast."

"You don't think there is? You may be right. All the same, you're going to tomorrow morning."

"What!"

"Six sharp. Don't be late."

"Don't be as ass, Adair. We've told you we aren't going to." . . .

"You've quite made up your minds?"

"Yes," said Stone.

"Right," said Adair quietly, and knocked him down.

He was up again in a moment. Adair had pushed the table back, and was standing in the middle of the open space.

"You cad," said Stone. "I wasn't ready."

"Well, you are now. Shall we go on?"

Stone dashed in without a word, and for a few moments the two might have seemed evenly matched to a not too intelligent spectator. But science tells, even in a confined space. Adair was smaller and lighter than Stone, but he was cooler and quicker, and he knew more about the game. His blow was always home a fraction of a second sooner than his opponent's. At the end of a minute Stone was on the floor again. . . .

"Will ten past six suit you for fielding-practice tomorrow?" said Adair.

"All right," said Stone.

"Thanks. How about you, Robinson?"

Robinson had been a petrified spectator . . . and it did not take him long to make up his mind. He was not altogether a coward. In different circumstances he might have put up a respectable show. But it takes a more than ordinarily courageous person to embark on a fight which he knows must end in his destruction. Robinson knew that he was nothing like a match even for Stone, and Adair had disposed of Stone in a little over one minute. It seemed to Robinson that neither pleasure nor profit was likely to come from an encounter with Adair.

"All right," he said hastily, "I'll turn up." (147–50)

London: Adam and Charles Black, 1909.

BEATINGS AND TORMENTS

John Betjeman's long, autobiographical poem *Summoned by Bells* describes his school days, first at a private school during World War I, and then at Marlborough, a prominent public school. Betjeman's memoir is unusual in being expressed in verse, but it is all too typical in its description of schoolboy life. There are friendships and simple pleasures in this world, but also profound fear and humiliation. There are beatings by masters and by other boys, often for mysterious and arbitrary reasons. In the first excerpt, Betjeman is beaten by a private school teacher, Gerald Haynes, for an offense he did not even commit. Note the way that the beating is treated almost as a rite of passage, a path to the respect of peers and superiors. In the second excerpt, Betjeman is beaten by the older boys—four captains and twelve friends known as "Big Fire" for their privileged places in comfortable chairs near the fire—at Marlborough. In the third excerpt, a boy named Angus is "basketed" for an offense unknown to Betjeman; for an entire afternoon, it is common knowledge throughout the school that the punishment is to take place, yet no one bothers to alert the intended victim. Each boy is simply glad that he himself is not the target.

JOHN BETJEMAN, *SUMMONED BY BELLS* (1960)

A gym-shoe in his hand, he stood about
Waiting for misdemeanors—then he'd pounce:
"Who's talking there?" The dormitory quailed.
"Who's talking?" Then, though innocent myself,
A schoolboy hero to the dorm at last,
Bravely I answered, "Please, sir, it was me."
"All right. Bend over." A resounding three
From the strong gym-shoe brought a gulp of pain.
"I liked the way you took that beating, John.
Reckon yourself henceforth a gentleman." (65)

• • •

Upper School captains had the power to beat:
Maximum six strokes, usually three.
My frequent crime was far too many books,
So that my desk lid would not shut at all:
"Come to Big Fire then, Betjeman, after prep."
I tried to concentrate on delicate points—
Ut, whether final or consecutive?
(Oh happy private-school days when I knew!)—
While all the time I thought of pain to come.
Swift after prep all raced towards "Big Fire,"
Giving the captain space to swing his cane:
"*One*,"they would shout and downward came the blow;
"*Two*" (rather louder); then, exultant, "*Three*!"
And some in ecstasy would bellow "*Four*."
These casual beatings brought us no disgrace,
Rather a kind of glory. In the dorm,
Comparing bruises, other boys could show
Far worse ones that the beaks and prefects made. (86–87)

• • •

Fellows walked past him trying to make it look
As if they didn't know his coming fate,
Though the boy's body called "Unclean! Unclean!"
And all of us felt goody-goody-good,
Nice wholesome boys who never sinned at all.
At ten to seven "Big Fire" came marching in
Unsmiling, while the captains stayed outside
(For this was "Unofficial"). Twelve to one:
What chance had Angus? They surrounded him,
Pulled off his coat and trousers, socks and shoes
And, wretched in his shirt, they hoisted him
Into the huge waste-paper basket; then
Poured ink and treacle on his head. With ropes
They strung the basket up among the beams,
And as he soared I only saw his eyes
Look through the slats at us who watched below.
Seven. "It's prep." They let the basket down
And Angus struggled out. "Left! Right! Left! Right!"
We stamped and called as, stained and pale, he strode
Down the long alley-way between the desks,
Holding his trousers, coat and pointed shoes.
"You're for it next," said H. J. Anderson.

"I'm not." "You are. I've heard." So all that term
And three terms afterwards I crept about,
Avoiding public gaze. (89)

London: John Murray, 1989.

JAPANESE SCHOOL CULTURE

If we assume that a school's rules and environment affect student behavior and personality, it would be advisable to look at a non-British school culture for the sake of contrast. In this interview, Noriko M——, a Japanese woman, looks at her own school environment as it existed in about 1972 to 1978. Like the British public school system, the Japanese schools allowed students a great deal of liberty as long as the students recognized the absolute authority of teachers. Unlike the British schools, however, which used beatings by peers and teachers to impose authority, the Japanese schools used academic competition and potential embarrassment to keep order. Another difference was in the degree of parental involvement. In British boarding schools, parents were by definition absent from day-to-day school decisions and discipline. In Japan, however, parents monitored their children's progress more closely. Ms. M—— discussed the fact that parents tended to believe teachers rather than their own children and recalled hearing of a recent case in which a boy with chronic discipline problems was actually killed by his father. The result is that, in Japanese schools, authority was less to be evaded or circumvented than avoided altogether, with constant self-censorship and self-monitoring preventing students from breaking the rules at all. Conflicts, which tended in the British schools to be external, were thus internalized in the Japanese system.

FROM AN INTERVIEW WITH NORIKO M——, "JAPANESE
SCHOOL CULTURE" (SEPTEMBER 9, 1999)

KO: The first question I'd like to ask is what the students' relationship with the teachers was. In other words, did you think of them as the enemy or did you think of them as—

NM: It all depends. Depending on what kind of teacher. But you can't really say things . . . to the teacher.

KO: What do you mean?

NM: It's seniority and respect. So . . . you can't talk back.

KO: What would be considered talking back? What's something that might be considered disrespectful?

NM: Well, it's kind of hard to say, but maybe, [if the] teacher makes a mistake, [you] can't really . . . correct them in front of the class.

KO: Would you go to them after class?

NM: Yes, and—*indicate*—*very nicely* . . .

KO: What would be the disciplinary consequence if a student, for example, cheated on a test or did talk back to the teacher?

NM: You know, I really *don't know*, because they didn't do it. I have no recollection, because—

KO: Nobody that you know of ever did that?

NM: Not really.

KO: Why do you think that is?

NM: Because they all understood what's going to happen, or, you know, they will be shunned . . .

KO: Shunned by the other students?

NM: No, by the teachers . . . the grade is very important, you know? And the grading system in Japan is a little different from here. You have 1 to 5; 1 is the lowest, and 5 is the highest. You have certain numbers of people who can be in front. So—

KO: So it's . . . a percentage of the people who can get fives?

NM: Yes. So even though all the classmates got 100, someone will get 1. . . . If you get fives, you can go to college. . . . To get into high school, we needed to pass an exam. High school is not mandatory. . . . Well, to get in a good high school, you have to study in junior high, so, if you make a mistake, meaning, talk back to the teacher, [you would be penalized]. . . . At that time, the ranking [of students' scores] was on the board, one to a hundred, each test.

KO: So the consequences if you broke a rule were in your grades, or you feared they would be in your grades.

NM: . . . Those who don't want to go to college or don't want to go to a good school, they did a lot of things and teachers don't really care, because they know those students won't get a higher education.

KO: So they just kind of let those students do what they wanted?

NM: Yes. Of course, they have to go back to the teacher and—we called it *sekkyo*—which is, like, teacher will tell you why you were not good, and what you should do*—

KO: A lecture?

NM: Yeah.

KO: Was there ever any corporal punishment?

NM: Not in my era, but . . . my father, maybe in third grade, was [forced to stand] outside with buckets, holding [them up] . . . †

KO: Were there . . . a lot of extracurricular activities?

NM: We did have a lot of after-school activities. . . . Volleyball, softball, mostly physical things.

KO: Were sports important?

NM: Yes, or music . . . because if you do very well, you can go to a better college, you know? . . .

KO: If you had had a problem with another student, a personal problem or an academic problem, what would you have done to resolve that?

NM: Nothing.

KO: Nothing.

NM: Just—[kept it] inside. In your self. . . . That's mostly the case. That's probably why the suicide rate is so high in Japan.

KO: Would a boy have done the same thing?

NM: Yes, I think so.

---

*Later in the interview, Ms. M—— indicated that a *sekkyo* might involve a roomful of teachers watching as the unruly student was confronted by one faculty member. The student was thus made aware that all the teachers knew of his or her unacceptable behavior.

†Later, she remembered that in her junior high school, there were a few instances in which misbehaving students had to stand in the back of the classroom for several minutes as a punishment.

TOPICS FOR WRITTEN OR ORAL EXPLORATION

1. Which of the boys in *Lord of the Flies* knew each other before landing on the island? Does their previous acquaintance make a difference in their loyalties and behavior?

2. If all the boys had come from the same school, do you think the outcome would have been different?

3. Describe a time in your own life when you witnessed or participated in an act of cruelty. Did it happen at school?

4. If there were no grownups in the school today, what would you do? What do you think everyone else would do?

5. Would there be a different outcome if we put members of a non-British society on the *Lord of the Flies* island? What do you think would happen with American children? Japanese children?

6. Why do you think the *Lord of the Flies* boys mention their school lives more than their home lives?

7. Ask your parents or grandparents about school bullying and teasing in their day. Did they have it worse or better than you?

8. You have read above about nineteenth and early-twentieth-century British public school attitudes toward cheating, practical jokes, schoolwork, sports, bullying, and personal status within the school. In which respects do you think your school's attitudes are similar? In which respects are they different?

9. Many of the Victorian moralists who wrote school stories believed that one small dishonorable act, such as telling a lie to protect oneself from punishment, could lead to more and more serious moral crimes. Do you agree with this position? Do you think Golding agrees with this position? Give examples to support your views.

10. Think about your own school culture. How would you describe your school's rituals, traditions, power structure, anxieties, discipline, and rewards to someone from a different culture? How does your school affect the sort of person you are?

11. Read the excerpt about Flashman from *Tom Brown's Schooldays*. Why does Flashman's tyranny fail while Jack's succeeds?

12. Several authors, writing about the public school experience, have pointed out that verbal attacks often hurt worse than the physical ones. Do you agree?

NOTES

1. Jeffrey Richards. *Happiest Days: The Public Schools in English Fiction* (Manchester, UK: Manchester University Press, 1988), 54–55.

2. Ibid., 88.

3. Ibid.

4. Alec Waugh, *The Loom of Youth* (1917), quoted in Richards, *Happiest Days*, 235.

5. Anthony Barrett, "Memories of Golding as a Schoolmaster," *William Golding: The Man and His Books*, ed. John Carey. (London: Faber and Faber, 1986), 27–29.

6. Richards, *Happiest Days*, 2, 60, 88.

7. Ibid., 110–11.

8. Jonathan Gathorne-Hardy, *The Old School Tie: The Phenomenon of the English Public School* (New York: Viking, 1977), 219.

9. E. C. Mack, *Public Schools and British Opinion Since 1860* (1941), pp. 201–2, quoted in Richards, *Happiest Days*, p. 15.

10. P. G. Wodehouse, *Mike* (London: Adam and Charles Black, 1909), p. 179.

11. George Orwell, "Such, Such Were the Joys . . ." (1950), in *A Collection of Essays* (New York: Doubleday Anchor, 1954), 11–12.

12. Gathorne-Hardy, *The Old School Tie*, 41.

13. Ibid., 42.

14. Frederic William Farrar, *Eric; or, Little by Little* (1858; reprint, London: N.p., 1907), 189.

15. Gathorne-Hardy, *The Old School Tie*, 115–16.

16. Ibid., 119.

17. Wodehouse, *Mike*, 222.

18. Richards, *Happiest Days*, 272.

19. Thomas Hughes, *Tom Brown's Schooldays* (1857; reprint, New York: Thomas Y. Crowell, 1890), 275–76.

20. Ibid., 293.

21. Richards, *Happiest Days*, 149–50, 155.

22. Ibid., 94.

23. Ibid., 174.

24. Gathorne-Hardy, *The Old School Tie*, 123.

25. Ibid., 163.

26. Richards, *Happiest Days*, 81–86, 202, 237.

27. Ibid., 171.

28. Hughes, *Tom Brown's Schooldays*, 217.

29. Richards, *Happiest Days*, 221.

30. Gathorne-Hardy, *The Old School Tie*, 145.

31. J.E.C. Weldon, *Gerald Eversley's Friendship* (1895), quoted in Richards, *Happiest Days*, 204.

32. *The Atheneum*, October 14, 1899, quoted in Richards, *Happiest Days*, 162.

33. Richards, *Happiest Days*, 80, 91, 162, 171–72, 194, 202.

34. Hughes, *Tom Brown's Schooldays*, 162.

35. Alec Waugh, *The Loom of Youth* (1917), preface to 1954 edition, reprinted 1984, p. 9, quoted in Richards, *Happiest Days*, p. 230.

36. Alec Waugh, *The Loom of Youth*, 90, quoted in Richards, *Happiest Days*, 238.

37. J.E.C. Weldon, *Gerald Eversley's Friendship* (1895), quoted in Richards, *Happiest Days*, 204.

38. Richards, *Happiest Days*, 13.

39. G.W.E. Russell, *Sketches and Snapshots* (1910), quoted in Richards, *Happiest Days*, 203.

40. Richards, *Happiest Days*, 167.

41. Horace Vachell, *The Hill: A Romance of Friendship* (1905), quoted in Richards, *Happiest Days*, 198.

SUGGESTIONS FOR FURTHER READING

Connolly, Cyril. *Enemies of Promise*. Garden City, NY: Anchor Books, 1960.

Darwin, Bernard. *The English Public School*. London: Longmans, Green, 1929.

Forster, E. M. *The Longest Journey*. Edinburgh, UK: W. Blackwood, 1907.

Hilton, James. *Goodbye, Mr. Chips*. London: Hodder & Stoughton, 1934.

Kipling, Rudyard. *Stalky & Co*. London: Macmillan, 1899.

Maugham, Robin. *Escape from the Shadows*. London: Hodder & Stoughton, 1972.

Norton, Richard, Lord Grantley. *Silver Spoon*. London: Hutchison, 1954.

Raymond, Ernest. *Tell England*. London: Cassell, 1922.

Reed, Talbot Baines. *The Fifth Form at St. Dominic's*. London: The Office of "The Boy's Own Paper," 1887.

Rowling, J. K. *Harry Potter and the Sorcerer's Stone*. New York: Arthur A. Levine, 1998.

Vachell, Horace Annesley. *The Hill: A Romance of Friendship*. 1905. Reprint. London: J. Murray, 1942.

Waugh, Alec. *The Early Years of Alec Waugh*. London: Cassell, 1962.

———. *The Loom of Youth*. London: G. Richards, 1917.

———. *Public School Life*. London: W. Collins, 1922.

SUGGESTIONS FOR VIEWING

Goodbye, Mr. Chips (1939, 1969)
Housemaster (1938)
Tom Brown's Schooldays (1940)
Tell England (1931)

4

The Adventure Story

To die would be an awfully big adventure.
—James Barrie, *Peter Pan*

Ordinarily, a story that stranded a group of boys on an island would be a rollicking adventure tale. Free from parental restraint and influence, the boys would take daring chances, build shelters, gather food, hunt, fish, battle wild animals, and perhaps encounter pirates or hostile natives. *Lord of the Flies*, however, turns the traditional adventure tale inside out. Freed from parental restraint, the boys lose all sense of responsibility and foresight. They take daring chances but with tragic consequences. They hunt, indeed, but the hunt distracts them from attracting rescuers and rots their fragile society from within. The boys' haunting enemy, the beast, is no colorful band of buccaneers but a ghastly symbol of death, superstition, violence, and decay. As for hostile natives, the boys *are* the hostile natives.

Golding, as a father and a schoolteacher, was intimately familiar with children and with children's literature. He knew, for example, the works of R. M. (Robert Michael) Ballantyne, author of *The Madman and the Pirate, Digging for Gold, The Dog Crusoe: A Tale of the Western Prairies,* and *The Coral Island*. (Of these works, *The*

Coral Island is the most relevant to the study of *Lord of the Flies*, since it concerns castaway boys.) Furthermore, as a onetime boy, and as a teacher and parent of boys, he would certainly have been familiar with the adventure genre as a whole. Though many of the classic adventure stories were nineteenth-century in origin (or even earlier—*Robinson Crusoe* was written in the early eighteenth century), they remained popular reading among preteen and teen-age British boys. An 1888 survey of 790 boys revealed that their favorite book was *Robinson Crusoe; The Swiss Family Robinson* was second. A 1908 survey of 800 boys listed *Treasure Island*, *Robinson Crusoe*, and *The Coral Island* second, third, and eighth, respectively, with plenty of non-island adventures, including *Westward Ho!*, *Ivanhoe*, *King Solomon's Mines*, and *The Last of the Mohicans*, in the top twelve. The trend continued until at least 1940, when a survey of 1,570 boys revealed that *Treasure Island* and *Robinson Crusoe* were the first and second choices of twelve-year-olds, with thirteen-year-olds also claiming *Treasure Island* as their favorite novel.[1] If there were any remaining doubt about Golding's use of this genre as a model, he dispels it by having his characters overtly claim adventure stories as an ideal (34–35). *Coral Island* is in fact mentioned twice in *Lord of the Flies*, once during a meeting at the beginning of the book and once, pointedly, at the very end, when the naval officer refers to the boys' early camaraderie as a "[j]olly good show. Like the Coral Island" (202).

The parallels are clear enough already, but Golding made the connection explicit in a 1970 interview. According to the author, it was after reading a "God-awful" book to his son David—not *The Coral Island*, as it happened, and perhaps not even one of Ballantyne's books, but something similar—that he conceived *Lord of the Flies*. He remarked to his wife, " 'Oh, I'm so tired of this busi-ness. Wouldn't it be fun to write a book about boys on an island and see what really happens?' And she said, 'That's an awfully good idea. You do that.' "[2] Golding, therefore, consciously set out to subvert the formulaic adventure story. Not every adventure tale is the same, but many of the following elements can be found in standard adventure fare.

CHARACTERISTICS OF ADVENTURE STORIES

The Role of the Child

Since adventure stories are, for the most part, consumed by children, authors usually see fit to include one or more children among the major characters. For the same reason, if a child is present, chances are that he or she will be granted an unrealistic amount of power. A child reading a story about children will tend to identify with the children, and almost no one wants to identify with a victim when they can identify with a hero. A story with a heroic child will, therefore, be more appealing to children than a story with a useless, helpless child.

Literature for children and teenagers is full of young people endowed with power. Often, because children are smaller than adults, the power is intellectual or magical in nature, as it is in Roald Dahl's *Matilda* or the Animorphs series. The rare exception, such as *Pippi Longstocking*, in which sheer physical strength is the child's power, is unusual enough to be as subversive in its way as *Lord of the Flies*.

The adventure tale typically gives children power in one of two ways: either it removes all adults from power or existence, freeing the children to behave as they like and to indulge their imaginations, or it makes the child into a kind of honorary adult, permitted to enjoy adult freedoms and powers ahead of schedule. Examples of the first kind of power can be found in Louise Fitzhugh's *Harriet the Spy*, in which Harriet has her best adventures without adult presence and oversight; in *The Lion, the Witch, and the Wardrobe*, like *Lord of the Flies* a tale in which children are evacuated from a place of conventional dangers into a place of unconventional ones; and in the Oz books, in which both the chief heroine (Dorothy) and the ruler of Oz (Ozma) are little girls. Examples of the second kind of power also abound. Fictional "honorary adults" include Charles Wallace Murry, the genius preschooler from *A Wrinkle in Time*, and Encyclopedia Brown, whose mystery-solving capabilities outshine those of his chief-of-police father. Sometimes the author empowers children by setting the story in a time, such as the middle ages or colonial America, that treated thirteen- or fourteen-year-olds mostly like adults.

Harmless Danger

Adventure tales are to children what action movies are to adults: a chance to experience danger without actually coming into contact with its messy consequences. Action movies never, for example, show the terrorist's henchmen having dinner with their families or helping their children with homework. If they did, then the audience might actually feel sorry that the hero is gunning them down left and right, blowing them up with grenades, setting them on fire, or dropping nuclear warheads on them. "Bad guys" in action movies are usually from whatever group is already demonized and dehumanized by the media and popular opinion: Nazis, East Germans, Russians, South African whites, black or Hispanic gang members, or Arab terrorists, as the political climate dictates. They usually conform to stereotype and are given no more individuality than a signature line or a particularly inventive way of dispatching their foes. Adventure tales, likewise, stick to a standard set of stereotypical bad guys: cannibals and other assorted fierce natives, pirates, the enemy army, and so on. Authors and directors employ this tactic for the same reason that military propagandists demonize the enemy in wartime. They do not want the reader, or the viewer, or the soldier, to get distracted by things like sympathy. They want bodies that it is permissible to stab, or shoot, or blow up. The first rule of danger, then, is that the real danger always happens to the other guy, the bad guy, the guy without any feelings, the guy who, the reader or viewer or soldier has been told, deserves to die.

Another cardinal rule of both action movies and adventure tales is that none of the heroes, at any time, should be mortally wounded. Bad guys, by definition, have bad aim. Good guys, by definition, can shoot the nose off a fly two football fields away. Good guys handle a sword, or a cannon, or a flintlock, or an uzi, just that much better than the bad guys. Even superior firepower is inconsequential. The bad guy can have fourteen machine guns, while the good guy has only a Swiss Army knife and a paper clip, and the good guy will prevail with only a bruise and a broken fingernail to show for it because the good guy is smarter, stronger, and more virtuous than the bad guy. It is a rare adventure tale that will follow all the other conventions of the genre and then, at the last minute, kill off the hero's best friend.

There is also, usually, a justification for violence in adventure stories. Self-defense is a common reason, for nothing puts a hero in the right as easily as being attacked without provocation. Sometimes, the hero acts to rescue another or to avenge a wrong. This is the favorite device of action movies, in which the hero's wife, best friend, girlfriend, or child has been killed, assaulted, abducted, or threatened. In some cases, the hero acts to prove something to others or to himself. The danger and violence are portrayed as enlarging or honorable. A good cause, a certainty of ultimate victory, and a faceless enemy guarantee that the violence will be glamorized.

Removal from the Everyday

Transportation to a place outside ordinary experience is such a staple of children's literature that a list of examples would consume the remainder of this book. In a real child's everyday world, magic does not happen. Each day passes largely as the last, with meals, bedtimes, homework, and so on dictated by others. If magic and power and adventure are to happen, they must take place in another world entirely: Oz, Narnia, the Land of Knowledge from *The Phantom Tollbooth*, or Neverland.

Adventure stories stick to this formula, but they do so in a way that seems, at least superficially, more plausible. They remove the heroes to a place that resembles the real world in many details, but that differs enough from the child's everyday world to upset the everyday rules. This can be accomplished by any removal from civilization. The heroes of pulp westerns often inhabit a town in the middle of nowhere, surrounded by wasteland. The Merry Men live in the lawless, dark, dangerous world of Sherwood Forest. (Fairy-tale magic and Shakespearean romance, too, have their home in the forest.) Sometimes, the alien region is inhabited but still untamed, for example the Caribbean of the seventeenth century or California during the Gold Rush.

A struggle to survive in an unfamiliar place, unadorned by any other danger, is an adventure of the highest order, and plenty of authors have followed this formula. Any place that is wild and isolated accomplishes the necessary removal from the world. It can be a swamp (*Lost in the Everglades*), a mountain range (*My Side of the Mountain*), a cavern (*Journey to the Center of the Earth*), or an island (*Robinson Crusoe, Island of the Blue Dolphins, The Cay*). Islands are particularly popular in this type of fiction, for they offer guaranteed physical isolation and an easily visualized amount of land.

The ubiquity of island stories, from Defoe on, is among the great phenomena of popular culture. There was once a fake tree at Disneyland dressed up to look like the Swiss Family Robinson's treehouse (now converted into Tarzan's home). Endless *Gilligan's Island* reruns subvert the island-castaway archetype for comedic purposes, just as Golding subverts it for tragic ones. The name of Robinson Crusoe's servant, Friday, became a generic term for any useful assistant—"man Friday" or "girl Friday," the latter term destined for immortalization in a Cary Grant–Rosalind Russell movie title. The island-castaway scenario is a staple of one-panel cartoons, with its own iconography—the minuscule circle of sand, the vast ocean, one palm tree, a survivor or two in ragged pants. *Treasure Island*, perhaps the most fertile of all such stories, gave birth to at least eight movies (including a Muppet version with Kermit the Frog as Smollett). A fast-food chain was named Long John Silver's, its employees dressed in striped pirate shirts and red bandannas as they served up plates of fish and hush puppies. The Admiral Benbow Inn, the inn owned by Jim Hawkins's parents, has lent its name to a number of subsequent hotels, including a bed-and-breakfast in Newport, Rhode Island, and a franchised hotel chain in the south. A male porn star adopted a pseudonym based on Silver's moniker and was immortalized, ingloriously, during the hearings to confirm Supreme Court Justice Clarence Thomas. Not least, the Silver-style pirate with a peg leg and a talking parrot has become as much of an icon as the tiny island with one coconut palm that populates a thousand cartoons.

Male Bonding

Adventure stories are also, often, tales of male friendship. Adventure stories that feature girls are a product of the late twentieth century, which explains why, in Golding's time, adventure fiction was read mostly by boys. Women are often absent or unimportant in older adventure tales, and it is the male bond of respect and loyalty that is foremost. *Peter Pan*, for example, is nominally about the relationship between Peter and Wendy (or, more accurately, between the almost-woman Wendy and her vanishing childhood as embodied by Peter), but the friendships in the book are between boys: between Peter and the Lost Boys and between John and Michael and the seductive male society of Neverland. *Robin Hood* as interpreted by Hollywood is a story of romance between Robin and Maid Marian, but in many versions it is mostly about Robin's combat with authority and his close, life-or-death bond with the Merry Men. In Howard Pyle's version of the Robin Hood legend, Maid Marian never even appears, and Marian is in fact a late addition to the much older Robin Hood legend.[3] In *Robinson Crusoe*, the bond is between Crusoe and Friday; in *Treasure Island*, Jim Hawkins earns the respect of Captain Smollett, Doctor Livesey, Squire Trelawny, and even his adversary Long John Silver and is accepted wholeheartedly into the society of men, proven worthy by his bravery, cleverness, and loyalty. In *Lord of the Flies*, when Piggy pleads with Ralph not to reveal his embarrassing nickname to the other boys, it is a sign that he hopes to become part of such a group (11). In a boys' adventure story, Ralph would solemnly agree never to tell and would help the less agile boy become a full member of the group. Instead, Ralph immediately reveals the nickname, and Piggy is Piggy forever, an outsider and an easy victim.

Here, too, *Lord of the Flies* diverges from the traditional pattern of the adventure story, in which male-male aggression is usually romanticized. In boys' adventure stories, the relationship between hero and antagonist is often as close, if not closer, than the relationship between the hero and his friends. The struggle between hero and villain is glamorized, with the adversaries knowing each other's capabilities and even being able to predict the other's thoughts and actions. They are almost perfectly matched in skill or daring, so as to make the contest more entertaining for the reader, and the closeness of their abilities almost always results in a grudging respect on both sides. For examples, see the relationships between Jim and Silver or Peter Pan and Hook. In *Lord of the Flies*, male-male aggression is practiced by a strong group upon a weak individual. It is mean, cowardly, anything but glamorized.

SUBVERTING THE ADVENTURE TALE

William Golding could have used any genre for his tale of human weakness and evil, but, as it happened, he chose this one. Perhaps it is especially appropriate. The adventure story has never been especially true-to-life, and by imbuing it with realistic dialogue and human frailty, Golding lends it a credibility it usually lacks. Furthermore, a bit of the genre's unnatural simplicity, remaining intact by virtue of the setting, helps lend Golding's tale the quality of myth. The island reduces the world's resources and people to meat, fruit, fire, friend, foe.

Golding chooses an especially innocent genre—starring children, aimed at children, set in virgin country, showcasing ingenuity, and purposefully free of really scary violence—and manipulates the reader's expectations. The reader sees boys without parents, expects adventure, and gets vicious warfare and cruelty. The reader sees an opportunity for relatively harmless danger (the hunt or the expedition to the top of the mountain, for example) and gets murder, arson, and torture. The reader sees a tropical island full of fruit and pigs, expects a harvesting of the bounty and a careful accumulation of supplies, and gets waste, carelessness, and greed. The reader sees boys who want to like each other and be liked in return, expects friendship, and sees betrayal. Golding could hardly have chosen a better way to demonstrate the possibility of evil everywhere than to infiltrate the adventure story.

THE DETAILS OF SURVIVAL: *THE SWISS FAMILY ROBINSON*

It does not require a very extensive reading of *The Swiss Family Robinson* to understand why most children's adventures dispense with the parents at the outset. Father Robinson (not his real surname in the story, but the title's allusion to *Robinson Crusoe*) means well, no doubt, but he is awfully infuriating for someone who is clearly meant to be a model parent. He never misses an opportunity to point out a fault or a lack of knowledge.

The Swiss Family Robinson is annoying for another reason as well. Of all the works discussed in this chapter, it ranks second to *Gilligan's Island* for sheer unbelievability. The island, we are expected to believe, contains boa constrictors, rabbits, antelope, porcupines, bears, ostriches, buffalo, agoutis, penguins, onagers, parakeets, flax, cotton, strawberries, rubber trees, bamboo, rice, coconut and sago palms, potatoes, ginseng, and sugar cane. To be as gracious as possible to the authors—the novel was begun by Johann David Wyss and completed and edited by his son Johann Rudolph Wyss—part of the book's purpose was to educate children about a variety of creatures. Many editions carried detailed engravings of the plants and animals mentioned in the text, sometimes with captions giving both common and Latin names. Furthermore, the book was written at a time when huge swaths of the globe remained unexplored by Europeans, and the idea of so many disparate creatures sharing a single island home probably seemed less ridiculous in a time when new species and habitats were being discovered every year.

However, even once these concessions have been made, *The Swiss Family Robinson* still surpasses credibility. Wild animals are tamed within minutes by leashing them to tame livestock or by blowing tobacco smoke at them. Multiple houses are constructed, crops are sown and harvested, and game is captured without more than trivial setbacks. An ostrich and a buffalo are made into saddle beasts. The bamboo golf carts and copious wardrobes of *Gilligan's Island* are a stone's throw away from this preposterous fantasy. The castaways seldom express any dismay at finding themselves alone with no hope of rescue, and when rescue comes at last, four of the six family members choose to remain in "New Switzerland," as they have named it. There is a promise of future immigration, and thus civilization comes to the wilderness for good. No adventure tale could be more ripe for realistic subversion than this one.

Nonetheless, these castaways make interesting foils for *Lord of the Flies'* English schoolboys. Their meticulous use of the bounty of their island stands in stark contrast to the boys' lackadaisical approach. The Swiss family—father, mother, and four boys—are abandoned on their sinking ship by the entire crew. The boat runs aground on some rocks and stays there through the night. In the morning, the family gathers what it can find and prepares to head for a nearby island. In most English translations of *The Swiss Family Robinson*, the boys' names are rendered as Fritz, Ernest, Jack, and Franz; however, in the edition containing this excerpt, their names are given as Frederick, Ernest, Rudolph or Rudly, and Fritz.

FROM JOHANN DAVID WYSS, *THE SWISS FAMILY ROBINSON*
(1812–13)

Immediately we all began to explore the vessel. For my part, I first visited the caboose, where the provisions and fresh water were stored, for the thought troubled me how all my people would be fed. My wife and little Fritz went in search of the poultry and domestic animals, which, forgotten two whole days in the press of our misfortunes, were dying of hunger and thirst.

As soon as Frederick had discovered the powder-room, Ernest repaired to the carpenter's stores, and Rudly to the captain's cabin; but he had scarcely opened the door before two dogs burst forth, and in their joy at recovering their liberty, brought our little boy to the ground with their noisy caresses. . . . Frederick brought two fowling-pieces, some lead, and a small cask of gunpowder; Ernest carried an axe, a hammer, and a pair of pincers. He had filled his cap with nails of all sizes, and a chisel and half-a-dozen gimlets projected from his pockets. Not one of us but contributed something to the general store; even little Fritz presented a box in which he had found, he said, "some pretty hooks."

"Truly," said I, after I had examined his treasure-trove, "our youngest has made the best discovery; Fritz's 'little hooks' are good strong fish-hooks, which will, perhaps, do more to support our lives than anything else in the whole vessel. Thus it is, my children, that good fortune in this life often falls to those who seek and understand it least."

"As for me," said my wife, "I bring nothing but good news: I have found a cow, an ass, two goats, and seven sheep, as well as a fat sow, still alive; and as I have given them plenty of food, they will, perhaps, supply our wants if it be the will of God we should remain some time on this frail shelter." . . .

"Oh!" said Rudly, with chagrin, "if I had but the great tub mamma formerly used in her washing, and in which I paddled upon the lake at home, I would soon manage to carry you all ashore: I would go much farther than that with my boat."

His words fell on my mind like a ray of light.

"Blessed be the fortunate suggestion," I cried; "though it issued only from a child's mouth. My God, I thank thee! Follow me, children; come, saw, hammer, nails, gimlets! We are going to work, I can promise you."

In a few words I explained my idea, and we immediately descended into the hold, where I had noticed some large casks floating in the water with which it was filled. . . . Made of substantial oak, and bound with strong iron hoops, I found them well fitted for my object; and, with the help of my wife and eldest son, sawed them in halves. I thus obtained eight small tubs, each about three feet in diameter and four in height.

I then sought out a long flexible plank, on which I arranged my tubs, placing them side by side in a row. . . .

We awoke at daybreak, for Hope is no less an enemy to sleep than Sorrow or Despair. After our usual morning prayers and a frugal breakfast, I finished all my arrangements for our departure, advising my children to supply themselves with whatever they considered indispensable necessaries, and my wife to provide the live-stock on board with several days' fodder; "for," added I, "if our expedition succeeds, we shall probably return for them."

Our new ship's cargo consisted of a barrel of gunpowder; three fowling-pieces; three muskets; two pair of pocket-pistols; one pair of horse-pistols; ball, shot, and lead, as much as we could carry, and a bullet-mould.

In addition, my children and wife each bore a well-stocked game-bag, of which we had found several among the effects of the ship's officers. I placed a case of portable soup in the boat, another of biscuits, a barrel of herrings and other comestibles, with an iron pot, some fishing-tackle, a chest of nails, and one of carpenter's tools, and finally, enough canvas to make a tent. . . . [W]e went in quest of the poultry; and soon I had the satisfaction of seeing one of the tubs stocked with ten hens and two cocks, who were covered over with a cloth to prevent them from flying away. As for the geese, the ducks, and the pigeons, we gave them their freedom, convinced that they would reach the shore more quickly and more easily than ourselves, some by air, the others by water.

. . . Then I cut the cable, and pushed off. . . .

As we began to increase our distance from the wreck, the poor dogs whom Rudly had found in the captain's cabin, howled loudly their regret at our unexpected departure. Then springing into the sea, as if by a common impulse, they swam vigorously after us. . . .

Our landing was speedily accomplished. . . .

Our first care, when safely landed, was to fall on our knees, and with a feeling of the liveliest and tenderest gratitude, to thank our heavenly Protector, and commend our future to His almighty goodness. We then proceeded to unload our argosy. Ah, how rich we considered ourselves with the little we had contrived to save! My wife released the poultry, and set them free to follow their own devices, for as yet we had neither food for them nor shelter. I busied myself in selecting a suitable locality for our tent and our night quarters. Over a long spar, one end of which I thrust into a fissure of the rock, while the other extremity was supported by a forked pole planted firmly in the sand, I extended the canvas which we had brought with us. Thus, as if by magic, a tent was constructed of sufficient size to accommodate all my family. We steadied the sides by loading the edges of the sail with chests, barrels, and other heavy objects, while to the opening in front we fixed a few hooks, that we might close it during the night.

I now dispatched my sons to gather a quantity of grass and moss, and spread it on the sand to dry in the warm sunshine, that we might not be compelled to sleep upon the bare earth. Meanwhile, I sought along the bank of a stream for some large smooth stones, and with these erected a rude fire-place at a short distance from the tent. With a quantity of driftwood which the sea had cast upon the shore I kindled a glorious fire, whose crackling, leaping flames soon rejoiced our eyes. The iron pot filled with water was placed upon it; my wife, with little Fritz assisting in the character of cook, cut up a few cakes of portable soup, and prepared our dinner. . . .

Meanwhile Fred had loaded his gun, and proceeded along the seashore. Ernest, reflecting that it might be neither safe nor pleasant to penetrate into the recesses of a desert island, also directed his steps towards the sea, while Rudly commenced exploring the weedy rocks in search of mussels, whose existence he had noticed on landing. . . .

[After he caught a lobster that had pinched him, his mother determined that] Rudly should have the largest claw as his portion; "for, indeed, my boy," said she, passing her hand caressingly over his forehead, "you are the first, and as yet the only person, who has discovered anything good, and contributed it to the general stock of the community."

Ernest having returned from his walk empty-handed, seemed to feel a slight reproach in the eulogium bestowed on his brother.

"As for that," said he, "I also found some excellent provisions, but I could not secure them without wetting my feet, and—"

"Bah," cried Rudly, "I know what it was! Some filthy mussels not fit to eat! While, as for my lobster, that now is a first-rate dainty, is it not, mamma?"

"But if it was oysters," rejoined Ernest, "perhaps my treasure-trove would not be considered so despicable, and I should not be astonished if they *were* oysters from the manner in which they adhered to the rock, the shallowness of the water, and other signs—"

"Now, my dear professor"—for such was the title we sometimes bestowed on Ernest when he made an unnecessary display of his learning—"since you saw all these things so clearly," said his mother, "be good enough to go in search of some proof of your valuable discovery. In our position we must neglect nothing, and above all must not be afraid of wetting our feet, or of any other little inconvenience, when called upon to co-operate for the general good."

Ernest immediately started, accompanied by Rudly, who knew no greater pleasure than that of dabbling in the water: while his brother sought for a few stepping-stones, he plunged in boldly, and each being provided with an iron-pointed stick, they quickly loosened from the rocks a quantity of splendid oysters, returning with both their handkerchiefs well filled. When turning the rock, our young naturalist made another discovery: in a corner, from which the sea had receded, he caught sight of a white and shining substance. Having tasted it, he felt certain it was salt; and instead of satisfying himself with the mere pleasure of the discovery, resolved to profit by it; he filled a large mussel-shell, and brought it to his mother, who received this new acquisition with evident pleasure. "This indeed is a treasure!" she exclaimed; "thanks to you, Ernest, our soup will now be somewhat savoury." . . .

Having hauled ashore the various casks and chests which contained our goods and chattels, I now returned to the *cuisine*, where my wife was busily stirring her pot with a stick. Tasting its contents, she announced that the soup was ready. . . .

"Had we only a few cocoa-nuts," said Ernest, "we might convert the shells into capital soup-dishes."

"Ah, if it were only necessary to say, Had we this, or, Had we that, I should wish for nothing better immediately than a dozen good silver plates, or pewter, or even wood; but to what purpose repeat such idle words?"

"Well, well," remarked Ernest, examining one of the oysters he and Rudly had discovered, "I think this oyster-shell is large enough to serve as a spoon."

"A good idea!" exclaimed his mother; "but first we must wash them thoroughly, or the taste of the sea-water will spoil our soup."

While she was engaged in this operation, we heard Frederick's voice. He approached us shouting merrily, and we replied to him in the same manner. He advanced with his hands behind him, and with a countenance full of meaning.

"I have found nothing," he said to us.

"What? nothing at all?" I asked, a little surprised.

"Nothing at all," he repeated.

But his brothers had by this time gathered round him, and suddenly exclaimed, "Oh, a little sucking-pig! A sucking-pig!* Where did you find it? How did you capture it? Oh, let us see it!"

Laughingly the young man displayed before our eyes an animal which certainly bore some resemblance to a young pig.

"I think your hunt has turned out very successful," I remarked; "but why spoil my enjoyment with an improper pleasantry? Oh, my dear son, never sin against the truth, even in jest; the habit is all unworthy of an honourable nature, and will lead you eventually into a fatal course of falsehood, the meanest and most shameful of the vices."

Frederick listened to my reprimand with a blush, and promised to remember my counsel. . . .

"Come, come," interrupted my wife, ". . . have you forgotten that the soup is ready? . . ."

. . . [W]e all gladly plunged our improvised spoons into the smoking pottage prepared by our excellent housekeeper. This was not done, however, without severely scalding our fingers, and loud cries arose of pain or impatience. Ernest took the mussel-shell in which he had collected the salt, emptied it, cleaned it, approached the pot in silence, filled the shell—which was as large as an ordinary plate—with soup, and, quietly laughing, put his portion aside to eat when cool.

"You have thought only of yourself, Ernest," I remarked, "which is not very amiable. Could you not have procured each of us a similar dish? . . . I see with regret that you think only of yourself. Beware, my dear boy; selfishness is a terrible vice, which effectually shuts us out from the love and esteem of others. As a punishment for your egotism, I must beg of you to give the portion you have so prudently cooled to our poor servants the two dogs, who also stand in need of refreshment, and then come and burn your fingers along with us!"

My reproach wounded the lad to the quick. He obeyed, placed his shell before the dogs, who soon lapped up its contents, and returned much ashamed to take his place in our little circle. But while we were thus

*Later identified as an agouti.

occupied, the dogs having scented Frederick's agouti, which he had placed in the shade behind our tent, discovered its place of concealment, and set to work upon it with greedy teeth. My boys were transported with indignation at the sight. Frederick in his rage seized his musket, and would have shot the dogs had not Ernest held his arm. He hurled at them a volley of stones, and in his excess of anger flung his musket after them with so much violence that the stock was broken, and the gun spoiled. I followed the young madman, with whose threats and vociferations the rocks re-echoed; I represented to him how ridiculous as well as hateful was such an outbreak of fury, and how surprised and grieved his mother felt to see her eldest son yielding to such unbridled passion, and setting his brothers so bad an example. (23–39)

London: T. Nelson and Sons, 1871.

THE DETAILS OF SURVIVAL: *ROBINSON CRUSOE*

Most authors of island tales give their castaways some companions. It is, after all, more interesting to see the reactions of two or more people to a crisis, because they must react both to the situation and to each other. It is the anticipation of this interaction that makes people ask, "Who would you most like to be stranded on a desert island with?"

But sometimes isolation, not the presence of others, is the real test. Hence the second most popular desert-island question: "If you had to be stranded on a desert island, what one book (or two, or ten books) would you take with you?" It is solitude that tests Robinson Crusoe, for Daniel Defoe's whole novel (like many of his other works) is concerned with people struggling against their own weaknesses. In Crusoe's case, it is his impatience and dissatisfaction that damn him. Offered a comfortable life at home, he defies his parents and goes off to sea, where he is promptly punished by storms and then by being taken captive and sold into slavery by pirates. Escaping slavery, he founds a profitable farm in Brazil, yet leaves it behind to make some quick cash by running a slave ship to Africa. Punished again for his greed, he is cast ashore on an uninhabited island that has enough game and shelter for survival, but not enough for true comfort. He lives there alone for years, alternately blessing God for rescuing him from the sea and cursing the fate that left him alone, miserable, and deprived of his former wealth. Yet when at last he sees a human footprint other than his own, his reaction is not joy but fear of capture and execution by hostile natives. Every change of fortune brings new causes for dismay and regret.

Survival comes easily to the Swiss family Robinson, but it is harder for Crusoe. In the excerpt that follows, Defoe summarizes Crusoe's first days on the island in journal form.

FROM DANIEL DEFOE, *THE LIFE AND STRANGE ADVENTURES OF ROBINSON CRUSOE*, VOL. 1 (1719)

September 30, 1659.—I, poor miserable Robinson Crusoe, being shipwrecked, during a dreadful storm, in the offing, came on shore on this dismal unfortunate island, which I called the Island of Despair, all the rest of the ship's company being drowned, and myself almost dead.

All the rest of that day I spent in afflicting myself at the dismal circumstances I was brought to, viz., I had neither food, house, clothes, weapon, or place to fly to; and in despair of any relief, saw nothing but death before me; either that I should be devoured by wild beasts, murdered by savages, or starved to death for want of food. At the approach of night, I slept in a tree for fear of wild creatures, but slept soundly, though it rained all night.

October 1.—In the morning I saw, to my great surprise, the ship had floated with the high tide, and was driven on shore again much nearer the island; which, as it was some comfort on one hand, for seeing her sit upright, and not broken to pieces, I hoped, if the wind abated, I might get on board, and get some food and necessaries out of her for my relief; so, on the other hand, it renewed my grief at the loss of my comrades, who, I imagined, if we had all stayed on board, might have saved the ship, or at least that they would not have been all drowned as they were; and that had the men been saved, we might perhaps have built us a boat out of the ruins of the ship, to have carried us to some other part of the world. I spent great part of this day in perplexing myself on these things; but at length seeing the ship almost dry, I went upon the sand as near as I could, and then swam on board; this day also it continued raining, though with no wind at all.

From the 1st of *October* to the 24th.—All these days entirely spent in many several voyages to get all I could out of the ship, which I brought on shore, every tide of flood, upon rafts. Much rain also in these days, though with some intervals of fair weather; but, it seems, this was the rainy season.

Oct. 20.—I overset my raft, and all the goods I had got upon it; but being in shoal water, and the things being chiefly heavy, I recovered many of them when the tide was out.

Oct. 25.—It rained all night and all day, with some gusts of wind, during which time the ship broke in pieces, the wind blowing a little harder than before, and was no more to be seen, except the wreck of her, and that only at low water. I spent this day in covering and securing the goods which I had saved, that the rain might not spoil them.

Oct. 26.—I walked about the shore almost all day to find out a place to fix my habitation, greatly concerned to secure myself from an attack in the night, either from wild beasts or men. Towards night I fixed upon a proper place under a rock, and marked out a semicircle for my encampment, which I resolved to strengthen with a work, wall, or fortification made of double piles, lined within with cables, and without with turf.

From the 26th to the 30th I worked very hard in carrying all my goods to my new habitation, though some part of the time it rained exceeding hard.

The 31st, in the morning, I went out into the island with my gun to see for some food, and discover the country; when I killed a she-goat, and her kid followed me home, which I afterwards killed also, because it would not feed.

Nov. 1.—I set up my tent under a rock, and lay there for the first night, making it as large as I could, with stakes driven in to swing my hammock upon.

Nov. 2—I set up all my chests and boards, and the pieces of timber which made my rafts, and with them formed a fence round me, a little within the place I had marked out for my fortification.

Nov. 3.—I went out with my gun, and killed two fowls like ducks, which were very good food. In the afternoon went to work to make me a table.

Nov. 4.—This morning I began to order my times of work, of going out with my gun, time of sleep, and time of diversion, viz., every morning I walked out with my gun for two or three hours, if it did not rain; then employed myself to work till about eleven o'clock; then eat what I had to live on; and from twelve to two I lay down to sleep, the weather being excessive hot; and then in the evening to work again. The working part of this day and of the next were wholly employed in making my table; for I was yet but a very sorry workman, though time and necessity made me a complete natural mechanic soon after, as I believe it would do any one else. (77–79)

New York: The Jenson Society, 1907.

THE DETAILS OF SURVIVAL: *THE CORAL ISLAND*

There are plenty of superficial resemblances between *The Coral Island* and *Lord of the Flies*, not the least of which is that two of the principal characters are named Ralph and Jack. Hunting, weaponry, and religion play important roles in both novels, but the complex and realistic relationships of the boys in *Lord of the Flies* are absent in *The Coral Island*. Part of this is because Ballantyne's group of boys is smaller. There are only three boys on the island: eighteen-year-old Jack Martin, fifteen-year-old Ralph Rover, and fourteen-year-old Peterkin Gay. They know each other before their ship sinks, and in fact, Jack and Peterkin are the narrator Ralph's "special favourites."[4] Furthermore, Jack is decidedly older and more knowledgeable than the other two boys, so his leadership is unquestioned. There is, thus, no threat offered by any of the boys to the others. Dangers are purely external: sharks, pirates, and the obligatory "savages" (who menace our heroes until converted to Christianity by a missionary). Ballantyne's Ralph can say with perfect honesty that "I have spent many of the happiest months in my life on that Coral Island."[5] Golding's Ralph, though never menaced by a shark, a pirate, or a Fiji chieftain, could hardly do likewise.

FROM R. M. BALLANTYNE, *THE CORAL ISLAND* (1858)

Having now got ourselves into a very comfortable condition, we began to talk of a project which we had long had in contemplation—namely, to travel entirely round the island; in order, first, to ascertain whether it contained any other productions which might be useful to us; and, second, to see whether there might be any place more convenient and suitable for our permanent residence than that on which we were now encamped. Not that we were in any degree dissatisfied with it; on the contrary, we entertained quite a home-feeling to our bower and its neighbourhood; but if a better place did exist, there was no reason why we should not make use of it. At any rate, it would be well to know of its existence.

We had much earnest talk over this matter. But Jack proposed that, before undertaking such an excursion, we should supply ourselves with good defensive arms, for, as we intended not only to go round all the shore, but to ascend most of the valleys, before returning home, we should be likely to meet in with, he would not say *dangers*, but, at least, with everything that existed on the island, whatever that might be.

"Besides," said Jack, "it won't do for us to live on cocoanuts and oysters always. No doubt they are very excellent in their way, but I think a little animal food, now and then, would be agreeable as well as good for us; and as there are many small birds among the trees, some of which are probably very good to eat, I think it would be a capital plan to make bows and arrows, with which we could easily knock them over."

'First rate!' cried Peterkin. 'You will make the bows, Jack, and I'll try my hand at the arrows. The fact is, I'm quite tired of throwing stones at the birds. I began the very day we landed, I think, and have persevered up to the present time, but I've never hit anything yet.'

'You forget,' said I, 'you hit me one day on the shin.'

'Ah, true,' replied Peterkin, 'and a precious shindy you kicked up in consequence. But you were at least four yards away from the impudent paroquet I aimed at; so you see what a horribly bad shot I am.'

'But,' said I, 'Jack, you cannot make three bows and arrows before tomorrow, and would it not be a pity to waste them, now that we have made up our minds to go on this expedition? Suppose that you make one bow and arrow for yourself, and we can take our clubs?'

'That's true, Ralph. The day is pretty far advanced, and I doubt if I can make even one bow before dark. To be sure I might work by fire-light, after the sun goes down.'

We had, up to this time, been in the habit of going to bed with the sun, as we had no pressing call to work o' nights; and, indeed, our work during the day was usually hard enough,—what between fishing, and improving our bower, and diving in the Water Garden, and rambling in the woods; so that, when night came, we were usually very glad to retire to our beds. But now that we had a desire to work at night, we felt a wish for candles.

'Won't a blazing good fire give you light enough?' inquired Peterkin.

'Yes,' replied Jack, 'quite enough; but then it will give us a great deal more than enough of heat in this warm climate of ours.'

'True,' said Peterkin; 'I forgot that. It would roast us.'

'Well, as you're always doing that at any rate,' remarked Jack, 'we could scarcely call it a change. But the fact is, I've been thinking over this subject before. There is a certain nut growing in these islands which is called the candle-nut, because the natives use it instead of candles, and I know all about it, and how to prepare it for burning—'

'Then why don't you do it?' interrupted Peterkin. 'Why have you kept us in the dark so long, you vile philosopher?'

'Because,' said Jack, 'I have not seen the tree yet, and I'm not sure that I should know either the tree or the nuts if I did see them. You see, I forget the description.' . . .

' . . . I fear I can remember little about it. I believe the nut is about the size of a walnut; and I think that the leaves are white, but I am not sure.'

'Eh! ha! hum!' exclaimed Peterkin, 'I saw a tree answering to that description this very day.'

'Did you?' cried Jack. 'Is it far from this?'

'No, not half a mile.'

'Then lead me to it,' said Jack, seizing his axe.

In a few minutes we were all three pushing through the underwood of the forest, headed by Peterkin.

We soon came to the tree in question, which, after Jack had closely examined it, we concluded must be the candle-nut tree. Its leaves were of a beautiful silvery white, and formed a fine contrast to the dark-green foliage of the surrounding trees. We immediately filled our pockets with the nuts, after which Jack said:

"Now, Peterkin, climb that cocoanut tree and cut me one of the long branches."

This was soon done, but it cost some trouble, for the stem was very high, and as Peterkin usually pulled nuts from the younger trees, he was not much accustomed to climbing the high ones. The leaf or branch was a very large one, and we were surprised at its size and strength. Viewed from a little distance, the cocoanut tree seems to be a tall, straight stem, without a single branch except at the top, where there is a tuft of feathery-looking leaves, that seem to wave like soft plumes in the wind. But when we saw one of these leaves or branches at our feet, we found it to be a strong stalk, about fifteen feet long, with a number of narrow, pointed leaflets ranged alternately on each side. But what seemed to us the most wonderful thing about it was a curious substance resembling cloth, which was wrapped round the thick end of the stalk, where it had been cut from the tree. . . .

Jack now took one of the leaflets, and, cutting out the central spine or stalk, hurried back with it to our camp. Having made a small fire, he baked the nuts slightly, and then pealed off the husks. After this he wished to bore a hole in them, which, not having anything better at hand at the time, he did with the point of our useless pencil-case. Then he strung them on the coconut spine, and on putting a light to the topmost nut, we found to our joy that it burned with a clear, beautiful flame; upon seeing which, Peterkin sprang up and danced round the fire for at least five minutes in the excess of his satisfaction.

'Now, lads,' said Jack, extinguishing our candle, 'the sun will set in an hour, so we have no time to lose. I shall go and cut a young tree to make my bow out of, and you had better each of you go and select good strong sticks for clubs, and we'll set to work at them after dark.'

So saying he shouldered his axe and went off, followed by Peterkin, while I took up the piece of newly discovered cloth, and fell to examining its structure. So engrossed was I in this that I was still sitting in the same attitude and occupation when my companions returned.

'I told you so!' cried Peterkin, with a loud laugh. 'Oh, Ralph, you're incorrigible. See, there's a club for you. I was sure, when we left you looking at that bit of stuff, that we would find you poring over it when we came back, so I just cut a club for you as well as for myself.'

'Thank you, Peterkin,' said I. 'It was kind of you to do that, instead of scolding me for a lazy fellow, as I confess I deserve.' . . .

As it was now getting dark we lighted our candle, and placing it in a holder made of two crossing branches, inside of our bower, we seated ourselves on our leafy beds and began to work.

'I intend to appropriate the bow for my own use,' said Jack, chipping the piece of wood he had brought with his axe. 'I used to be a pretty fair shot once. But what's that you're doing?' he added, looking at Peterkin, who had drawn the end of a long pole into the tent, and was endeavouring to fit a small piece of the hoop iron to the end of it.

'I'm going to enlist into the Lancers,' answered Peterkin. 'You see, Jack, I find the club rather an unwieldy instrument for my delicately formed muscles, and I flatter myself I shall do more execution with a spear.'

'Well, if length constitutes power,' said Jack, 'You'll certainly be invincible.'

The pole which Peterkin had cut was full twelve-feet long being a very strong but light and tough young tree, which merely required thinning at the butt to be a serviceable weapon.

'That's a very good idea,' said I.

'Which—this?' inquired Peterkin, pointing to the spear.

'Yes,' I replied.

'Humph!' said he; 'you'd find it a pretty tough and matter-of-fact idea, if you had it stuck through your gizzard, old boy!'

'I mean the idea of making it is a good one,' said I, laughing. 'And, now I think of it, I'll change my plan, too. I don't think much of a club, so I'll make me a sling out of this piece of cloth. I used to be very fond of slinging, ever since I read of David slaying Goliath the Philistine, and I was once thought to be expert at it.' . . .

While we were thus engaged, we were startled by a distant but most strange and horrible cry. It seemed to come from the sea, but was so far away that we could not clearly distinguish its precise direction. Rushing out of our bower, we hastened down to the beach and stayed to listen. Again it came quite loud and distinct on the night air,—a prolonged, hideous cry, something like the braying of an ass. The moon had risen, and we could see the islands in and beyond the lagoon quite plainly, but there was no object visible to account for such a cry. A strong gust of wind was blowing from the point whence the sound came, but this died away while we were gazing out to sea.

'What can it be?' said Peterkin, in a low whisper, while we all involuntarily crept closer to each other.

'Do you know,' said Jack, 'I have heard that mysterious sound twice before, but never so loud as to-night. Indeed it was so faint that I thought I must have merely fancied it, so, as I did not wish to alarm you, I said nothing about it.'

We listened for a long time for the sound again, but as it did not come, we returned to the bower and resumed our work.

'Very strange,' said Peterkin, quite gravely. 'Do you believe in ghosts, Ralph?'

'No,' I answered, 'I do not. Nevertheless I must confess that strange, unaccountable sounds, such as we have just heard, make me feel a little uneasy.'

'What say you to it, Jack?'

'I neither believe in ghosts nor feel uneasy,' he replied. 'I never saw a ghost myself, and I never met with any one who had; and I have generally found that strange and unaccountable things have almost always been accounted for, and found to be quite simple, on close examination. I certainly can't imagine what *that* sound is; but I'm quite sure I shall find out before long—and if it's a ghost I'll—I'll—'

'Eat it,' cried Peterkin.

'Yes, I'll eat it! Now, then, my bow and arrows are finished; so if you're ready we had better turn in.' . . .

Although thus prepared for a start on the morrow, we thought it wise to exercise ourselves a little in the use of our weapons before starting, so we spent the whole of the next day in practising. And it was well we did so, for . . . Jack found that the bow was much too strong, and he had to thin it. Also the spear was much too heavy, and so had to be reduced in thickness, although nothing would induce Peterkin to have it shortened. My sling answered very well, but I had fallen so much out of practice that my first stone knocked off Peterkin's hat, and narrowly missed making a second Goliath out of him. However, after having spent the whole day in diligent practice, we began to find some of our former expertness returning—at least Jack and I did. As for Peterkin, being naturally a neat-handed boy, he soon handled his spear well, and could run full tilt at a cocoanut, and hit it with great precision once out of every five times.

But I feel satisfied that we owed much of our rapid success to the unflagging energy of Jack, who insisted that, since we had made him Captain, we should obey him; and he kept us at work from morning till night, perseveringly, at the same thing. Peterkin wished very much to run about and stick his spear into everything he passed; but Jack put up a cocoanut, and would not let him leave off running at that for a moment, except when he wanted to rest. We laughed at Jack for this, but we were both convinced that it did us much good. (50–61)

London: J. M. Dent & Co. 1907.

THE IMPOSSIBLE POWER OF THE CHILD

Perhaps the quintessential stranded-on-an-island tale is *Treasure Island*, written in 1883 by Robert Louis Stevenson. It is the story of an eighteenth-century boy, Jim Hawkins, who discovers a treasure map in a dead pirate's sea chest. Unlike many children's adventure tales, *Treasure Island* is well populated by grown-ups. Jim, in fact, is the only child among them. But in many ways, the grown-ups might just as well be absent. Some, like the map's original possessor Billy Bones, are habitually drunk. Others, like the sharp-shooting blabbermouth Squire Trelawny, are simply idiots. The most competent of the adult heroes, Captain Smollett, is the only one who seeks to rein in Jim's daring behavior, and Smollett is removed as an authority figure late in the book when he sustains a serious wound. The most competent of the villains, Long John Silver, treats Jim more or less as an equal, and, as the book's principal spokesman for the anarchic life of a "gentleman of fortune" (i.e., pirate), is hardly a stickler for order or seniority. His own authority among the pirates, unlike Smollett's among the seamen, derives not from duty or class but from common consent. The pirates choose a leader much the way children would choose captains for a baseball game and switch leaders as freely when they feel the job is being done poorly.

   In its lack of true adult authorities, then, the book is quite characteristic of the child's adventure tale. By creating an absence of strong leadership, the author makes it slightly more plausible that Jim Hawkins is treated as if he were an adult. Hawkins goes to sea as a cabin boy, so he is of an age to be apprenticed. In the eighteenth century, that makes him, if not an adult, a working man learning a trade. Nevertheless, he is given a ridiculous amount of latitude and assures the success of the treasure-hunting venture almost singlehandedly. He finds the treasure map, turns it over to the local squire and doctor-magistrate, and is cut into the adventure apparently as a full partner. It is the squire, not Jim, whose talkativeness and naïveté lead to the hiring of a nearly all-buccaneer crew to sail for the island. Aboard the ship, the *Hispaniola*, it is Jim who discovers the impending treachery of Long John and the pirates. On the island, after the pirates' mutiny, Jim's befriending of castaway Ben Gunn leads directly to the conquest of the pirates and to the recovery of the treasure. When those faithful to Captain Smollett flee the *Hispaniola* and take refuge in a stockade on Treasure Island, Jim finds them and aids in the defense of the stockade. He then slips away, takes Ben Gunn's small boat, sneaks up to the *Hispaniola*, cuts her adrift from her moorings to harass the pirates, climbs aboard, subdues its last living pirate crewman, singlehandedly sails around the island to run the ship aground in a convenient spot, outwits the pirate's attempt to kill him, and shoots the pirate. Back on the island, he is captured by the remaining mutineers but saves his skin with a daring, even impudent, announcement of his own accomplishments. He manages by this speech to make Silver dependent on his good will, and later Jim's friend Doctor Livesey makes the sort of announcement every adventurous child lives to hear: "There is a kind of fate in this. . . . Every step, it's you that saves our lives" (256).

The only surprise, after this catalogue of triumphs, is that Jim does not sail the schooner alone to England, win a war singlehandedly, invent the steam engine, and become thrice Lord Mayor of London. The fact is that real children are seldom permitted to do *one* outstandingly brave and stupid thing, let alone a dozen in a row. When they do, the consequences are often tragic, as in 1212 when a twelve-year-old named Stephen organized a children's crusade to Jerusalem, only to have his entire group kidnapped and sold into slavery by the sailors who had volunteered to transport them. Golding's fictional children are, in this sense, real children. They ridicule, torment, and persecute. Confronted by Long John Silver, as Jim Hawkins is in the following passage they would likely join the pirates to save their skins or for the sheer pleasure of an anarchic, violent life. However, Jim Hawkins is a pure fiction and an honorary adult, granted thrillingly impossible powers by his creator.

FROM ROBERT LOUIS STEVENSON, *TREASURE ISLAND*,
CHAPTER 28 (1883)

"Well," said I, "I am not such a fool but I know pretty well what I have to look for. Let the worst come to the worst, it's little I care. I've seen too many die since I fell in with you. But there's a thing or two I have to tell you," I said, and by this time I was quite excited; "and the first is this: here you are, in a bad way: ship lost, treasure lost, men lost; your whole business gone to wreck; and if you want to know who did it—it was I! I was in the apple barrel the night we sighted land, and I heard you, John, and you, Johnson, and Hands, who is now at the bottom of the sea, and told every word you said before the hour was out. And as for the schooner, it was I who cut her cable, and it was I that killed the men you had aboard of her, and it was I who brought her where you'll never see her more, not one of you. The laugh's on my side. I've had the top of this business from the first; I no more fear you than I fear a fly. Kill me, if you please, or spare me. But one thing I'll say, and no more; if you spare me, bygones are bygones, and when you fellows are in court for piracy, I'll save you all I can. It is for you to choose. Kill another and do yourselves no good, or spare me and keep a witness to save you from the gallows."

I stopped, for, I tell you, I was out of breath, and, to my wonder, not a man of them moved, but all sat staring at me like as many sheep. And while they were still staring, I broke out again:

"And now, Mr. Silver," I said, "I believe you're the best man here, and if things go to the worst, I'll take it kind of you to let the doctor know the way I took it."

"I'll bear it in mind," said Silver, with an accent so curious that I could not, for the life of me, decide whether he were laughing at my request, or had been favorably affected by my courage.

"I'll put one to that," cried the old mahogany-faced seaman—Morgan by name—whom I had seen in Long John's public-house upon the quays of Bristol. "It was him that knowed Black Dog."

"Well, and see here," added the sea-cook, "I'll put another to that, by thunder! for it was this same boy that faked the chart from Billy Bones. First and last, we've split upon Jim Hawkins!" (233–34)

Philadelphia: David McKay, c. 1917.

GLAMORIZED VIOLENCE

A characteristic of the adventure story is that violence, when present, is viewed through a Teddy Roosevelt–style, what-the-hell-let's-invade-Cuba, what-a-bully-idea sort of lens. Danger threatens the hero at times, but the reader seldom feels any real apprehension. Death, when it occurs, is always (1) justified because it was a "bad guy" who got killed, (2) mitigated because the victim died in a good cause or was "only" a "savage," or (3) avenged by the victim's compatriots. The sheer brutal uselessness of Simon's and Piggy's deaths is seen nowhere in the tales that inspired *Lord of the Flies*.

In the following passage, Doctor Livesey tells how, after unloading some supplies from the *Hispaniola*, he, Smollett, and some loyal crewmen (including a converted mutineer, Abraham Gray) made their way to the island's stockade.

FROM ROBERT LOUIS STEVENSON, *TREASURE ISLAND*, CHAPTER 18 (1883)

We made our best speed across the strip of wood that now divided us from the stockade; and at every step we took the voices of the buccaneers rang nearer. Soon we could hear their footfalls as they ran, and the cracking of the branches as they breasted across a bit of thicket.

I began to see we should have a brush for it in earnest, and looked to my priming.

"Captain," said I, "Trelawny is the dead shot. Give him your gun; his own is useless."

They exchanged guns, and Trelawny, silent and cool as he had been since the beginning of the bustle, hung a moment on his heel to see that all was fit for service. At the same time, observing Gray to be unarmed, I handed him my cutlass. It did all our hearts good to see him spit in his hand, knit his brows, and make the blade sing through the air. It was plain from every line of his body that our new hand was worth his salt.

Forty paces farther we came to the edge of the wood and saw the stockade in front of us. We struck the enclosure about the middle of the south side, and almost at the same time, seven mutineers—Job Anderson, the boatswain, at their head, appeared in full cry at the southwestern corner.

They paused, as if taken aback; and before they recovered, not only the squire and I, but Hunter and Joyce from the blockhouse, had time to fire. The four shots came in rather a scattering volley; but they did the business: one of the enemy actually fell, and the rest, without hesitation, turned and plunged into the trees.

After reloading, we walked down the outside of the palisade to see the fallen enemy. He was stone dead—shot through the heart.

We began to rejoice over our good success, when just at that moment a pistol cracked in the bush, a ball whistled close past my ear, and poor Tom Redruth stumbled and fell his length on the ground. Both the squire and I returned the shot; but as we had nothing to aim at, it is probable we only wasted powder. Then we reloaded, and turned our attention to poor Tom.

The captain and Gray were already examining him; and I saw with half an eye that all was over.

I believe the readiness of our return volley had scattered the mutineers once more, for we were suffered without further molestation to get the poor old gamekeeper hoisted over the stockade, and carried, groaning and bleeding, into the log-house.

Poor old fellow, he had not uttered one word of surprise, complaint, fear, or even acquiescence, from the very beginning of our troubles till now, when we had laid him down in the log-house to die. He had lain like a Trojan behind his mattress in the gallery; he had followed every order silently, doggedly, and well; he was the oldest of our party by a score of years; and now, sullen, old, serviceable servant, it was he that was to die.

The squire dropped down beside him on his knees and kissed his hand, crying like a child.

"Be I going, doctor?" he asked.

"Tom, my man," said I, "you're going home."

"I wish I had had a lick at them with the gun first," he replied.

"Tom," said the squire, "say you forgive me, won't you?"

"Would that be respectful like, from me to you, squire?" was the answer. "Howsoever, so be it, amen!"

After a little while of silence, he said he thought somebody might read a prayer. "It's the custom, sir," he added, apologetically. And not long after, without another word, he passed away.

In the meantime the captain, whom I had observed to be wonderfully swollen about the chest and pockets, had turned out a great many various stores—the British colors, a Bible, a coil of stoutish rope, pen, ink, the log-book, and pounds of tobacco. He had found a longish fir-tree lying felled and cleared in the enclosure, and, with the help of Hunter, he had set it up at the corner of the log-house where the trunks crossed and made an angle. Then, climbing on the roof, he had with his own hand bent and run up the colours.

This seemed mightily to relieve him. He reëntered the log-house, and set about counting up the stores, as if nothing else existed. But he had an eye on Tom's passage for all that; and as soon as all was over, came forward with another flag, and reverently spread it on the body.

"Don't you take on, sir," he said, shaking the squire's hand. "All's well with him; no fear for a hand that's been shot down in his duty to captain and owner. It mayn't be good divinity, but it's a fact."

Then he pulled me aside.

"Dr. Livesey," he said, "in how many weeks do you and squire expect the consort?"

I told him it was a question, not of weeks, but of months; that if we were not back by the end of August, Blandly was to send to find us; but neither sooner nor later. "You can calculate for yourself," I said.

"Why, yes," returned the captain, scratching his head, "and making a large allowance, sir, for all the gifts of Providence, I should say we were pretty close hauled."

"How do you mean?" I asked.

. . . "As for the powder and shot, we'll do. But the rations are short, very short—so short, Dr. Livesey, that we're perhaps as well without that extra mouth."

And he pointed to the dead body under the flag.

Just then with a roar and a whistle, a round shot passed high above the roof of the log-house and plumped far beyond us in the wood.

"Oho!" said the captain. "Blaze away! You've little enough powder already, my lads."

At the second trial the aim was better, and the ball descended inside the stockade, scattering a cloud of sand, but doing no further damage.

"Captain," said the squire, "the house is quite invisible from the ship. It must be the flag they are aiming at. Would it not be wiser to take it in?"

"Strike my colors!" cried the captain. "No, sir, not I;" and, as soon as he had said the words, I think we all agreed with him. For it was not only a piece of stout, seamanly good feeling; it was good policy besides, and showed our enemies that we despised their cannonade.

All through the evening they kept thundering away. Ball after ball flew over or fell short, or kicked up the sand in the enclosure; but they had to fire so high that the shot fell dead and buried itself in the soft sand. We had no ricochet to fear; and though one popped in through the roof of the log-house and out again through the floor, we soon got used to that sort of horse-play, and minded it no more than cricket. (146–50)

Philadelphia: David McKay, c. 1917.

TOPICS FOR WRITTEN OR ORAL EXPLORATION

1. Read *The Swiss Family Robinson* or the excerpt in this chapter. How would the Robinson boys deal with their island if their parents were not present? Write a scenario in which only the boys survive the ship's crash.

2. Compare Golding's treatment of the details of survival—finding food and shelter—with the treatments by Defoe or Wyss.

3. Read *The Coral Island* or the excerpt in this chapter. Compare the ways in which the boys make decisions in *The Coral Island* and in *Lord of the Flies*. Which version is more realistic? Why?

4. Read the excerpts from *Swiss Family Robinson*, *Robinson Crusoe*, or *The Coral Island*. How are the hunting scenes similar or different?

5. Rewrite the *Treasure Island* battle reprinted in this chapter as if Golding had written it.

6. There's an old saying, "Idle hands are the devil's workshop." Do the *Lord of the Flies* boys confirm or refute this saying?

7. Compare a more traditional adventure tale, such as *Tom Sawyer*, *Robin Hood*, or *Peter Pan*, to *Lord of the Flies*. How do the characters in each story react to their freedom from authority? Do they try, like the *Lord of the Flies* boys, to create a new system of authority? Do they succeed or fail?

8. How do you think you and your classmates would get along if you were dropped on a tropical island with no adults and no apparent chance of rescue?

9. Read *The Cay*, by Theodore Taylor, which uses the island motif for a story of redemption rather than a tragedy. Is it more or less realistic than *Lord of the Flies*?

10. Compare the behavior of the *Lord of the Flies* boys to the behavior of characters in another type of adventure tale—for example, old movie westerns.

11. Devise a desert-island cartoon based on *Lord of the Flies*.

12. Look at examples of desert-island cartoons, for example in *Far Side* or *New Yorker* collections. Are there rules that govern such cartoons, such as the rules that govern "castaway" stories? Are the cartoons funny because they follow the rules, or because they subvert the rules?

13. Pick another book or film type (genre), such as the western, or the romance novel. Think of several examples of this genre. Then list what they have in common. Can you discover the "rules" of this

genre? Can you think of books or movies in this genre that break the rules?

14. Research a particular island's climate and wildlife. Assume it is uninhabited and pretend you have been marooned there after a sea or air disaster. Write a diary like Robinson Crusoe's, describing how you survive. Make sure not to give yourself skills you don't already have. Stick as closely as possible to what you think would *really* happen.

15. In the passage from *The Swiss Family Robinson* reprinted in this chapter, what similarities (especially in the boys' behavior) to *Lord of the Flies* do you notice? What keeps these boys from behaving like Golding's boys? Is their behavior realistic?

16. *The Coral Island's* Jack is named "Captain," while *Lord of the Flies'* Jack wants to be "Chief." What connotations do these two titles carry? Why do you think Golding chose "chief" over "captain"?

17. Read *Island of the Blue Dolphins*, *The Cay*, or *Alive*. How does the book you chose conform to the conventions of the adventure story? How does it depart from those conventions?

18. Read a non-island adventure novel, such as *Tom Sawyer*, *Last of the Mohicans*, or *Robin Hood*. Are the conventions the same as for island-based adventure tales?

19. Read *Peter Pan*. How are Golding's boys "lost boys"? Is there more than one way to be lost?

NOTES

1. Jeffrey Richards, *Happiest Days: The Public Schools in English Fiction* (Manchester, UK: Manchester University Press, 1988), 59–60.

2. Jack I. Biles, *Talk: Conversations with William Golding* (New York: Harcourt Brace Jovanovich, 1970), 60.

3. J. C. Holt, *Robin Hood* (1982; reprint, London: Thames and Hudson, 1991), 37.

4. R. M. Ballantyne, *The Coral Island* (1858; reprint, London: J. M. Dent & Co., 1907), 7.

5. Ibid., 172.

SUGGESTIONS FOR FURTHER READING

Barrie, J. M. *Peter Pan*. 1911. Reprint. New York: Signet, 1987.

O'Dell, Scott. *Island of the Blue Dolphins*. 1960. Reprint. New York: Yearling, 1987.

Orwell, George. "Boys' Weeklies," *A Collection of Essays*. Garden City, NY: Doubleday & Company, 1954.

Pyle, Howard. *The Merry Adventures of Robin Hood*. 1883. Reprint. New York: Troll, 1992.

———. *The Story of King Arthur and His Knights*. 1903. Reprint. New York: Atheneum, 1991.

———. *The Story of the Grail and the Passing of Arthur*. 1910. Reprint. New York: Dover, 1993.

Ransome, Arthur. *Swallows and Amazons*. 1931. Reprint. Lincoln, MA: David R. Godine, 1986.

Taylor, Theodore. *The Cay*. 1969. Reprint. New York: Camelot, 1995.

Twain, Mark. *The Adventures of Tom Sawyer*. 1876. Reprint. New York: Viking, 1987.

SUGGESTIONS FOR VIEWING

Captain Blood (1935)
Crusoe (1989)
Robin Hood (1938)
The Sea Hawk (1940)
Swiss Family Robinson (1960)
Treasure Island (1934)
Treasure Island (1989)

5

Religion

In the 1530s, Henry VIII, an English monarch whom the Pope had granted the title *Fidei Defensor* (Defender of the Faith) for his published refutation of Lutheranism, turned his back on papal authority, proclaimed himself head of the Church of England, and profoundly and permanently affected England's relationship to every other country in Europe. England's Protestantism affected its enmities, alliances, and national character, and though eventually the Anglican Church lost its absolute monopoly on the souls and public life of the English, it remained and still remains a powerful force in British culture. Even outside the Church of England, its influence can be seen. Thanks to movies, television, books, and personal contact, even people who are not Anglican think of the archetypal marriage ceremony as the one that begins, "Dearly beloved, we are gathered together in the sight of God . . . to join together this man and this woman in holy matrimony." This ceremony, with its poetic series of contrasts, "for better for worse, for richer for poorer, in sickness and in health," is in fact the Anglican wedding service from the Book of Common Prayer. One need not be Anglican to have had one's ideas shaped by the Church of England.

Golding, then, whatever his personal religious beliefs, could hardly have escaped the influence of Protestantism generally and of Anglicanism specifically. As a native of England, a resident of England, an English-speaking person, and a well-educated man who took a degree from Oxford in English literature, he simply had to be aware of these institutions. Even though Golding's father was an atheist, Golding himself, in interview after interview, attested to his own belief in God and in some of the most basic principles of Protestantism. Most important to the study of *Lord of the Flies*, he said that he was "convinced of original sin"—the doctrine that people are born naturally inclined to sin, a condition descending in most Christian theology from the fault of Adam and Eve in eating the fruit of the tree of knowledge. Intriguingly, Golding links original sin not to disobedience and forbidden knowledge, but to ignorance and selfishness:

> I think that because children are helpless and vulnerable, the most terrible things can be done by children to children. The fact that they are vulnerable, and ignorant of their own nature—can push the twin away from the breast without knowing that they are injuring themselves, without knowing that it's an antisocial action—that is ignorance. And we confuse it with innocence. I do myself. But I still think that the root of our sin is there, in the child. As soon as it has any capacity for acting on the world outside, it will be selfish; and, of course, original sin and selfishness—the words could be interchangeable. . . . You can only learn unselfishness by liking and loving.[1]

In another interview, Golding elucidated the experiences of World War II in a deeply religious manner. Humanity, he argued, was steeped in sin, yet there was hope for redemption.

> Golding: We all saw a hell of a lot in the war that can't be accounted for except on the basis of original evil. Man is born to sin. . . .
>
> Interviewer: But didn't the war also provide evidence on the other side?
>
> Golding: I believe, you see, that good can look after itself; it is self-propagating. The weight of any investigation must be in asking why man commits evil, rather than why he sometimes does good.[2]

Golding, it is clear, shared the concern of theologians over the nature and origin of sin. Yet he himself conceded that what he personally believed was not as important as what was present in the texts of his novels. As interviewer Jack Biles, who was acquainted with Golding, pointed out, Golding was not a Calvinist— a follower of John Calvin, whose rather terrifying teachings about sin, election, and salvation influenced some of England's strictest sects, including the Puritans. Yet in a conversation with Biles, Golding distinguished between himself and his works:

> [M]en don't write the books they should, they write the books they can. Now I don't think it's true I'm a Calvinist, but I'm willing to believe that my capacity for writing, such as it is, and my general make-up and my experience have made my books shape themselves so that Calvinism could be deduced from them.[3]

Golding, in summary, was a religious man from a historically Protestant nation who accepted that his works could be read as Calvinist. These factors make a religious reading of his novels particularly interesting.

CHRISTIANITY IN *LORD OF THE FLIES*

Lord of the Flies is a perfect example of the necessity of familiarity with the Bible to any serious study of Western literature. Allusions to the Old and New Testaments are profuse within its pages. The island is an Eden, with fruit thick on the trees, yet the boys, like Adam and Eve, yearn for the tempting, illicit food—in Adam and Eve's case, the fruit of the Tree of the Knowledge of Good and Evil, in the boys' case, the meat of the island's pigs. In both cases, the source of the temptation is ever-present and possession of it comes at a very high price. There are further religious allusions, not the least of which is the name of the pigheaded beast, whose name, "Lord of the Flies," is a rough English translation of the Hebrew name of the devil Beelzebub. Evoking the devil in a different form, the beast is identified by the littluns as a "snake-thing" (35), and it is several times afterward referred to as a snake (36, 46, 52), calling to mind the story of Adam and Eve once again. Perhaps the best illustration of the links between Christianity and *Lord of the Flies*, however, lies in the life and death of a single character.

In *Lord of the Flies*, as in the Bible, innocents are repeatedly slaughtered. The birthmarked boy dies in the fire, and Piggy is deliberately murdered near the novel's end, but the boy whose execution has the most Christian parallels is Simon. Even his name is significant, for the disciple Peter's name before his conversion is Simon, and it is Simon the Cyrenian who carries Christ's cross on the road to Golgotha. The cross episode is retold several times in the Bible, though it is the wording in Luke that is most ambiguous and intriguing: "[T]hey laid hold upon one Simon, a Cyrenian, coming out of the country, and on him they laid the cross, that he might bear it after Jesus" (Luke 23:26). In context, the use of the word *after* is clear enough; Simon follows Jesus in the procession, carrying the cross. However, as a possible source of inspiration for Golding's Simon, the use of the word *after* takes on a new meaning. In this case, Simon, the novel's Christ-figure, carries the cross of truth not geographically, but chronologically, after Christ—picking up, in a way, where Christ left off.

Simon resembles Jesus in other ways. Like Christ, he engages in prophecy. Christ repeatedly predicts his own death. Simon, by comparison, predicts not his own death but Ralph's survival (111). Simon never specifically predicts his own brutal fate, but it is worth noting that he always says that "you" (Ralph) will "get back all right," not that "we" will.

Like Christ, who feeds his followers with loaves and fishes (Matthew 15:32–38; Mark 6:34–44, 8:1–9; John 6:5–13), Simon feeds the littluns with fruit from the island's trees, handing fruit "back down to the endless, outstretched hands" (56). Like Christ, who early in his ministry "withdrew himself into the wilderness, and prayed" (Luke 5:16), Simon retreats into the wilderness to be alone with his thoughts (56–57). Later, he climbs the island's mountain and subjects himself to a fast of sorts, just as Christ does for forty days and nights. Subjected to physical discomfort, Simon maintains his vigil despite heat and thirst and flies on his face (132–33, 138) and, like Christ, is tempted by a devil on a mountain. This devil, though, does not offer kingdoms or demand demonstrations of heavenly favor (143–44). Simon's devil does not promise or tempt but threatens, warning of the sorts of torments that would most impress a young boy—the disapproval of his peers, the disapproval of an apparent authority figure, the hopelessness of the boy's cause, physical violence, and death. Simon collapses in an epileptic fit but, like Christ in Gethsemane, recovers himself and goes on to meet his doom. "What else is there to do?" (145) he asks aloud, with the anxious resignation of Christ subjecting himself to the will of God.

That doom is a re-enactment of the crucifixion, foreshadowed midway through the novel when Simon walks into a tree and injures his forehead, blood trickling down his face in imitation of the crown of thorns (104). Simon, like Christ being subjected to the mocking reverence of Pilate's men, is ridiculed by the boys, who call him "batty" and "cracked" (132). Most significantly, in the very act of bringing the truth of the beast's nature to the boys, he is mistaken for the beast and executed (152–53).

True to the words in Luke 23:34, "Father, forgive them, for they know not what they do," the boys seem somewhat unaware of their act in the frenzy of their dance. Yet there is a hint that they kill Simon knowingly. There is one single reference to him by name in the midst of the murder, implying that they do not wholly mistake him for a beast. Afterward, like Pilate conscious of guilt but unwilling to admit it, they wash their hands of the whole business, pretending they were not even present (156–58). In the context of the story, "something about a body on the hill" clearly means the paratrooper whose corpse is rotting on the mountaintop, but in the context of the novel's religious imagery, the wording is particularly appropriate. After all, the central visual image of Christianity is that of a body on a hill, suspended on a cross instead of a tree. And, like Christ's, the paratrooper's body in *Lord of the Flies* is spirited away, with only fear, doubt, and faith to show that it was ever there.

NON-CHRISTIAN RELIGION IN *LORD OF THE FLIES*

Not all of the religious imagery in *Lord of the Flies*, however, is Christian in nature. The explicitly Christlike Simon's visions of truth, in which he sees the essence of the beast in its physical (paratrooper) and metaphorical (human evil) manifestations, are in direct opposition to the worship of the beast. This primitive appeasement of an evil spirit may resemble popular British opinion of non-Christian religious practice, but it corresponds even more closely to accounts in the Old Testament (or Hebrew Bible)[4] of the worship of idols and gods in the Middle East's ancient polytheistic pantheon. The beast is Baal, Ashtaroth, the golden calf, a

"god" of revelry and decadence, burnt offerings, and human sacrifice.

This pagan worship evolves despite the fact that Jack and his
band were, as choirboys, certainly involved in church services at
home. Jack would seem therefore to be a likely focal point for the
establishment of Christianity on the island, but none of the boys
seem inclined to extend the reach of the Church of England to
their little kingdom. Even Simon remains a Christ figure without
Christianity per se. He never demands that the other boys revere
him or submit to the will of any god. His doctrine, such as it is, is
that there may be a beast on the island, but that it is neither god
nor monster but the dark side of human nature, the fear and greed
and envy and will to harm that roil like magma in the psyche, ready
to erupt at any moment and present below the surface even when
unseen.

Into this void of faith steps the beast, whose existence is accepted by most if not all of the littluns but doubted by the bigger
boys until they have reliable evidence. Even Jack repudiates the
beast (83). He accepts it as real only when two things occur: the
encounter of Samneric with the paratrooper's corpse, which they
insist is an animal, and Jack's own realization that a hunt for the
beast will give him a distinct edge over Ralph (100). For the rest
of the boys, with the notable exception of Simon, the convincing
piece of evidence is the nighttime encounter of Ralph and the
hunting party with the corpse on the mountain (123). From that
point, the infant religion grows rapidly. Once there is something
tangible to fear, something that can perhaps be appeased and thus
diminish the boys' larger and less specific fears, the trappings of
religious ritual develop. Thus there is a gift or offering to the beast
(the pig's head), a special ceremony (the hunt dance), and a ritual
chant ("*Kill the beast!*") (137, 152, 160–61). Typical of hunting
societies, the object of worship is associated with the success or
failure of the hunt, and Jack is intrigued by the idea that the beast
might be a hunter of some kind (126).

Why does Golding have his characters abandon one religion and
set up another in its place? A number of possible answers suggest
themselves. He may, as a Christian, wish to reserve only positive
associations for his own faith, while associating evil with "savage"
pagan beliefs. He may wish to demonstrate that religion is a natural
part of human existence and that, in the absence of an existing

religious hierarchy, a new one will arise in its place. He may be trying to demonstrate the role of religion in quieting people's existential fears and enabling them to go about their lives in something approximating peace of mind. He may be exploring the natural outcome of the imposition of an alternative code of morality.

One interesting explanation is that he is, throughout the novel, examining the role of authority in human society. Religion, like parents, teachers, police, the military, and governmental bureaucracy, is a source of authority in human communities. The boys on the island have had every type of authority stripped from them. It should be a child's dream, to be free of the demands of all those parents and substitute parents. Yet they immediately begin trying to recreate authority, by electing a chief, by investing the conch with symbolism, by establishing rules, and by inventing a religion. All the boys, even those who say they are not, are to some extent anxious in the absence of strong leadership. Lacking a strong enough internal morality, they look to an external figure to provide them with guidance.

In a way, the gods that humans have worshipped throughout recorded history have a strong resemblance to the parents of small children. Parents, like gods, punish unless certain forms are followed, demand obedience, control food supply, impose taboos, have sanctuaries and mysteries, seem sometimes to be capricious, possess vast knowledge, and offer bounty in reward for good behavior. Gods, like parents, are often called "Mother" or "Father" and bear a parental relationship to their followers. It is natural, then, that a group of children, absent from their parents and terrified about the future, should fashion a god from their fears and hopes.

BIBLICAL ALLUSIONS: THE OLD TESTAMENT

There are fewer allusions to the Old than to the New Testament in *Lord of the Flies*, but this hardly means that they are entirely absent. Original sin is central to the novel's theme, which makes the story of Adam and Eve particularly relevant. The Old Testament is also rife with injustice, persecution, and murder, of which the slaying of Abel by his jealous older brother Cain is only the first example. Though these passages do not offer the kind of direct correspondence to Golding's text that the gospels do, they are illustrative of the idea that sin arises from the most trivial stimuli and sometimes seem to well unbidden out of the depths of human nature. The fact that a serpent tempts Eve is also significant in light of the form that the beast takes in the littluns' dreams.

The Old Testament is also of interest for its treatment of pigs. Pork is *trefe*, a nonkosher food, in Judaism, and the swine is a powerful Old Testament symbol of filth and forbiddenness. The parallels to *Lord of the Flies*, in which pigs are associated with some of the darkest aspects of human behavior, are obvious.

Another apparent parallel is that between the boys' crazed and murderous feast dance and that of the Israelites in the desert as they worship the golden calf. Both grow out of the worship of false idols, both have an atmosphere of total abandon and revelry, both are accompanied by feasting, and both result in violence. In this episode, Simon can be seen both as Jesus—the innocent sacrifice—and as Moses, who brings wisdom down from the mountain only to find barbarous ignorance among his people.

All the following passages and those in the New Testament section that follows are from the King James Version of the Bible.

THE OLD TESTAMENT

ORIGINAL SIN

And the Lord God planted a garden eastward in Eden; and there he put the man whom he had formed. And out of the ground made the Lord God to grow every tree that is pleasant to the sight, and good for food; the tree of life also in the midst of the garden, and the tree of knowledge

of good and evil. . . . And the Lord God took the man, and put him into
the garden of Eden to dress it and to keep it. And the Lord God commanded the man, saying, Of every tree of the garden thou mayest freely
eat: But of the tree of the knowledge of good and evil thou shalt not eat
of it, for in the day that thou eatest thereof thou shalt surely die.

. . . And they were both naked, the man and his wife, and were not
ashamed.

Now the serpent was more subtil than any beast of the field which the
Lord God had made. And he said unto the woman, Yea, hath God said,
Ye shall not eat of every tree of the garden? And the woman said unto
the serpent, We may eat of the fruit of the trees of the garden; But of the
fruit of the tree which is in the midst of the garden, God hath said, Ye
shall not eat of it, neither shall ye touch it, lest ye die. And the serpent
said unto the woman, Ye shall not surely die: For God doth know that
in the day ye eat thereof, then your eyes shall be opened, and ye shall
be as gods, knowing good and evil. And when the woman saw that the
tree was good for food, and that it was pleasant to the eyes, and a tree
to be desired to make one wise, she took of the fruit thereof, and did
eat, and gave also unto her husband with her; and he did eat. And the
eyes of them both were opened, and they knew that they were naked;
and they sewed fig leaves together, and made themselves aprons. . . .

And the Lord God said, Behold, the man is become as one of us, to
know good and evil: and now, lest he put forth his hand, and take also
of the tree of life, and eat, and live for ever: Therefore the Lord God sent
him forth from the garden of Eden, to till the ground whence he was
taken. So he drove out the man; and he placed at the east of the garden
of Eden Cherubims, and a flaming sword which turned every way, to keep
the way of the tree of life. (Genesis 2:8–9, 15–17, 21–22, 25; 3:1–7, 22–
24)

THE FIRST MURDER

And Adam knew Eve his wife; and she conceived, and bare Cain, and
said, I have gotten a man from the Lord. And she again bare his brother
Abel. And Abel was a keeper of sheep, but Cain was a tiller of the ground.
And in process of time it came to pass, that Cain brought of the fruit of
the ground an offering unto the Lord. And Abel, he also brought of the
firstlings of his flock and of the fat thereof. And the Lord had respect
unto Abel and to his offering: But unto Cain and to his offering he had
not respect. And Cain was very wroth, and his countenance fell. And the
Lord said unto Cain, Why art thou wroth? and why is thy countenance
fallen? If thou doest well, shalt thou not be accepted? and if thou doest
not well, sin lieth at the door. And unto thee shall be his desire, and
thou shalt rule over him. And Cain talked with Abel his brother: and it

came to pass, when they were in the field, that Cain rose up against Abel his brother, and slew him.

And the Lord said unto Cain, Where is Abel thy brother? And he said, I know not: Am I my brother's keeper? And he said, What hast thou done? the voice of thy brother's blood crieth unto me from the ground. (Genesis 4:1–10)

SWINE

And the swine, though he divide the hoof, and be clovenfooted, yet he cheweth not the cud; he is unclean to you. Of their flesh shall ye not eat, and their carcase shall ye not touch; they are unclean to you. (Leviticus 11:7–8)

And the swine, because it divideth the hoof, yet cheweth not the cud, it is unclean to you: ye shall not eat of their flesh, nor touch their dead carcase. (Deuteronomy 14:8)

As a jewel of gold in a swine's snout, so is a fair woman which is without discretion. (Proverbs 11:22)

I have spread out my hands all the day unto a rebellious people, which walketh in a way that was not good, after their own thoughts; A people that provoketh me to anger continually to my face; that sacrificeth in gardens, and burneth incense upon altars of brick; Which remain among the graves, and lodge in the monuments, which eat swine's flesh, and broth of abominable things is in their vessels; Which say, Stand by thyself, come not near to me; for I am holier than thou. These are a smoke in my nose, a fire that burneth all the day. Behold, it is written before me: I will not keep silence, but will recompense, even recompense into their bosom. Your iniquities, and the iniquities of your fathers together, saith the Lord, which have burned incense upon the mountains, and blasphemed me upon the hills: therefore will I measure their former work into their bosom. (Isaiah 65:2–7)

He that killeth an ox is as if he slew a man; he that sacrificeth a lamb, as if he cut of a dog's neck; he that offereth an oblation, as if he offered swine's blood; he that burneth incense, as if he blessed an idol. Yes, they have chosen their own ways, and their soul delighteth in their abominations. (Isaiah 66:3)

They that sanctify themselves, and purify themselves in the gardens behind one tree in the midst, eating swine's flesh, and the abomination and the mouse, shall be consumed together, saith the Lord. (Isaiah 66:17)

THE GOLDEN CALF

And when the people saw that Moses delayed to come down out of the mount, the people gathered themselves together unto Aaron, and said unto him, Up, make us gods, which shall go before us; for as for this Moses, the man that brought us up out of the land of Egypt, we wot not what is become of him. And Aaron said unto them, Break off the golden earrings, which are in the ears of your wives, of your sons, and of your daughters, and bring them unto me. And all the people brake off the golden earrings which were in their ears, and brought them unto Aaron. And he received them at their hand, and fashioned with it a graving tool, after he had made it a molten calf: and they said, These be thy gods, O Israel, which brought thee up out of the land of Egypt. And when Aaron saw it, he built an altar before it; and Aaron made proclamation, and said, To morrow is a feast to the Lord. And they rose up early on the morrow, and offered burnt offerings, and brought peace offerings; and the people sat down to eat and to drink, and rose up to play.

And the Lord said unto Moses, Go, get thee down; for thy people which thou broughtest out of the land of Egypt, have corrupted themselves. . . .

And Moses turned, and went down from the mount, and the two tables of the testimony were in his hand. . . . And when Joshua heard the noise of the people as they shouted, he said unto Moses, There is a noise of war in the camp. And he said, It is not the voice of them that shout for mastery, neither is it the voice of them that cry for being overcome: but the noise of them that sing do I hear.

And it came to pass, as soon as he came nigh unto the camp, that he saw the calf, and the dancing: and Moses' anger waxed hot, and he cast the tables out of his hands, and brake them beneath the mount. And he took the calf which they had made, and burnt it in the fire, and ground it to powder, and strawed it upon the water, and made the children of Israel to drink of it. . . .

And when Moses saw that the people were naked; (for Aaron had made them naked unto their shame among their enemies:) Then Moses stood in the gate of the camp, and said, Who is on the Lord's side? let him come unto me. And all the sons of Levi gathered themselves together unto him. And he said unto them, Thus saith the Lord God of Israel, Put every man his sword by his side, and go in and out from gate to gate throughout the camp, and slay every man his brother, and every man his companion, and every man his neighbour. And the children of Levi did according to the word of Moses: and there fell of the people that day about three thousand men. (Exodus 32:1–7, 15–20, 25–28)

BIBLICAL ALLUSIONS: THE NEW TESTAMENT

The similarities between Simon and Christ have already been outlined; below are three relevant passages. In the first, Christ goes into the wilderness to fast and is confronted by the devil, who tempts him to abandon his ministry. It corresponds to Simon's confrontation with the Lord of the Flies. In the second, Christ defends himself against the charge that his powers of exorcism come from the devil; the significance of this passage is that the devil in question is named "Beelzebub," literally, the "Lord of the Flies." In the third, Christ drives a horde of demons from a madman into a herd of Gadarene swine, which then commit suicide by plunging into the sea. This passage is interesting because of the link between devils and pigs and, to some extent, because of the role of the sea. To boys stranded on an island, and possessed in a way by devils, the sea might be a similarly ominous presence.

THE NEW TESTAMENT

TEMPTATION IN THE WILDERNESS

Then was Jesus led up of the Spirit into the wilderness to be tempted of the devil. And when he had fasted forty days and forty nights, he was afterward an hungred. And when the tempter came to him, he said, If thou be the Son of God, command that these stones be made bread. But he answered and said, It is written, Man shall not live by bread alone, but by every word that proceedeth out of the mouth of God. Then the devil taketh him up into the holy city, and setteth him on a pinnacle of the temple, And saith unto him, If thou be the Son of God, cast thyself down: for it is written, He shall give his angels charge concerning thee: and in their hands they shall bear thee up, lest at any time thou dash thy foot against a stone. Jesus said unto him, It is written again, Thou shalt not tempt the Lord thy God. Again, the devil taketh him up into an exceeding high mountain, and sheweth him all the kingdoms of the world, and the glory of them; And saith unto him, All these things will I give thee, if thou wilt fall down and worship me. Then saith Jesus unto him, Get thee hence, Satan: for it is written, Thou shalt worship the Lord thy God, and him only shalt thou serve. Then the devil leaveth him, and, behold, angels came and ministered unto him. (Matthew 4:1–11)

BEELZEBUB

Then was brought unto him one possessed with a devil, blind, and dumb: and he healed him, insomuch that the blind and dumb both spake and saw. And all the people were amazed, and said, Is not this the son of David? But when the Pharisees heard it, they said, This fellow doth not cast out devils, but by Beelzebub the prince of the devils. And Jesus knew their thoughts, and said unto them, Every kingdom divided against itself is brought to desolation; and every city or house divided against itself shall not stand: And if Satan cast out Satan, he is divided against himself; how shall then his kingdom stand? And if I by Beelzebub cast out devils, by whom do your children cast them out? therefore they shall be your judges. But if I cast out devils by the Spirit of God, then the kingdom of God is come unto you. (Matthew 12:22–28)

THE GADARENE SWINE

And they came over unto the other side of the sea, into the country of the Gadarenes. And when he was come out of the ship, immediately there met him out of the tombs a man with an unclean spirit, Who had his dwelling among the tombs; and no man could bind him, no, not with chains: Because that he had been often bound with fetters and chains, and the chains had been plucked asunder by him, and the fetters broken in pieces: neither could any man tame him. And always, night and day, he was in the mountains, and in the tombs, crying, and cutting himself with stones. But when he saw Jesus afar off, he ran and worshipped him, And cried with a loud voice, and said, What have I to do with thee, Jesus, thou Son of the most high God? I adjure thee by God, that thou torment me not. For he said to him, Come out of the man, thou unclean spirit. And he asked him, What is thy name? And he answered, saying, My name is Legion: for we are many. And he besought him much that he would not send them away out of the country. Now there was there nigh unto the mountains a great herd of swine feeding. And all the devils said besought him, saying, Send us into the swine, that we may enter into them. And forthwith Jesus gave them leave. And the unclean spirits went out, and entered into the swine: and the herd ran violently down a steep place into the sea, (they were about two thousand;) and were choked in the sea. (Mark 5:1–13)

ORIGINAL SIN

One of the early Protestant theorists was John Calvin, a French theologian who was one of the most influential figures of the sixteenth-century Reformation. Based primarily in Geneva, Switzerland, he published his views, founded the University of Geneva, and encouraged the founding of Protestant churches throughout Europe. Informed by "optimism as to God despite pessimism as to man,"[5] Calvinism was expressed most fully in the book *Institutes of the Christian Religion*. In it and in his other writings, Calvin argued for the majesty of God, the profound sinfulness of man, the salvation of the elect (certain virtuous souls predestined for paradise), and the need to honor God regardless of one's saved or damned status. An activist, aggressive, austere faith, Calvinism spread to France, the Netherlands, England, Scotland, and New England.

Typical of Calvin's beliefs about human nature is his assertion, reiterated in one way or another throughout the *Institutes*, "that all men are overwhelmed with an inevitable calamity, from which they can never emerge unless they are extricated by the mercy of God."[6] That "inevitable calamity" is the damnation that must result from humanity's abominable inclination to commit acts hateful to God—in other words, from original sin. Of all Calvin's theories, this is the one most relevant to the study of *Lord of the Flies*. Though Calvin was hardly the first to discuss the concept of original sin, which had been a principal tenet of Christianity for centuries, he gave it new emphasis. As a Protestant, he was attempting to distinguish his faith from Catholicism, with its reliance on confession, indulgences, and good works to wash away or mitigate sin. Sects based on Calvinist doctrine often harped even more on this string than Calvin himself, leading to some very severe views of human nature and a permanent association between Calvin and original sin. Calvin's own words on the subject, though not as harsh as those of some of his followers, make it no surprise that Golding is often mistaken for a Calvinist.

FROM JOHN CALVIN, *INSTITUTES OF THE CHRISTIAN RELIGION* (1536)

To remove all uncertainty and misunderstanding on this subject, let us define original sin. It is not my intention to discuss all the definitions given by writers; I shall only produce one, which I think perfectly consistent with the truth. Original sin, therefore, appears to be an hereditary pravity and corruption of our nature, diffused through all the parts of the soul, rendering us obnoxious to the Divine wrath, and producing in us those works which the Scripture calls "works of the flesh." And this is indeed what Paul frequently denominates *sin*. The works which proceed thence, such as adulteries, fornications, thefts, hatreds, murders, revellings, he calls in the same manner "fruits of sin;" although they are also called "sins" in many passages of Scripture, and even by himself. These two things therefore should be distinctly observed: first, that our nature being so totally vitiated and depraved, we are, on account of this very corruption, considered as convicted and justly condemned in the sight of God, to whom nothing is acceptable but righteousness, innocence, and purity. And this liableness to punishment arises not from the delinquency of another; for when it is said that the sin of Adam renders us obnoxious to the Divine judgment, it is not to be understood as if we, though innocent, were undeservedly loaded with the guilt of his sin; but, because we are all subject to a curse, in conseuqence [*sic*] of his transgression, he is therefore said to have involved us in guilt. Nevertheless we derive from him, not only the punishment, but also the pollution to which the punishment is justly due. . . . And therefore infants themselves, as they bring their condemnation into the world with them, are rendered obnoxious to punishment by their own sinfulness, not by the sinfulness of another. For though they have not yet produced the fruits of their iniquity, yet they have the seed of it within them; even their whole nature is as it were a seed of sin, and therefore cannot but be odious and abominable to God. . . . The other thing to be remarked is, that this depravity never ceases in us, but is perpetually producing new fruits, those works of the flesh which we have before described, like the emission of flame and sparks from a heated furnace, or like the streams of water from a never failing spring. Wherefore those who have defined original sin as a privation of the original righteousness, which we ought to possess, though they comprise the whole of the subject, yet have not used language sufficiently expressive of its operation and influence. For our nature is not only destitute of all good, but is so fertile in all evils that it cannot remain inactive. Those who have called it *concupiscence* have used an expression not improper, if it were only added, which is far from being conceded by most persons, that every thing in man, the understanding and will, the soul and body, is polluted and engrossed by this concupiscence; or, to express it more briefly, that man is of himself nothing else but concupiscence. (229–30)

Philadelphia: Presbyterian Board of Publication, 1841.

THE ANGLICAN BAPTISM

The text of the Anglican infant baptism, as rendered in the Book of Common Prayer, makes it clear that the concept of original sin did not die with Calvin but continued to flourish in Protestant churches. This portion of the baptismal service has a more hopeful ring to it than Calvin's doctrines, but the central idea is intact: People are born bad, and only Christ can make them good.

FROM THE ANGLICAN BOOK OF COMMON PRAYER

Dearly beloved, forasmuch as all men are conceived and born in sin, and that our Saviour Christ saith, None can enter into the kingdom of God, except he be regenerate and born anew of water and of the holy Ghost; I beseech you to call upon God the Father, through our Lord Jesus Christ, that of his bounteous mercy he will grant to this child that thing which by nature he cannot have, that he may be baptized with water and the holy Ghost, and received into Christs holy Church, and be made a lively member of the same. . . .

Almighty and everlasting God, who of they great mercy didst save Noah and his family in the ark from perishing by water, and also didst safely lead the children of Israel they people through the red sea, figuring thereby the holy baptism; and by the baptism of thy wel-beloved Son Jesus Christ in the River Jordan didst sanctifie water to the mystical washing away of sin; We beseech thee for thine infinite mercies that thou wilt mercifully look upon this child; wash him and sanctifie him with the holy Ghost, that he being delivered from thy wrath, may be received into the ark of Christs Church; and being stedfast in faith, joyful through hope, and rooted in charity, may so pass the waves of this troublesom world, that finally he may come to the land of everlasting life; there to reign with thee world without end, through Jesus Christ our Lord. Amen.

Almighty and immortal God, the aid of all that need, the helper of all that flee to thee for succour, the life of them that believe, and the resurrection of the dead; We call upon thee for this infant, that he coming to thy holy baptism, may receive remission of his sins by spiritual regeneration. (1251–54)

London: Ecclesiastical History Society, 1850, vol. 2.

TOPICS FOR WRITTEN OR ORAL EXPLORATION

1. What is the position of your religion, or your personal philosophy, on the nature of humanity? Are we inherently good, evil, or neither?

2. What are your personal views about good and evil? Where do good and evil come from? Why does one triumph or fail in a given set of circumstances?

3. In *Lord of the Flies*, which of the boys is most guilty of evil?

4. Now that the boys have been rescued, should they atone somehow for what they have done on the island? How?

5. Jack's invention of a beast-god seems to imply that, in Golding's view, religion is a natural element of human society and that, in the absence of an established religion, some sort of religion will be created to replace it. Do you agree with this view? Is the presence of some kind of religion an essential part of humanity?

6. What is the purpose of religion in human society?

7. It is tempting, when reading any book with religious symbolism, to see any immersion in water as a potential baptism. Read the passages in *Lord of the Flies* that feature the boys swimming. Do these swims in the ocean constitute a symbolic baptism? Why or why not?

8. Research a religion other than your own. What are its views on the origin, punishment, and expiation of sin?

9. Jack's behavior with regard to the beast might be considered superstitious. What is the difference between superstition and religion?

10. Read the story of the expulsion of evil from the Garden of Eden in the book of Genesis. What is the forbidden fruit in *Lord of the Flies?* Does eating it bring a knowledge of good and evil?

11. Compare the depiction of pigs in the Bible with the depiction of pigs in *Lord of the Flies*.

12. Is the paratrooper's body a symbol of good? Evil? Something else?

13. List the similarities between the golden calf episode in Exodus and *Lord of the Flies*.

14. Research the religion of a real-life hunting/gathering society. Compare and contrast it to the boys' worship of the beast.

15. How does the hunt dance and its aftermath compare to the Greek story of the death of Orpheus?

NOTES

1. William Golding, "William Golding Talks to John Carey," in *William Golding: The Man and His Books*, ed. John Carey (London: Faber and Faber, 1986, 175.

2. William Golding, interview with Maurice Dolbier, *New York Herald Tribune*, May 20, 1962.

3. William Golding, in Jack I. Biles, *Talk: Conversations with William Golding* (New York: Harcourt Brace Jovanovich, 1970), 86.

4. Most Christians, in their religious practice, would call these chapters of the Bible the Old Testament. Jews and religious scholars often prefer the term "Hebrew Bible." Of the two terms, I have chosen to use "Old Testament" throughout this chapter as being in wider lay use and as reflecting Golding's explicitly Christian sensibility.

5. Roland H. Bainton, *The Reformation of the Sixteenth Century* (1952; reprint, Boston: Beacon Press, 1985), 112.

6. John Calvin, *Institutes of the Christian Religion*, Book II, Chapter III (1536; reprint, Philadelphia, PA: Presbyterian Board of Publication, 1841), 262.

6

Biology, Evolution, and *Lord of the Flies*

The population of Iceland, an island nation in the north Atlantic, is relatively small and has been kept so throughout history by repeated calamities such as plague, smallpox, and volcanic eruption. The country's physical isolation and small population has meant that eventually, over the last thousand years or so, almost everybody on the island became related to one another. As a result, a surprising number of Icelanders share a particular mutation of a particular gene known as BRCA2, a mutation that has been traced back to their sixteenth-century ancestor Einar. The reason anyone cares is that this particular mutation of BRCA2 causes breast cancer in both men and women.[1]

Scientists traced the mutation back to Einar by following the advice of Charles Darwin, who wrote that "when naturalists observe a close agreement in numerous small details of habits, tastes, and dispositions between two or more domestic races, or between nearly allied natural forms, they use this fact as an argument that they are descended from a common progenitor who was thus endowed."[2] In other words, if you share a trait with someone, odds are that at some point you have a common ancestor, whether the ancestor is your mother or an Australopithecus or a proto-mammal. In fact, Darwin goes on to say, the very points of resemblance can be assembled to draw a kind of theoretical picture of what that ancestor might have looked like. All humans, for example, have noses. That makes it likely that the first humans had noses, too.

Suppose for a moment that the BRCA2 mutation had instead occurred in Africa at the time when humans were just beginning to flourish. Suppose that when they spread to other parts of the world, they took the mutation with them. Assuming that they survived and multiplied through the ensuing millennia, we would today consider early death from breast cancer to be common, even normal. As it happened, early humans did not pass on this particular mutation, but they left other legacies. They were social creatures, not lone wanderers, and to survive, they needed to cooperate and to settle disputes. They gathered and later cultivated plant food, but they also hunted, and to hunt, as well as to contend for leadership, they needed teamwork and carefully channelled aggression.

Early humans, then, needed both aggression and cooperation to survive, and modern humans retain these characteristics. Charity, the anger felt when someone cuts in line, the sense that babies are cute and ought to be protected, the urge to rescue someone in danger, and unreasonable fury at fellow drivers can all be seen as manifestations of a genetic legacy. Similarly, Piggy's desire for fairness, Simon's curiosity, and Ralph's need to maintain leadership of the group can be traced to traits that enabled early humans to survive.

Yet it is Jack's urge to hunt that seems most primitive and fundamental. Hunting is simple: kill, eat, and survive, or fail, starve, and die. Even though there is abundant fruit on the island, the hunting instinct is so strong, so unavoidable, that the hunt surpasses everything in importance. It becomes more important than friendship, civilization, rescue, and human life. Even before Jack has had a successful hunt, he has a hard time valuing rescue over a kill (53).

Hunting brings status, awarded both for the hunter's mysterious skill and for the valuable commodity the hunt provides. In Jack's case, hunting provides him with a means of gaining power over the other boys and over his own fears. He can barely tolerate losing the election for leader, yet he and Simon and Ralph get along splendidly on their exploration of the island until they startle and fail to kill a pig. Simon is only mildly troubled by the escape of the pig because he seems to have no interest in political leadership. Ralph is only somewhat embarrassed because he is already the leader and has little to prove. But Jack has already suffered one recent failure, and it is he who turns defensive (31). Jack knows already that there is something special about hunting, something that ought to be instinctive and that would enable him to prove himself to the others. The failure to hunt is a failure of a principal biological mechanism, and it causes "a madness" in Jack (51). Golding always presents the desire to hunt and the desire to eat meat as overwhelming urges, so irresistible that even Piggy and Ralph are drawn to the feast. The author sees clear ties between the bare essence of humanity and the desire to kill and eat prey.

A desire for fairness, by contrast, is hard to trace to survival, though the connection can be made: In one tribe, people agree to certain basic rules and thus spend less time arguing, while in a rival tribe, the people are so torn by internal disagreements and conflicts that they are overwhelmed by their neighbors, or fail to gather enough food and so die of hunger, or kill each other out of sheer spite. The tribe that understands fairness passes on its legacy—its own kind of mutation—to the next generation. The tribe that turns on itself is the subject of Golding's novel. *Lord of the Flies* can be seen as a case study of a genetic dead end: a tribe in which aggression overcomes social skills.

The novel leaves its readers with a host of biological questions. Are all humans potentially violent? Is violence more powerful than altruism or justice? If Jack's behavior is "natural," in the sense that it is a common genetic legacy, what does society do about that? Is the hunting instinct stronger in some people than in others? Is altruism stronger in some people than in others? Once the aggressive instinct is switched on and given free rein, as it is in Jack's case, how can it be switched off again? These questions arise from a profound change in biological theory that took place in the century prior to the publication of *Lord of the Flies*.

THE THEORY OF EVOLUTION

For nearly as long as humans have been capable of considering such questions, it was an accepted truth that species did not change without divine intervention. Creation stories from various cultures explained the origins of animals, humans, natural phenomena, and so on, and these creatures and phenomena were presumed to be consistent throughout history. A horse was a horse, and had been a horse in its present form since the dawn of time.

In the nineteenth century, however, some scientists were beginning to question this ancient wisdom. European and American explorers were poking their way into parts of the globe previously unfamiliar to them, discovering new species of plants and animals. Excavators were uncovering strange bones that belonged to outlandish creatures unknown in modern times. Stockbreeders and farmers had been, since the eighteenth century, experimenting with developing new breeds of crops and animals simply by cross-breeding individuals or varieties with desirable characteristics. Such discoveries indicated that life was much more varied than had been suspected, that animals and plants were extremely well adapted to their particular circumstances, that some species had once existed but had ceased to exist, and that some species could be altered artificially by human selection. The monolithic idea of unchanging, eternal forms for species began to show cracks.

Then along came a man with an intellectual jackhammer. Charles Darwin, in 1859, published *The Origin of Species*, proposing that natural conditions "selected" the best-adapted species and favored adaptive change, just as stockbreeders selected the fattest cows and woolliest sheep. The best-adapted creatures, he reasoned, would survive longer and reproduce more prolifically, resulting in more of their kind in succeeding generations. Poorly adapted creatures would die early and leave fewer offspring to carry their genes. Darwin's work was popular as well as revolutionary, with the first printing of his book selling out in a single day.

Darwin's theory of "natural selection," also called "survival of the fittest," met with hostility from religious individuals and groups. After all, if creatures had evolved from primitive ancestors, diversifying and changing as circumstances warranted, then humans must have evolved in the same manner. They must have descended from apelike ancestors as the result of chance and adaptation rather than divine molding from Edenic clay. Humans must, indeed, be no better than clever apes themselves. It was a horrifying concept for a British, Christian, Victorian audience that heartily believed that humans were the pinnacle of creation, that Christianity was the one true religion, and that Britons were the most civilized and advanced group of humans on the planet. Even though Darwin made haste to argue that women were intellectually and physically inferior to men and that "savages" were morally inferior to Europeans, the fact remained that he had challenged one of the fundamental beliefs of his society. Darwin's theories threatened assumptions about human and European superiority, and at the same time, they reduced the story of Adam and Eve to one more creation myth. The publication of *The Origin of Species* was as radical and revolting to a great many people as the much earlier idea that the Earth revolved around the Sun.

Perhaps the most frightening aspect of evolutionary theory was its lack of moral absolutes. The God-given good and evil of theology were replaced, suddenly, with adaptive and non-adaptive behaviors. Behaviors and traits (in the scientific realm at least) were not good or bad; they were simply reproductively successful or unsuccessful. Many feared that a logical amorality would replace traditional, religiously or philosophically derived morality. This is, in fact, part of the creepiness of *Lord of the Flies*: its portrait of a triumph of biology over culture.

Yet, as the decades passed, evolutionary theory became widely accepted. Evidence in a wide range of scientific disciplines emerged to support it. All over the world, botanists, zoologists, entomologists, and geneticists documented the behavior, traits, reproductive cycles, and interdependencies of plants and animals. Fossilized remains of early hominids provided a glimpse of humankind's African infancy. Darwinian theory was used (and abused) to explain everything from world politics to segregation; all too often, "survival of the fittest" was invoked, in the form of Social Darwinism, to justify imperialism, sexism, poverty, and racism. Many who might once have felt afraid of the consequences of Darwinian theory embraced a version in which humanity had evolved, growing progressively better, smarter, stronger, and more successful with each generation, toward the inevitable goal: rich, white, male, Victorian and Edwardian Britons, who as masters of the world's largest empire, were apparently the Darwinian victors.

SOCIOBIOLOGY

If the late-nineteenth-century debate on evolution centered around its validity as a theory, the mid- to late-twentieth-century debate has centered on how far the theory should be taken. How much of human behavior is "nature" (i.e., genetic programming) and how much is "nurture" (culture or environment)? What are the origins of anger, love, and fear? Is marriage a cultural invention or the result of ancestral females choosing specific mates—males who would linger, form bonds, and help to provide for their offspring? Is it more natural for humans to cooperate or to compete? Under what circumstances do people display aggression?

In the twentieth century, a whole new discipline, sociobiology, arose to help answer such questions. Sociobiology attempts to trace social behaviors and patterns to their evolutionary roots. As with Darwinism, it has been widely used and abused. It has been criticized, particularly by feminists, for its emphasis on biology rather than culture. Some theorists or politicians have also used sociobiology to justify the status quo, without recognizing evolution as a process that extends into the future as well as the past. Furthermore, people's biases or political agendas sometimes color their views of animal studies or cause them to derive farfetched conclusions from sketchy or conflicting data. So controversial has the field become that some sociobiologists have adopted the label "evolutionary psychologists" instead.

Yet sociobiology offers some intriguing explanations for human and animal behavior. Dogs, for example, evolved as social carnivores with a dominance hierarchy to allow for efficient hunting. Even today, with thousands of years of careful breeding separating them from their wolf ancestors, they often exhibit pack behavior: pining for their "pack leader" or owner when absent, staying close to the "pack leader" when present, indicating submission to the "pack leader" by dropping the tail and ears, and guarding the hunting territory by leaving scent markers (in the form of widely scattered small amounts of urine), fighting other dogs to protect or expand their territory, and growling and raising the hackles, ears, and tail at intruders. Clear evolutionary justifications can be given for every single one of these behaviors. Surely humans, having evolved in a land full of large predators, and themselves lacking extraordinary speed, large teeth, sharp claws, hard scales, or horns, must have faced intense evolutionary pressures. Exactly which skills—mathematics, speech, complex social relationships, tool use—turned the tide in favor of a marginal species of African primates remains a mystery and probably always will. But it is absurd to deny that no trace of those skills remains in our psychology today, just as it is absurd to say that a dog's submission to its owner bears no relationship to its origin as a pack hunter.

Indeed, a sociobiologist reading *Lord of the Flies* could recommend two dog-based strategies to Ralph: either submit quickly to Jack's authority and wait for an opportunity to seize power (the strategy that Jack uses so successfully), or put up a better front of aggression when threatened. Ralph never raises his hackles, never growls. When Jack begins to lure away the majority of boys, Ralph sticks to quiet logic—the morally superior strategy, but a largely ineffective one (150–51). Jack, sensing weakness, barges right into Ralph's territory and accomplishes the dog-equivalent of urinating all over it, stealing the fire and Piggy's glasses, and terrorizing the littluns. The raid makes Jack the chief (168), giving him control of both the hunt and the fire. In Golding's world, aggression is an all-too-successful way of life.

Male Bonding and Aggression

One of the world's more controversial sociobiologists, Lionel Tiger, has achieved most of his notoriety by asserting the importance of bonding and aggression between men. Tiger, who admits that *Lord of the Flies* made a deep impression on him, asserts that behavior is at least in part determined by biology; that hunting influenced human development by requiring cooperation and the founding of all-male work groups; and that aggression toward the environment, other species, and other humans is a natural human, but especially masculine, characteristic. In his book, *Men in Groups*, he claims that in the prehistoric past, successful human hunting groups would have been entirely male because women would have been weighed down by pregnancy, lactation, and child care. "Any who did take part," he states, "would be at least marginally more prone than their sisters to loss of offspring."[3] Therefore, hunting females would produce fewer children, grandchildren, and so on, either because they had less time to care for their babies or because of accidents or injury to themselves. He argues that women would make inferior hunters anyway because they would be "less fleet, generally less strong, possibly more prone to changes in emotional tonus as a consequence of the estrous cycle, and less able to adapt to changes in temperature than males. Also, they could interfere with the co-operative nature of the group by stimulating competition for sexual access."[4] He concludes that men who let women hunt would have been less successful hunters and would also have produced fewer offspring.

Tiger proposes that reproductively successful males were capable of cooperating in the hunt, subordinating themselves to dominant males, and asserting authority when and if they got their own chance to dominate. The male-male bond, he argues, was as integral to sustaining the species as the male-female one, and to it he attributes such diverse phenomena as men's dominance in politics and the military, the existence of all-male clubs and secret societies, "[t]he dares which young boys issue each other," drinking contests, barroom brawls, men's willingness to barbecue, and the brutality of fraternity initiations and military academies. He considers aggression and hierarchical male bonding inseparable. True to this belief, in a several-page literary analysis of *Lord of the Flies*, Tiger focuses intently on the hunting episodes: success in the hunt determining the right to rule, hunting as a regression to a more basic (or "savage") form of existence, and the "species-specific patterns . . . of coalition, aggression, violence, and the savour of blood."[5]

Tiger's work has been criticized for its underemphasis of cultural influence and its overemphasis of hunting. In contemporary hunting-gathering societies, for example, plant gathering often produces a greater percentage of the diet than hunting does. *Men in Groups* was also written in the late 1960s, and there have obviously been significant culturally wrought changes in both male and female behavior since that time. Tiger's belief that women probably are incapable of attracting a substantial political following seems particularly ironic given the subsequent rise to power, in his own country, of Margaret Thatcher. His sense of the inappropriateness of men raising children, and his warnings about the "perhaps hazardous social change with numerous latent consequences should women ever enter politics in great numbers" seem comically dated. Yet *Men in Groups* remains an interesting guess about how certain types of behavior may have been encouraged by natural selection. It also reflects assumptions about maleness and femaleness that were prevalent at the time Golding wrote *Lord of the Flies*.

Altruism

Fortunately for the real world, there is more to evolution than aggression. Even Tiger concedes that "violence isn't necessary, nor indeed are coalition and hostility; this depends upon the social and economic circumstances in which people find themselves. After all, in reality constitutional government is possible."[6] While aggression is a successful strategy, so is altruism. If there were no evolutionary reason for effort on behalf of others, even at great cost to oneself, there would today be no charity, no celibate clergy, no adoption of unrelated offspring, no working so that a sibling can attend college, no risking one's life to save that of another. Piggy's concern for the littluns is as much the result of evolution as Jack's bloodlust. In fact, Ralph's and Piggy's desire to be rescued, even if it means forsaking meat in the short term, is a sounder evolutionary strategy than Jack's shortsighted hunting policy; without girls on the island, only a rescue will enable the surviving boys to reproduce. It is an accident of fate and an authorial need that brings a ship within sight of the island just when Jack is attempting to smoke out Ralph. Without that fortuitous ship, Ralph is killed, and Jack's boys likely die on the island, their genetic material withdrawn from the human pool.

If altruism and aggression are both valid evolutionary strategies, then a yearning toward both must exist in human nature. Evolution does not preclude the possibility of morality; it simply defines it more exactly. Good may be what benefits others with absolutely no genetic benefit to oneself and may be a natural and extreme consequence of evolutionary altruism. Evil, like that embodied by Jack, may be what penalizes oneself and others and may be a natural and extreme consequence of evolutionary aggression. Everything in between involves a balancing of benefits to oneself and others and is a more pragmatic merging of the moral and the biological.

SEXUAL SELECTION AND AGGRESSION

Darwin, in *The Origin of Species*, mentions "human selection," the selective breeding of livestock or crops by farmers. He also refers frequently to "natural selection," a term invented by Herbert Spencer. Natural selection describes the environmental forces that cause one variation in a species to be more successful than another. A particular family of birds, for example, might have stronger beaks than their neighbors in the next tree. Stronger beaks might enable them to break open tougher seeds and nuts, thus offering them a more copious food supply. The young birds in this family might therefore grow up stronger and healthier than their neighbors. They can thus survive longer, attract more or better mates, and produce more offspring with strong beaks.

Darwin also refers to "sexual selection," by which he means selection favoring a sex-linked characteristic. Such characteristics include gaudy plumage in male birds (for attracting mates and advertising good health) and drab plumage for female birds (for camouflage in nesting), tusks and horns for combat among males prior to mating, and differences between males and females in size or strength. According to Darwin, such characteristics, which relate specifically to mating or a sexual division of labor, are passed only to the sex that needs them.

At the time Golding wrote *Lord of the Flies*, interest in hunting, superior physical strength, and most types of aggression would have been considered male characteristics. Think about whether you would consider them the results of natural selection (the struggle to survive), sexual selection (the struggle to reproduce), or both.

FROM CHARLES DARWIN, *THE ORIGIN OF SPECIES* (1859)

This leads me to say a few words on what I have called Sexual Selection. This form of selection depends, not on a struggle for existence in relation to other organic beings or to external conditions, but on a struggle between the individuals of one sex, generally the males, for possession of the other sex. The result is not death to the unsuccessful competitor, but few or no offspring. Sexual selection is, therefore, less rigorous than natural selection. Generally, the most vigorous males, those which are best fitted for their places in nature, will leave most progeny. But in many cases, victory depends not so much on general vigor, as on having special weapons, confined to the male sex. . . . [M]ale salmons have been observed fighting all day long; male stag-beetles sometimes bear wounds from the huge mandible of other males; the males of certain hymenopterous insects have been frequently seen by that inimitable observer M. Fabre, fighting for a particular female who sits by, an apparently unconcerned beholder of the struggle, and then retires with the conqueror. The war is, perhaps, severest between the males of polygamous animals, and these seem oftenest provided with special weapons. The males of carnivorous animals are already well armed; though to them and to others, special means of defence may be given through means of sexual selection, as the mane of the lion, and the hooked jaw to the male salmon; for the shield may be as important for victory, as the sword or spear.

Amongst birds, the contest is often of a more peaceful character. All those who have attended to the subject, believe that there is the severest rivalry between the males of many species to attract, by singing, the females. The rock-thrush of Guiana, birds of paradise, and some others, congregate; and successive males display with the most elaborate care, and show off in the best manner, their gorgeous plumage; they likewise perform strange antics before the females, which, standing by as spectators, at last choose the most attractive partner. . . . [I]f man can in a short time give beauty and an elegant carriage to his bantams, according to his standard of beauty, I can see no good reason to doubt that female birds, by selecting, during thousands of generations, the most melodious or beautiful males, according to their standard of beauty, might produce a marked effect. Some well-known laws, with respect to the plumage of male and female birds, in comparison with the plumage of the young, can partly be explained through the action of sexual selection on variations occurring at different ages, and transmitted to the males alone or to both sexes at corresponding ages; but I have not space here to enter on this subject.

Thus it is, as I believe, that when the males and females of any animal have the same general habits of life, but differ in structure, colour, or ornament, such differences have been caused mainly by sexual selection:

that is, by individual males having had, in successive generations, some slight advantage over other males, in their weapons, means of defence, or charms, which they have transmitted to their male offspring alone. (108–10)

New York: D. Appleton and Company, 1915.

EVOLUTIONARY AGGRESSION AND ALTRUISM

Edward O. Wilson's *Sociobiology: The New Synthesis* quickly became a classic analysis of evolutionary influences on animal and human behavior. Two of Wilson's subjects are altruism and aggression—specifically, the evolutionary benefits and hazards of each, and some of the forms in which they are found. In the case of altruism, he asks how self-sacrificing acts could possibly have evolved. How does it benefit an individual to sacrifice its food, shelter, or safety for another? Wouldn't such individuals be weeded out of the gene pool, prevented from producing offspring by their own generosity? As the saying goes, "no good deed goes unpunished."

Wilson's answer is that while an individual may suffer reproductively by sacrificing itself, it tends to perform altruistic acts on behalf of its relatives. Its relatives, of course, share some of its DNA—including, perhaps, the tendency to altruism. A bee, or lemming, or human that sacrifices itself but ensures its kin's survival indirectly passes on its genetic material to future generations.

Aggression, too, even murderous aggression, can serve evolutionary purposes. Throughout the animal world, creatures engage in aggression, in the form of displays and threats, nonlethal "tournaments," fights, and killing. Clearly, aggression serves an evolutionary purpose, allowing some creatures to gain better access to resources (food, nesting or breeding sites, mates, etc.) for themselves or their relatives. Still, aggression has its evolutionary costs as well as benefits. Overly aggressive animals may waste time that could be better spent gathering food. They also make themselves vulnerable to injury or to predation by other animals. The trick seems to be finding the perfect balance between aggression and pacification, a balance that can shift as conditions change.

Scientists have different ways of categorizing aggression. Sociobiologist David Barash, for example, lists several reasons for aggression:

"The Darwin Club," a 1915 cartoon by Rea Irvin from a series entitled "Clubs We Do Not Wish to Join." This satirical drawing is typical of the attacks on Darwinism. Tracing the origins of human behavior and characteristics to ancient ancestors, it was feared, would make men seem no better than animals. Reproduced from the collections of the Library of Congress (USZ62-88147)

to acquire a resource

to resist the loss of a resource (for example, by defending a hunting territory)

to protect a nesting or breeding site

to compete for mates

in response to crowding (in *some* species—among rats, for example, but not among schooling fish)

to establish a place in a dominance hierarchy, especially if the existing social system has been disrupted, either by the removal of the dominant members or by the introduction of new members

in response to pain or frustration

to defend offspring

because, for a particular individual, aggression has been a successful strategy in the past.[7]

Wilson's list is similar but not identical. He notes several causes of aggression, including the appearance of a stranger, food scarcity, crowding, seasonal changes, previous experiences, and hormone levels.[8] In one of the following excerpts, he offers a list of purposes or types of aggression. However, though sociobiologists may differ about the numbers and types of reasons for aggression, they generally agree that aggression must serve some purpose. When it ceases to have a purpose, it becomes counterproductive and actually decreases an individual's genetic fitness.

As you read the passages that follow, think about whether the boys in *Lord of the Flies* are acting according to nature and according to evolutionary imperatives. Is behavior such as theirs the kind that saves a community or the kind that destroys it? Is what happens "survival of the fittest," or merely "survival of the most aggressive"?

FROM EDWARD O. WILSON, *SOCIOBIOLOGY: THE NEW SYNTHESIS* (1975)

CHAPTER 5, "GROUP SELECTION AND ALTRUISM"

When a person (or animal) increases the fitness of another at the expense of his own fitness, he can be said to have performed an act of *altruism*. Self-sacrifice for the benefit of offspring is altruism in the conventional but not in the strict genetic sense, because individual fitness is measured by the number of surviving offspring. But self-sacrifice on behalf of second cousins is altruism at both levels; and when directed at total strangers such abnegating behavior is so surprising (that is, "noble") as to demand some kind of theoretical explanation. In contrast, a person who raises his own fitness by lowering that of others is engaged in *selfishness*. While we cannot publicly approve the selfish act we do understand it thoroughly and may even sympathize. Finally, a person who gains nothing or even reduces his own fitness in order to diminish that of another has committed an act of *spite*. The action may be sane, and the perpetrator may seem gratified, but we find it difficult to imagine his rational motivation. We refer to the commitment of a spiteful act as "all too human"—and then wonder what we meant.

The concept of kin selection to explain such behavior was originated by Charles Darwin in *The Origin of Species*. Darwin had encountered in the social insects the "one special difficulty, which at first appeared to me insuperable, and actually fatal to my whole theory." How, he asked, could the worker castes of insect societies have evolved if they are sterile and leave no offspring? . . . To save his own theory, Darwin introduced the idea of natural selection operating at the level of the family rather than of the single organism. In retrospect, his logic seems impeccable. If some of the individuals of the family are sterile and yet important to the welfare of fertile relatives, as in the case of insect colonies, selection at the family level is inevitable. With the entire family serving as the unit of selection, it is the capacity to generate sterile but altruistic relatives that becomes subject to genetic evolution. To quote Darwin, "Thus, a well-flavoured vegetable is cooked, and the individual is destroyed; but the horticulturist sows seeds of the same stock, and confidently expects to get nearly the same variety; breeders of cattle wish the flesh and fat to be well marbled together; the animal has been slaughtered, but the breeder goes with confidence to the same family" (*The Origin of Species*, 1859: 237). . . .

. . . A genetically based act of altruism, selfishness, or spite will evolve if the average inclusive fitness of individuals within networks displaying it is greater than the inclusive fitness of individuals in otherwise comparable networks that do not display it.

Consider, for example, a simplified network consisting solely of an individual and his brother. If the individual is altruistic he will perform some sacrifice for the benefit of the brother. He may surrender needed food or shelter, or defer in the choice of a mate, or place himself between his brother and danger. The important result, from a purely evolutionary point of view, is loss of genetic fitness—a reduced mean life span, or fewer offspring, or both—which leads to less representation of the altruist's personal genes in the next generation. But at least half of the brother's genes are identical to those of the altruist by virtue of common descent. Suppose, in the extreme case, that the altruist leaves no off-spring. If his altruistic act more than doubles the brother's personal representation in the next generation, it will ipso facto increase the one-half of the genes identical to those in the altruist, and the altruist will actually have gained representation in the next generation. Many of the genes shared by such brothers will be the ones that encode the tendency toward altruistic behavior . . .

The evolution of selfishness can be treated by the same model. Intuitively it might seem that selfishness in any degree pays off so long as the result is the increase of one's personal genes in the next generation. But this is not the case if relatives are being harmed to the extent of losing too many of their genes shared with the selfish individual by common descent. . . .

Finally, the evolution of spite is possible if it, too, raises inclusive fitness. The perpetrator must be able to discriminate relatives from non-relatives, or close relatives from distant ones. If the spiteful behavior causes a relative to prosper to a compensatory degree, the genes favoring spite will increase in the population at large. True spite is commonplace in human societies, undoubtedly because human beings are keenly aware of their own blood lines and have the intelligence to plot intrigue. Human beings are unique in the degree of their capacity to lie to other members of their own species. They typically do so in a way that deliberately diminishes outsiders while promoting relatives, even at the risk of their own personal welfare (Wallace, 1973). Examples of spite in animals may be rare and difficult to distinguish from purely selfish behavior. This is particularly true in the realm of false communication. As Hamilton drily put it, "By our lofty standards, animals are poor liars." Chimpanzees and gorillas, the brightest of the nonhuman primates, sometimes lie to one another (and to zookeepers) to obtain food or to attract company (Hediger, 1955: 150, van Lawick-Goodall, 1971). The mental capacity exists for spite, but if these animals lie for spiteful reasons this fact has not yet been established. Even the simplest physical techniques of spite are ambiguous in animals. Male bowerbirds sometimes wreck the bowers of the neighbors, an act that appears spiteful at first (Marshall, 1954). But bowerbirds are polygynous, and the probability exists that the destructive bird is able to attract more females to his own bower. Hamilton (1970) had cited cannibalism in the corn ear worm (*Heliothis zea*) as a possible example of spite. The first caterpillar that penetrates an ear of corn eats all subsequent rivals, even though enough food exists to see two or more of the caterpillars through to maturity. Yet even here, as Hamilton concedes, the trait might have evolved as pure selfishness at a time when the *Heliothis* fed on smaller flowerheads or small corn ears of the ancestral type . . .

Reciprocal Altruism

The theory of group selection has taken most of the good will out of altruism. When altruism is conceived as the mechanism by which DNA multiplies itself through a network of relatives, spirituality becomes just one more Darwinian enabling device. The theory of natural selection can be extended still further into the complex set of relationships that Robert L. Trivers (1971) has called reciprocal altruism. The paradigm offered by Trivers is good samaritan behavior in human beings. A man is drowning, let us say, and another man jumps in to save him, even though the two are not related and may not even have met previously. The reaction is typical of what human beings regard as "pure" altruism. However, upon reflection one can see that the good samaritan has much to gain by his act. Suppose that the drowning man has a one-half chance of dying if he is not assisted, whereas the rescuer has a one in twenty chance of dying. Imagine further that when the rescuer drowns the victim also drowns, but when the rescuer lives the victim is always saved. If such episodes were extremely rare, the Darwinist calculus would predict little or no gain to the fitness of the rescuer for his attempt. But if the drowning man reciprocates at a future time, and the risks of drowning stay the same, it will have benefitted both individuals to play the role of rescuer. Each man will have traded a one-half chance of dying for about a one-tenth chance. A population at large that enters into a series of such moral obligations, that is, reciprocally altruistic acts, will be a population of individuals with generally increased genetic fitness. The trade-off actually enhances personal fitness. . . .

In its elementary form the good samaritan model still contains an inconsistency. Why should the rescued individual bother to reciprocate? Why not cheat? The answer is that in an advanced, personalized society, where individuals are identified and the record of their acts is weighed by others, it does not pay to cheat even in the purely Darwinist sense. Selection will discriminate against the individual if cheating later has adverse affects [*sic*] on his life and reproduction that outweigh the momentary advantage gained. Iago stated the essence in *Othello*: "Good name in man and woman, dear my lord, is the immediate jewel of their souls." (117–120)

• • •

CHAPTER 11, "AGGRESSION"

The essential fact to bear in mind about aggression is that it is a mixture of very different behavior patterns, serving very different functions. Here are its principal recognized forms:

1. *Territorial aggression.* The territorial defender utilizes the most dramatic signaling behavior at its disposal to repulse intruders. Escalated fighting is usually employed as a last resort in case of a standoff during mutual displays. The losing contender has submission signals that help it to leave the field without further physical damage, but they are not ordinarily so complex as those employed by subordinate members of dominance orders. By contrast, females of bird species entering the territories of males often use elaborate appeasement signals to transmute the aggressive displays of the males into conciliation and courtship.

2. *Dominance aggression.* The aggressive displays and attacks mounted by dominant animals against fellow group members are similar in many respects to those of the territorial defenders. However, the object is less to remove the subordinates from the area than to exclude them from desired objects and to prevent them from performing actions for which the dominant animal claims priority. In some mammalian species, dominance aggression is further characterized by special signals that designate high rank, such as the strutting walk of lemmings, the leisurely "major-domo" stroll with head and tail up of rhesus macaques, and the particular facial expressions and tail postures of wolves. Subordinates respond with an equally distinctive repertory of appeasement signals.

3. *Sexual aggression.* Males may threaten or attack females for the sole purpose of mating with them or forcing them into a more prolonged sexual alliance. Perhaps the ultimate development in higher vertebrates is the behavior of male hamadryas baboons, who recruit young females to build a harem and continue to threaten and harass these consorts throughout their lives in order to prevent them from straying.

4. *Parental disciplinary aggression.* Parents of many kinds of mammals direct mild forms of parental aggression at their offspring to keep them close at hand, to urge them into motion, to break up fighting, to terminate unwelcome suckling, and so forth. In most but not all cases the action serves to enhance the personal genetic fitness of the offspring.

5. *Weaning aggression.* The parents of some mammal species threaten and even gently attack their own offspring at the weaning time, when the young continue to beg for food beyond the age when it is necessary for them to do so. Recent theory . . . suggests that under a wide range of

conditions there exists an interval in the life of a young animal during which its genetic fitness is raised by continued dependence on the mother, while the mother's fitness is simultaneously lowered. This conflict of interests is likely to bring about the evolution of a programmed episode of weaning aggression.

6. *Moralistic aggression.* The evolution of advanced forms of reciprocal altruism carries with it a high probability of the simultaneous emergence of a system of moral sanctions to enforce reciprocation (see Chapter 5). Human moralistic aggression is manifested in countless forms of religious and ideological evangelism, enforced conformity to group standards, and codes of punishment for transgressors.

7. *Predatory aggression.* . . .

8. *Antipredatory aggression.* A purely defensive maneuver can be escalated into a full-fledged attack on the predator. In the case of mobbing the potential prey launches the attack before the predator can make a move. The intent of mobbing is often deadly and in rare instances brings injury or death to the predator. (242–43)

• • •

The evidence of murder and cannibalism in mammals and other vertebrates has now accumulated to the point that we must completely reverse the conclusion advanced by Konrad Lorenz in his book *On Aggression*, which subsequent popular writers have proceeded to consolidate as part of the conventional wisdom. Lorenz wrote, "Though occasionally, in the territorial or rival fights, by some mishap a horn may penetrate an eye or a tooth or an artery, we have never found that the aim of aggression was the extermination of fellow members of the species concerned." On the contrary, murder is far more common and hence "normal" in many vertebrate species than in man. I have been impressed by how often such behavior becomes apparent only when the observation time devoted to a species passes the thousand-hour mark. But only one murder per thousand hours per observer is still a great deal of violence by human standards. In fact, if some imaginary Martian zoologist visiting Earth were to observe man as simply one more species over a very long period of time, he might conclude that we are among the more pacific mammals as measured by serious assaults or murders per individual per unit time, even when our episodic wars are averaged in. If the visitor were to be confined to . . . 2900 hours and one randomly picked human population comparable in size to the Serengeti lion population, . . . he would probably see nothing more than some playfighting—almost completely limited to juveniles—and an angry verbal exchange or two between adults. Incidentally, another cherished notion of our wickedness starting to crumble is that man alone kills more prey than he needs to eat. The Serengeti lions, like the hyenas described by Hans Kruuk, sometimes kill wantonly if it is convenient for them to do so. (246–47)

Cambridge, MA: Belknap Press of Harvard University Press, 1975.

TOPICS FOR WRITTEN OR ORAL EXPLORATION

1. There are no female characters in *Lord of the Flies*, except for absent aunties and mothers. Why do you think Golding omits female characters?

2. Darwin proposes that many animals have sex-linked characteristics—characteristics that attached to males or females to make them more attractive or available to the opposite sex. What are humans' sex-linked characteristics? Make a list, then eliminate all traits that are shared by both men and women. Can you think of an evolutionary reason for the others?

3. Have men and women become more alike since Golding's day or have they stayed about the same?

4. What traits that sociobiologists call male-linked do Golding's boys display? Do all the boys display these "male" traits?

5. If there were girls on the island, which boy or boys do you think they would prefer? Why?

6. Would *Lord of the Flies* be a different novel if there were some girls, or all girls, on the island?

7. Rewrite an episode from the novel making the boys into girls. Try to stay as close to Golding's style as possible, but resolve the situation the way you think girls would resolve it.

8. Piggy is picked on by the boys because he is fat, asthmatic, and near-sighted. If this were a primitive hunting community, what would be Piggy's probable fate? Is scapegoating the weak or different justifiable from an evolutionary perspective? From a moral perspective?

9. Can something be evolutionarily sound and morally reprehensible at the same time? Give examples, either from *Lord of the Flies* or from the real world.

10. Does your school have dominance hierarchies? Are there "top dogs" and "lesser dogs"? How do the dominant kids get or stay that way? Do girls use different strategies than boys? Do girls and boys have the same hierarchy, separate and parallel ones, or multiple and over-lapping hierarchies depending on who they are with?

11. Is it harder to be a girl trying to establish a social place among other girls, or a boy trying to establish a social place among other boys? Which sex is rougher on those who do not fit in?

12. If you have a pet, log its behavior for a week. How often does it display aggression? Under what circumstances? Why, from an evolutionary point of view, does it display aggression at these times?

13. Whose approach to governing the island is more evolutionarily sound, Jack's or Ralph's?

14. Give some examples from *Lord of the Flies* and from real life when culture overcomes aggression. What do you think this means, and why?

15. List some statements of morality (rules of behavior derived from religion or philosophy). How many of them can be justified in evolutionary terms? Remember to think not just of the evolutionary success of individuals but also that of related groups.

16. Faced with no external enemies, the boys seem compelled to invent enemies: the beast and each other. Does a group have to have enemies of some kind? Will it invent them? Why?

17. What are some ways that individuals contribute to a group's survival? Think, for example, of a nuclear or extended family.

18. If the point of evolution is to pass on one's genetic material, why do many people adopt children unrelated to themselves?

19. Some situations in the real world mimic the all-male society of *Lord of the Flies*. In prison, for example, many of the rules of the external world no longer apply, and reproduction within the community is not an option. Do some research on prison conditions. How do such communities resemble that on the island? How do they differ?

20. Give some examples of violence, in real life or literature, against those who rebel or differ from the group.

21. There is no lack of food on the island, and no competition for possible mates. Do you think that the hunters aggress out of biological habit, or does some other kind of stress cause them to behave this way?

22. Look at Wilson's categories of aggression. Which of them do humans practice? Give examples. Which of these types of aggression do Golding's characters display? Give examples, with page numbers, from the text.

23. Read the short story "The Most Dangerous Game" by Richard E. Connell. Compare General Zaroff and Rainsford to Jack and Ralph.

24. Think of a human example of each type of aggression in either Barash's or Wilson's list.

25. Read some books about behavior in single-sex societies (for example, prisons). Does the behavior there resemble that of the boys in *Lord of the Flies*? Why or why not?

NOTES

1. Michael Specter, "Decoding Iceland," *The New Yorker*, January 18, 1999, 40.

2. Charles Darwin, *The Descent of Man, and Selection in Relation to Sex*, vol. 1, 2nd ed., (1874; reprint, New York: P. F. Collier & Son, 1905) 238–39.

3. Lionel Tiger, *Men in Groups* (New York: Random House, 1969), 45.

4. Ibid., 45.

5. Ibid., 162.

6. Ibid.

7. David P. Barash, *Sociobiology and Behavior* (New York: Elsevier, 1977).

8. Edward O. Wilson, *Sociobiology: The New Synthesis* (Cambridge, MA: The Belknap Press of Harvard University Press, 1975) 248–54.

SUGGESTIONS FOR FURTHER READING

Barash, David P. *Sociobiology and Behavior*. New York: Elsevier, 1977.

Bowler, Peter J. *The Norton History of the Environmental Sciences*. New York: W. W. Norton & Company, 1993.

Connell, Richard E. "The Most Dangerous Game." *In Exciting Short Stories*. Ed. Greta A. Clark. New York: Hart Publishing Co., 1960.

Darwin, Charles. *The Descent of Man, and Selection in Relation to Sex*. 1871. Reprint. Princeton, NJ: Princeton University Press, 1981.

Gilligan, Carol. *In a Different Voice: Psychological Theory and Women's Development*. Cambridge, MA: Harvard University Press, 1982.

Hrdy, Sarah Blaffer. *The Woman That Never Evolved*. Cambridge, MA.: Harvard University Press, 1981.

Lorenz, Karl. *On Aggression*. New York: Bantam, 1967.

Sunday, Suzanne R. "Biological Theories of Animal Aggression." In *On Peace, War, and Gender: A Challenge to Genetic Explanations*. Ed. Anne Hunter. New York: The Feminist Press at the City University of New York, 1991.

Tiger, Lionel. *Men in Groups*. New York: Random House, 1969.

Wright, Robert. *The Moral Animal: The New Science of Evolutionary Psychology*. New York: Pantheon Books, 1994.

7

War and Postwar

Let us therefore brace ourselves to our duties and so bear ourselves that if the British Empire and its Commonwealth last for a thousand years men will still say, "This was their finest hour."

—Winston Churchill, June 18, 1940

World War II Timeline

1933	Hitler's Nazi regime constructs its first concentration camps.
1939	Germany invades Poland.
	Britain issues a White Paper limiting Jewish settlement in Palestine and withdrawing its support for a Jewish state.
Sept. 1	Government-organized evacuation of children, pregnant women, the blind, and others begins in Britain. Between 1 and 1.5 million people will be evacuated in the next four days.
	Britain's armed forces are mobilized. Hospitals and mortuaries are readied for expected casualties. Nighttime blackouts begin.

Sept. 3	Britain's declaration of war against Germany is announced on the radio. Listening evacuees realize that they won't be going home as soon as they thought.
1940	Another wave of British evacuations moves nonessential inhabitants from coastal to inland areas.
	The Children's Overseas Reception Board (CORB) begins sending British children ages 5 to 16 abroad, offering free passage to places like Canada, the United States, and South Africa.
May	Winston Churchill replaces Neville Chamberlain as Britain's prime minister.
May 10	One aircraft attacks two Kentish villages in the first German assault on British soil.
May 14	The Germans bomb the Dutch city of Rotterdam, killing 980, destroying 20,000 buildings, and making 78,000 people homeless.[1]
July	The Battle of Britain, with Royal Air Force (RAF) planes striving to keep German bombers away from British soil, begins.
Sept. 7	The Blitz of London begins, with heavy casualties throughout September. The Blitz will continue until May 1941.
Sept. 13	The transport ship *City of Benares* is sunk with almost all of the CORB children aboard killed. CORB ships in port are stopped, and further overseas evacuations are suspended.
Nov. 14–15	449 Luftwaffe planes fire-bomb the English city of Coventry, killing 380 and burning the town's cathedral.
1944 Sept. 8	London is first bombed by V2 rockets.
1945 Jan. 27	The Soviet Army liberates the concentration camp at Auschwitz.
Feb. 13–14	The German city of Dresden is bombed in a three-wave attack by British and American forces.
April 12	American forces liberate the Buchenwald concentration camp.
May 7	Germany surrenders.
July	Churchill is replaced as prime minister by Clement Attlee.

Aug. 6	An atomic bomb is dropped on Hiroshima, Japan, leveling 60 percent of the city.
Aug. 9	A second atomic bomb is dropped on Nagasaki, Japan.
Aug. 10	Japan surrenders.

The fifteen years preceding the publication of *Lord of the Flies* may have included, to paraphrase Churchill, some of Britain's finest hours. However, there were dark hours as well—bleakly, miserably, and, often literally, dark hours. Ignore for the moment the obvious costs of World War II: the soldiers killed by disease and battle and the money and labor devoted to military rather than peaceful purposes. A thousand incidents, large and small, conspired to undermine the morale of the British during the years 1939 to 1954.

Even the taste of the eventual Allied victory was soured by atrocities on both sides, such as the firebombing of Dresden, the wholesale exterminations in Nazi concentration camps such as Bergen-Belsen and Auschwitz, the human rights violations in Japanese-occupied territories, and the bombings of Hiroshima and Nagasaki. For Golding, who served as a naval officer during the war, "Belsen and Hiroshima and all the rest of it"[2] provided proof of the depths to which humans could sink.

War and its consequences permeate *Lord of the Flies*. The boys land on the island in the first place because they are being evacuated from a war zone. In keeping with 1950s anxiety about atomic weapons, Golding makes it a nuclear war; Piggy asks about the atom bomb early in the novel (14). However, it is Britain's most recent war, World War II, that is uppermost in Golding's mind. After the defeat of the Nazis and the revelation of atrocities, the question everyone—not only Golding—was asking was, "How could this have happened?" How could people have permitted someone like Hitler to come to power, and how could they have gone along with him once they saw what he was doing with his power?

Once Jack is seen as a Hitler stand-in, it becomes easy to assign roles to the various actors. Ralph is Britain's prewar prime minister, Neville Chamberlain, who let Hitler invade the Sudetenland in the hope that it would stop there. Or perhaps Ralph is Germany's pre-Nazi government, which failed to understand the danger represented by giving the Nazis any sort of power at all. Piggy is the Jews and other "undesirables" persecuted by Hitler's regime; at first he is merely disliked, then silenced, then robbed, then killed. Significantly, he is given the same name as the hunters' prey. The torturer Roger, who exults in death and feels "powerful" (175) in flinging stones at people, is the Gestapo, Hitler's secret police, or perhaps the SS, who ran the concentration camps. Samneric are the decent Germans cowed by fear and torture; their quiet resistance and ultimate helplessness are made clear by their warning to Ralph to run before he is killed (188). The littluns and the unnamed older boys are the great mass of the people, the ones influenced by a mixture of fear, desire for glory, greed, and sheer unwillingness to stand up for anything.

Jack rises to power partly by offering something for nothing—meat and fun with no fire-tending—and partly by treading on established rules and getting away with it. At one of the boys' meetings, he attacks the very symbol of parliamentary order and individual rights (101–12). Golding's point is not that every speaker has something worthwhile to say, but that the right to speak, or at least the illusion of the right, is essential to order and justice. The boys, however, do not realize this or, if they do realize it, are not prepared to defend it vigorously enough. Jack is told to sit, but he stands and continues to talk, and this, like every other rupture of the rules, eventually encourages other transgressions. In the same way, Roger proceeds from little cruelties to great ones, encouraged at each episode by his tribe's approval or, at least, lack of condemnation. The society as a whole, by failing to resist strongly enough at the right times, is carried along the same road, escalating from the accidental killing of the littlun in the fire to the frenzied killing of Simon to the deliberate but largely unpremeditated killing of Piggy to the conscious, intentional hunting of Ralph.

Jack's true public-relations coup also follows Hitler's pattern. Wanting to rule everyone, he implies that he will only rule those he deems worthy (140). By employing exclusivity, he guarantees that everyone will want to be one of the chosen few. Once they join, he imposes a dictatorship, with no voting and no conch (133).

Of course, his paint provides him with courage as well, by giving him a uniform and subsuming him in something larger than himself. With paint on his face, he finds it easier to be simultaneously more anonymous and more important, and while the paint is, to Golding, a savage throwback, it is also a battle uniform. When Jack first paints himself, he offers the justification that it is "[f]or hunting. Like in the war" (63). With the last four words, he recognizes that, in the adult world, it's okay to disguise oneself to hunt and kill other humans.

The island in *Lord of the Flies* may be small, and its few characters may be armed largely with spears and fire, but it is as much about nations in conflict and weapons that can destroy entire cities. War is the excuse for the boys' isolation, their state of existence for the last third or so of the novel, and, perhaps, the entire raison d'être of the novel. It intrudes again at the end, when the boys are rescued by a warship, which seems curiously more peaceful than the boys themselves. Jack, like the postwar Nazis, is curiously deflated by the arrival of a stronger force than himself, and becomes "a little boy" (201) again. Oddly, given his occupation, the naval officer who rescues the boys sees yet does not understand their activities. He assumes that the chase is a game, (201) without recognizing that their war and his own differ only in scale.

WARTIME SUFFERING

Air-Raids

The war, though met by the British with a stubborn and admirable determination, seemed perfectly designed to chip away at the nation's confidence. There was an assumption, even before war was declared, that violence would come to British shores. On the eve of the war, signposts were taken down to hinder German agents from gathering information or obtaining directions, and 44,000,000 gas masks were issued, with a special style called the "Mickey Mouse" mask made in bright colors for toddlers.[3] German bombings interrupted the pace of daily life, forcing residents of affected towns to hide their household lights behind black curtains and their families indoors or in bomb shelters. Air-raid and all-clear sirens punctuated waves of destruction and damage assessment; in all, 458,000 homes were destroyed, to say nothing of businesses and homes that were damaged but not razed. Sixty thousand people were killed.[4]

The emotional cost to those who lived through the air-raids is impossible to calculate. One girl left her family home after an unexploded incendiary fell on the roof. She made it to a shelter, but "the next day we learned that most of my school chums and their families had been killed." Another girl found that a friend had been killed by a bomb that sliced the house in half. "One could see fireplaces and curtains waving about at the gaping holes where windows used to be. I imagined the body of my friend being still down in the crater." D. I. Parkes, a reception officer in Leeds, noted that mothers and children who had lived through the bombings showed signs of intense stress: "Life had been very hard for them for some months. The big difficulty we found was that at the sound of an aeroplane, without waiting for the siren, everyone silently vanished. No panic, no noise, they just disappeared under anything that would give them shelter."[5]

Early in the war, the air forces of both sides discovered the value of fire. Blackouts made it harder to locate targets visually, but if parts of a city could be set on fire, the light from the fire would illuminate potential targets, even as it destroyed other buildings. Thus the first wave of planes would drop glowing markers on desirable targets; the second wave would drop incendiaries near the markers to start the fires, and bombers would follow with high explosives to destroy what the fire did not. City after city fell prey to this strategy, despite the employment of various defense tactics. Anti-aircraft batteries threw "flak" at incoming planes; fighters met bombers in the air and tried to shoot them down; and workers on the ground set out "decoy" markers to draw bombers away from the real targets.

London was the target of a prolonged, vicious bombing campaign, but it was the German city of Dresden that suffered most dramatically. Dresden was not a militarily significant city, a fact that had left it untouched by air-raids for most of the war. It had some industry, some communications value, and not much else. It was, moreover, a haven for refugees from the Russian front and the site of POW camps. By early 1945, its flak batteries had been moved eastward in an attempt to halt the Soviet advance.[6] Yet on the night of February 13–14, 1945, it was attacked by three waves of planes. A wave of markers and incendiaries set the city ablaze. Then, a few hours later, when power outages prevented many of the city's air-raid sirens from sounding, and when relief crews from nearby cities were working feverishly to put out the fires, a second wave of planes bombarded the city. They were met with no flak, few fighters, and only a pitiful, poorly planned set of decoy markers. Of 1,400 RAF Bomber Command planes involved, only 6 were lost, and they dropped almost 650,000 incendiaries on the city. The bomber crews, hardened as they were, spoke of feeling "sorry for the Germans."[7] Retreating planes could see the glow of the blazing city for at least 150 miles. The blaze violently drew air from surrounding areas, blowing over railway trucks and sucking people, including a woman pushing a baby carriage, into the fire. Shortly after noon, a force of 1,350 American planes (minus at least one group that went astray and bombed Prague by mistake) delivered a daylight bombardment and strafed crowds with machine-gun fire. In all, 1,600 acres of Dresden were leveled, and 135,000 people were killed, so many casualties that "for the first time in the history of the war, an air raid had wrecked a target so disastrously that there were not enough able-bodied survivors left to bury the dead."[8]

Evacuations

Bombings, shifting employment opportunities, and the other upheavals of wartime resulted in a mobile population, with the average civilian moving almost 1.6 times during the war years.[9] Schoolboy Simon Raven, for example, was uprooted from his boarding school in 1940 when his parents felt that nearby areas might be bombed. He "was not sorry," he later wrote, "to be gone. The feeling in the air in those early days of the war was all of movement, and it would have been invidious to be left static. (Later on one would pray for nothing else, but that is another story.)"[10] In real life, the relocations were sometimes a blessing, sometimes unspeakably horrific, and always a bit chaotic.

In literature, the evacuations often crop up with similarly mixed results. In one of the most famous children's books of the twentieth century, C. S. Lewis's *The Lion, the Witch, and the Wardrobe*, there is magic in evacuation. Here, the often-used device of children's books—mysterious entry into another world—is preceded by dislocation of a more mundane kind. Four brothers and sisters are "sent away from London during the war because of the air-raids" and billeted with "an old Professor who lived in the heart of the country."[11] The transportation of Peter, Susan, Edmund, and Lucy into Narnia is no less revelatory and astounding than was the transportation of some of the evacuees—fed poorly and seldom, accustomed to relieving themselves wherever they liked (even in a corner of the dining room), and infested with lice and scabies—to loving homes in the countryside.

Golding's interpretation of evacuation is less rosy and magical than Lewis's and must have resonated with those who experienced the opposite side of evacuation. Plenty of children went from secure, loving homes to unfamiliar places where they experienced rejection, discrimination, neglect, abuse, and sexual assault. Cockney speech was incomprehensible to some hosts, whose dialects were in turn incomprehensible to the evacuees. The country had bedbugs, mud, few shops, and sometimes no running water. Children were sometimes placed with families of different faiths, and some Jewish children were placed with Christian hosts who still believed that Jews had horns. Village schools were overrun, while London schools were closed, allowing those children who had not evacuated to run around half the day unsupervised. While plenty of hosts and evacuees formed affectionate bonds, in many cases the relationship was a nightmare on one or both sides.[12] In *Lord of the Flies*, the boys, like Simon Raven, are also being relocated for their safety during a war. Like so many of the real evacuees, separated from everything they know, they begin by feeling exhilarated but soon give way to less thrilling emotions: shame, disgust, fear, loneliness, anger, and hatred.

Even before the war began, the British government prepared to evacuate potentially dangerous areas of the country. In general, this meant large cities, whose industrial production made them likely bombing targets in the event of war with Germany. The first evacuations actually began as early as 1938, well before the outbreak of hostilities.[13] In the weeks prior to Germany's invasion of Poland, practice drills were held in the London schools. Parents scrambled to purchase the items on school-provided lists, and the children carried these sacks of clothes and supplies in "rehearsal" evacuations, dutifully trudging to the train stations and back again.[14] Not all the evacuees were to be unattended children. About 20 percent of them were children ages five to fifteen, who left with school groups. About 80 percent were children under age

Schoolchildren being evacuated during World War II. Used with the permission of the Trustees of the Imperial War Museum, London (HU 36238)

five, whose mothers were encouraged to accompany them. Other evacuees included pregnant women and the blind.[15]

On August 31, 1939, the order came to begin the real evacuation on the following day.[16] Schoolchildren were labeled with large tags bearing their names, and each was given a gas mask in a cardboard box with a carrying string.[17] Weeping mothers lined the streets to the seventy-two embarkation stations, though in many cases the children did not understand the cause of the distress. To them, it seemed at first like a grand holiday, a chance to see a countryside that had, for many urban children, been nothing but a rumor.[18] By the end of their train rides (boats and double-decker buses were also used, but trains were the most common means of transport, with over 4,000 trains used in the 1939 evacuation),[19] most children's enthusiasm had waned. Some parents had had the foresight to pack food in their children's satchels,[20] but hunger and thirst tormented many, as did the lack of toilet facilities. Many children had accidents. On at least one train, the boys urinated out the windows[21]; on another, the children practically rioted and forced the train to stop so that they could relieve themselves.[22] The evacuees arrived at their destinations exhausted, dispirited, and dirty.

Upon arrival, the evacuees were often herded into some sort of meeting-hall, where locals arrived and chose individuals or groups to board. The heedless comments of the volunteer hosts and their obvious preference for attractive children deeply wounded the feelings of those chosen last. Curly-haired angels and older boys ideal for farm work went first. Children in groups of three or more and those who had pimples, glasses, or weight problems were the last to be selected. Often, despite the admonitions of parents at departure, siblings were separated. In one village, the last two girls to be chosen sat together in profound misery, when a lady came in and asked, "Is that all you have left?" The leftovers in each town were hauled door-to-door until someone finally agreed to take them in.[23]

Despite the efficiency of the first departures from London, the evacuations were a constant exercise in improvisation. Should evacuation be mandatory? (The answer to that, throughout the war, was "no."[24]) How much should hosts be paid to take in each child? How much of that fee should come from the government, how much from the parents? What should be done with children who ran away from their billets and walked or hitchhiked back to London? What should be done with children orphaned while staying with host families? Should villagers be forced to accept evacuees? (At first, the answer was "no," then "yes, according to the size of their houses.") This caused a wave of evasions, usually by moving to smaller houses, and outcries that the rich were not being forced to accept commensurate numbers of evacuees.[25] With all the human death and physical destruction of the war, some of the most absurd, yet touching, stories of evacuation concern the pets. There was the evacuation of hundreds of dogs to the Duchess of Hamilton's estate in Shaftesbury[26] and the heartbreaking euthanization of hundreds of pets whose entire families were evacuating to the countryside. One woman remembered, as a girl, "a long queue at the vet's" prior to her family's departure. She freed her tortoise but had to have her cat and canary put to sleep: "I can tell you how much I hated Hitler."[27]

For a time after the first evacuations, there was relative peace in London during the "phoney war" of 1939–1940. Then, with the Battle of Britain, more residents fled the city, and some evacuees who had returned to their homes fled anew.[28] It was at about this time that the government began evacuating children overseas. Volunteer hosts in various English-speaking countries were found. Adult escorts to accompany the children to their destinations were trained and assembled. Passage on ships was, with some difficulty, arranged. At first there was great popular enthusiasm for the program, then anger that the system seemed to favor the wealthy, then apprehension for the safety of those on the transport ships. Armed escort ships accompanied the transports for part of the way, but many of the evacuation ships were nevertheless sunk or bombarded. The death-knell of the overseas evacuation program was the sinking of the *City of Benares*, in which more than eighty children were killed.[29]

POSTWAR TROUBLES

If Golding and his compatriots had seen absolute evil during the war, the years from 1946 to 1954 offered them a taste of something more ordinary but, in its own way, just as disappointing. In the United States, with its untouched industrial base, the postwar years were ones of unprecedented general prosperity. Americans celebrated the end of rationing by buying cars, radios, nylon stockings, meat, sugar, and long dresses. In Britain, where the bombings had been devastating, rationing continued with little respite. Food, fuel, and clothing were scarce. What food was available was bad. Petty crime flourished, with two-thirds more crimes committed in 1947 than in 1938.[30] There was, on the whole, a more tolerant attitude toward bending or even breaking the rules, exemplified in the black market that circumvented the rationing laws. Since the early years of the war, those who could afford to buy illicit goods had been doing so. Simon Raven recalled, in 1941, "eating black market choccies, [being] warmed by black market coal," and reading a book he had shoplifted.[31]

In Britain, rationing continued well into the 1950s. Shops were not even permitted to hold sales until 1948. Newspapers were smaller (to conserve paper) until about 1949. In the late 1940s, those who wanted to buy a bottle of SDI squash (a soft drink) had to return an empty bottle first.[32] Piggy's nostalgic reminiscences about his aunt's candy store and his unlimited access to sweets (13) must have resonated particularly strongly in Britain.

Even the elements seemed inimical. The winter of 1946–1947 was unusually cold. Big Ben froze, people attending plays had to wrap themselves in blankets, business was done by candlelight, and hundreds of cars were stranded in a huge snowfall on February 5, 1947.[33] It would have been easy enough, in such times, to be a pessimist, or at least to be capable of writing a profoundly pessimistic novel.

Political Worries

Britain's postwar political position was no sunnier than the weather. The menace of fascism was rapidly being replaced by that of communism. While the Soviet Union was generally admired in Britain immediately after the war, even the leaders of the left-leaning Labour party did not want communism in Britain, and eventually there was widespread disillusionment with the U.S.S.R.[34] As eastern European nations fell within Soviet influence, the terms "iron curtain" and "cold war" came into common usage. In 1948, Berlin was unsuccessfully blockaded by the Communists, adding further tension to an atmosphere already thick with anxiety, and in 1949, China went Communist, and the U.S.S.R. was found to have nuclear capability. In this context, it makes perfect sense that the war in *Lord of the Flies* is an "atom" war against the "Commies" (162).

Internal politics gave cause for concern as well. The British Empire, until the war a dominant force in world politics, was crumbling from within. One by one, its colonies were fleeing its control and declaring independence: Transjordan (later Jordan) in 1946; Burma (Myanmar), India, and Pakistan in 1947; Palestine (Israel) in 1948. The transitions were not always peaceful. Severe rioting and even wars accompanied independence in several former colonies, notably Palestine, India, and Pakistan. In Kenya, which was seeking independence as Golding wrote, a violent uprising known as the Mau Mau rebellion was directed at European settlers.

In short, it could very well seem to an inhabitant of these times—especially a British inhabitant—that the world was going to hell at a rapid pace. Little wonder that Golding, looking at humanity, saw murderousness, stupidity, short-sightedness, and illogic. Little wonder that his audience found in *Lord of the Flies* a reflection of their own fears for the state of their species.

LIFE IN POSTWAR BRITAIN

In the account that follows, T.E.B. Howarth describes the mood of Britain in the years immediately following World War II. It could hardly be more different than the buoyant materialism of America's postwar period. Note how something as simple as a shortage of certain goods invades every aspect of everyday life, from shopping to morality. Particularly important to the study of *Lord of the Flies* are the generally dark mood of the nation and the ways in which stress caused breakdowns of civility and law.

FROM T.E.B. HOWARTH, *PROSPECT AND REALITY: GREAT BRITAIN, 1945–1955* (1985)

Despite years of blackout and privation and the loss of 60,000 lives in air-raids, the morale of the civilian population had remained astonishingly high until the winter of 1944–5, during which 6500 tons of flying bombs and rockets descended on them, and the war, which had seemed virtually over in the summer, dragged on into its sixth year. At what seemed a snail's pace, restrictions were lifted, as peace at long last came into sight. That winter you were allowed to have a radio in your car and buy a large scale map. You could release a racing pigeon without police permission. The blackout was partially lifted and then totally abolished and, as the curtains were torn down they released a cascade of dust and dead bats and spiders. . . .

When the street lamps reappeared in London, children who had never seen such a sight were dazzled and burst into tears of alarm. Grown-ups were thereby increasingly made aware of their desperate shabbiness. Harold Nicolson found that up to July 1943 all his clothes, of whatever vintage, maintained a high level of neatness, 'and then suddenly in some wild Gadarene rush, they all disintegrated simultaneously and identically within the space of a week', his shirts splitting from top to bottom 'with a sharp sigh of utter weariness', while his pyjamas 'assumed the form of pendant strips, such as might be worn by some zany in a morality play'. He gloomily concluded that by 1947 he would have nothing to wear except his Defence Medal. If you were able to save enough clothing coupons to buy a shirt you would find it had a short tail cut away with horizontal abruptness and cost at least five times more than a much superior pre-war one. Statistics in *The Economist* in September 1944 indicated that Harold Nicolson was not exaggerating: they revealed that the average yearly purchase of shirts was 1.41; of pants 0.69; of pyjamas 0.14; of boots and shoes 1.21. Such modest purchases were to supplement an average surviving wardrobe of 4 shirts, 2.4 pants, 1.4 pyjamas and 3.8 pairs of boots and shoes. Clothes rationing was to last till 1949. For a decade the nation was on its uppers.

The civilian population was not only shabby, but immensely tired, few more so than the King himself, who wrote to his brother the Duke of Gloucester at the beginning of 1946: 'I have been suffering from an awful reaction from the strain of war, I suppose, and have felt very tired . . . Food, clothes and fuel are the main topics of us all.' There seemed no great likelihood of relaxation. The rival political leaders were at pains to emphasize the stern path of duty. Churchill told the nation on 13 May 1945 that: 'You must be prepared for further efforts of mind and body and further sacrifices to great causes,' and that he would be unworthy of their confidence and generosity if he did not still cry: 'Forward, unflinching, unswerving, indomitable, till the whole task is done and the whole world is safe and clean.' Ten months later [Prime Minister Clement] Attlee had the same message, couched in more prosaic tones: 'I know that most people are feeling the strain of the last six years. I know how many things there are which irritate and worry you. I know how trying it is not to be able to get the goods which you want from the shops, and to have to wait in queues for them. But there is only one way to fill the shops and get back to plenty and that is to produce more.'

In the weeks and months following VE day and VJ day layer after layer of hopeful illusion was stripped away. Harold Nicolson, once again reporting a Paris Peace Conference, as he had in 1919, summed up the post-war world: 'There is one great difference between 1919 and today which hangs like a fog in the air. . . . In 1919 we all of us possessed faith and hope. There is no faith or hope to be found in the Luxembourg today. They do not believe in what they are doing—they do not believe in each other—they do not believe even in themselves.' Admittedly such bitterness and disillusionment as there was only occasionally expressed itself in outbursts induced by unusually severe frustration and irritation— indeed, Alistair Cooke returning to Britain after eight years early in 1946 thought that behind the grime and fatigue the country had never had such dignity. For the most part, conditioned over the years to grin and bear it, the British tacitly decided to shoulder a new set of burdens with a grim fatalism. And such fatalism would be very necessary, especially for the housewife engaged on a shopping expedition in the peace-time summer of 1945 which would characteristically develop like this*:

*From the unpublished letters of W. H. Haslam in the Imperial War Museum.

Request	Answer
Children's sandals, size one	(8 shops) None at present
Plain straw hat for school	Board of Trade doesn't allow them
Ladies' shoes, size 6	All gone. No more yet
Bicycle bell	Try at end of week
No. 8 battery	No such thing
Glucose on doctor's note	All sold already
Any parsley?	None
What about the grapefruit allocation?	No sign of it
Any chocolate peppermint creams?	Had some two weeks ago
Can you clean this blazer?	If you join the queue at nine o'clock. . . . (44–47)

One of the most widely read novelists at the time was Angela Thirkell, who achieved after the war a more or less annual production line of would-be Trollopean novels, depicting life in a twentieth-century Barsetshire. Her pages were frequently devoted to the related themes of rationing, shopping, food and clothing. Her characters would sit down at the end of the war to a Sunday lunch comprising 'beef substitute, flannel Yorkshire pudding made with dried eggs, tough potatoes, damp greens, a pie with a leather crust and watery custard powder mess'. At a time when the meat ration was so small that butchers' shops were closed five days a week, she describes a hot day in Barchester with vividly authentic realism: 'Even the bluebottles outside the butcher's were dozing upon a bloodstained placard bearing the inscription "SORRY NO OFFAL TODAY. A REFUSAL OFTEN OFFENDS".' Refusals for that matter were often curt. The camaraderie of wartime was beginning to wear thin. . . . Coffee continued to consist primarily of a far from stimulating bottled essence called Camp and even tea was not what it had been, though as Mrs Thirkell testified, it continued to hold its secure place in the affection of the nation: 'England, our beloved country, battered and bullied by THEM, still has one source of real comfort in every affliction. THEY have rationed it; they have caused it to be made of dust and bits of black straw; they allow government offices to glut themselves on it while the working housewife with a husband and children hardly knows how to last till the end of the week; but as long as a spoonful of tea is to be had, England will keep her heart.'

Tea and sugar did not come off the ration until 1952. Although milk was finally de-rationed in 1950, butter, fats, bacon and meat were still rationed in 1954. Potatoes were rationed in 1947 and came off in 1948 with jam and bread. The weekly quantities of cheese, bacon and cooking fat were minute. In May 1945 bacon came down from four ounces to three ounces and soon dropped to two; in November 1948 it was reduced from two ounces a week to two ounces a fortnight. The cheese ration tended to be three ounces of what was universally known as mousetrap. The annual allocation of fresh eggs for 1946–7 was eighty-seven per person. Just after Christmas of 1950 the meat ration was lower than it had ever been and it was not encouraging for the populace to learn that henceforth it would have to include a proportion of the greatly disliked ewe and wether mutton. In April 1949 sweets were de-rationed and visitors to Blackpool were observed buying rock in eight pound chunks. This encouraging relaxation was, however, rescinded by the middle of August and it was 4 February 1953 before the children could celebrate as a red letter day the availability of sweets in the shops without coupons, after being restricted to three ounces or so a week as long as they could remember. A civic welcome greeted the arrival of the first post-war banana ship at Bristol in January 1946, but for a long time greengrocers had only exiguous quantities. Home-made 'cream' to go with a banana was a mixture of flour, milk, margarine and a little sugar.

Three years after the war an average man's allowance per week was thirteen ounces of meat, six ounces of butter and margarine, one and a half ounces of cheese, one ounce of cooking fat, eight ounces of sugar, one egg and two pints of milk. In general these privations were accepted with a stoicism which was as remarkable as it was admirable, especially as everyone knew substantial quantities of food were being diverted to Germany and India. Indeed, while we were setting out to dismantle German heavy industry, 60,000 people volunteered to reduce their own rations to make up German food parcels. . . . (49–51)

In those early post-war queues the vagaries of human nature were sharply exposed. Shopping, an activity which before the war had brought women together except at the sales, had now become disagreeably competitive. It was not even a question of anything so simple as the early bird being favoured with a highly treasured piece of offal. The shops opened at different times, so that, if you staked your morning campaign on being at the head of the grocer's queue at 8.30, you might have to hang about for a couple of hours before the fishmonger opened, and it was a matter of pure guesswork to determine when the second delivery of bread would arrive at the baker's. More and more, the wartime spirit of 'all mucking in together' gave way to a niggling wave of envy that one's neighbour had inexplicably acquired a quarter of an ounce more mar-

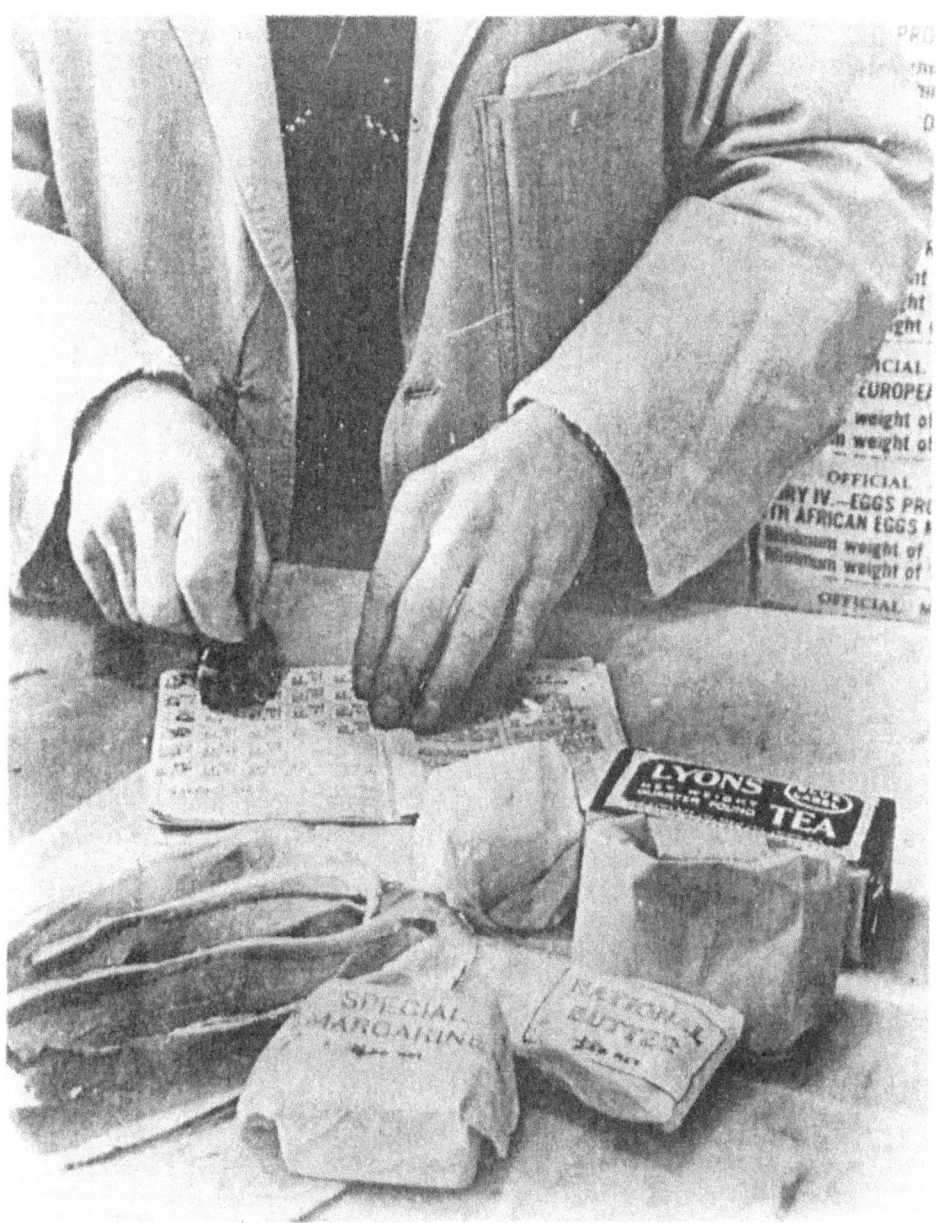

A shopkeeper cancels the coupons in a British housewife's ration book for one week's worth of tea, sugar, cooking fat, and bacon in April 1943. Rationing of many goods in Britain would continue until the 1950s. Reproduced from the collections of the Library of Congress (USZ62-107647)

garine than one had oneself. In such circumstances it was not surprising that normally law-abiding citizens were increasingly prone to listen to the siren voices of black marketeers possessed of a dozen eggs or half a pound of steak or a pair of nylons on offer at fancy prices. (54)

London: William Collins & Sons Ltd., 1985.

GOLDING'S ACCOUNT OF THE WAR

World War II had a significant impact on Golding's opinion of the human race. He disliked giving interviews, feeling that his work ought to speak for itself, but he sat down for a series of conversations with Jack Biles, which were published in 1970. Not all of Golding's stories of the war are grim; he tells one rather funny anecdote about going into danger and finding that the anxiety had fixed an immovable grin on his face, with unintended consequences among his men. However, in the excerpt below, he attempts to trace the effects of the war on his views about people. He claims to have been influenced not only by the grossest outrages of the war but also by its revelation of all sorts of human weakness.

FROM JACK I. BILES, *TALK: CONVERSATIONS WITH WILLIAM GOLDING* (1970)

Biles: Shall we turn to the military, apropos of *Lord of the Flies*? What occurred during the war that changed your thinking, other than the evident fact that everyone grew up a bit in those days? If my information is correct, and it has been gathered haphazardly, you were involved in a number of actions. Weren't you at the sinking of the Bismarck?

Golding: Uh huh.

Biles: Then, there is the practically unpronounceable Dutch place, Walcheren Island.

Golding: Uh huh.

Biles: Were these incidents specifically involved in changing your views? You were in no occupation force. Your statement was that up to, say, September 1939 or thereafter, like everyone else you had heard the reports about horrible events in Germany and you were literally unable to believe them. Then, when the war was over, you did believe those things and had apparently decided that, as Huxley says, since society is a collection of individuals, what the individuals are is what society is. You plainly thought so, when you wrote *Lord of the Flies*. To repeat the question, what happened during the war that changed your mind?

Golding: I don't think I can answer that question, except in general terms and by putting it this way: in a way one saw during the war much more . . . what *happened*. All this has nothing to do, directly, with Nazis or anything; it has much more to do with *people*. One had one's nose rubbed in the human condition.

It is too easy a thing to say that before the war I believed one thing and after the war I believed another. It was not like that. I was gradually coming up against people and I was understanding a bit more what people were like; and, also gradually, learning that the things I hadn't really believed, that I had taken as propaganda, were, in fact, *done*. This kind of thing, for example: only about fifteen miles down there [near Bowerchalke], meeting some people who were working on the drops into France, the occupied territory; going there twice—meeting a man one time and the next time not meeting him, and being told that he was probably being tortured to death at that moment. This kind of thing one gradually began to see, and, at the end, I *fully* believed in [the fact of] Nazism; one couldn't do anything else. Finally, there were films of it, and there it was.

I had to equate that, on the one side, with what I knew about people, on the other side. Now it would be terribly flattering to me to make out that I suddenly saw how horrific people could be, as compared to the nice people I had known for the last five years of the war [Golding's term of service], but it wasn't so. I had seen enough in the last five years to know that these people [the "nice people"] are capable of that, too; that really this was an extension of the human condition; that what the Nazis were doing, they were doing because certain capacities in them, certain deficiencies, certain anything you like in them, had been freed, and they were just people like us, in different circumstances.

So I saw that it was no good saying, "Well, fine. America, Britain, France, China, have all won. Against the dirty swine." Because I just didn't believe it. I saw that humanity had been fighting against itself in a kind of endless war. But what had been fighting and what had been doing all these things? On the whole, *only* on the whole—I wouldn't like this to be misunderstood, as I'm *sure* it would be—if you could take the people out of the concentration camps and make concentration-camp guards of them, the situation would not be altered materially. Can you see at all what I'm talking about?

It was a much more gradual process than the kind of snap things I have said about it because I wanted to say snap things; one's got to account for things somehow. One can say "before the war, after the war," but it was a long and slow process, it was growing up to adolescence. . . .

But when I was thrown, like millions of other people—and I don't want to exaggerate this—was thrown into contact with my "own brothers," I began to find them much more complicated—and much less self-aware, this is the important thing. I could listen to people talking about "bloody Nazis," people who I knew *were* Nazis. Do you see, they were in fact Nazis; only they didn't happen to live in the Nazi social system. Of course, I got round to the point where I said to myself, "There must be an explanation of why there is a Nazi system in one place and not in another, because even if they were held back only by certain social sanctions or social prohibitions, the social prohibitions were there." (33–36)

New York: Harcourt Brace Jovanovich, 1970.

THE NUREMBERG TRIALS

Of all the crimes committed during World War II, none was more
revolting to world opinion than the Holocaust. Hitler's regime
spent much of the 1930s revoking the rights of Germans it felt
were less than fully human, including Jews and the mentally and
physically handicapped. Members of undesirable groups were pe-
nalized in marriage, education, and employment. For Christabel
Bielenberg, an Englishwoman married to a German man, the
harshness of the discriminatory Nuremberg Laws first struck her
when her children's pediatrician, Professor Bauer, sat up late one
night with her son Nicky. Bauer asked if she intended to keep
bringing her children to him, pointing out that he was a Jew and
that his clinic had been seized by the government and given to an
Aryan doctor. "He had received threatening letters bidding him to
keep his hands off Aryan children." Shortly afterward, the doctor,
broken-hearted over the loss of his practice, tried to emigrate to
the Netherlands and soon died, some said by his own hand.[35]

Anti-Semitic violence, for centuries a problem in Europe, especially around Easter, was tolerated and even encouraged by the
Nazis. Eventually, Jews, Gypsies, homosexuals, Communists, and
others were rounded up, catalogued, and sent to concentration
camps. As Germany began to attack its neighbors, Czechoslovakian,
Polish, and Hungarian citizens were seized as well. In camps with
names like Treblinka, Auschwitz, Bergen-Belsen, and Sobibor, people were sorted, starved, worked to death, shot, bludgeoned,
hanged, gassed, burned, tortured, subjected to medical experi-
ments, and forced to watch their entire families murdered in front
of them. Their property, their labor, and their bodies were put
into the service of those who had imprisoned them. The sheer size
of the crime, the number of victims, the number of perpetrators,
the number of silently complicit townsfolk and neighbors, left the
world wondering how such a thing could happen. The idea that
justice, law, and order could be reversed, could indeed be made
to serve a monumental criminal system, seemed to defy civilization
itself.

There was also a certain amount of worldwide, retroactive guilt.
During the 1930s, the Nazi government had permitted, even en-

couraged, Jewish emigration, but several countries had refused entry to many of the refugees. Kenya, for example, limited Jewish immigration to twenty-five families per year.[36] Britain was in an especially difficult ethical position. For most of the first half of the twentieth century, its official policy had been that a Jewish homeland in Palestine was desirable. However, when Jewish immigration to Palestine rose rapidly between 1933 and 1939, Arab hostility to this immigration caused the British government to rethink its policy. In 1939, it issued a White Paper reneging on its intention to create a Jewish state in Palestine and imposing immigration limits for Jews. Approximately 75,000 Jews were to be admitted over the next five years, with no more admitted after that time unless the Arab residents of Palestine agreed.[37] After the war, when they considered the millions of Jews displaced, robbed, beaten, tortured, and murdered under the Nazi regime, Britain's politicians and bureaucrats must have felt uneasy indeed.

Golding's comment about Belsen, the concentration camp in which Anne Frank died, was a typical summing-up of the proof of human evil. The mere existence of a place like Belsen seemed to defy explanation, and its name and the details of its executions were common knowledge enough that Golding, in an interview, could utter that one word and summon up for his auditor all the horrific imagery of years of calculated torture and murder. In *Lord of the Flies*, his use of black and silver uniforms and a columned marching formation for the entrance of the choirboys (19) is a similarly eloquent shorthand; to a mid-twentieth-century audience, such details would necessarily call to mind, at least subliminally, the SS, which was principally responsible for carrying out the Holocaust.

In the 1940s, the event that called greatest attention to the Holocaust was the series of trials of military criminals at Nuremberg, Germany, shortly after the war. A few excerpts from the trial transcripts give some idea of what the world was hearing in the years between the war and publication of *Lord of the Flies*.

TRIALS OF WAR CRIMINALS BEFORE THE NUERNBERG [SIC]
MILITARY TRIBUNALS UNDER CONTROL COUNCIL LAW NO. 10.
VOL. 5. U.S. v. OSWALD POHL, AUGUST FRANK, GEORG LERNER,
HEINZ KARL FANSLAU, HANS LOERNER, JOSEF VOGT, ERWIN
TSCHENTSCHER, RUDOLF SCHEIDE, MAX KIEFER, FRANZ
EIRENSCHMALZ, KARL SOMMER, HERMAN POOK, HANS
HEINRICH BAIER, HANS HOHBERG, LEO VOLK, KARL
MUMMENTHEY, HANS BOBERMIN, AND HORST KLEIN, TRIED IN
NUREMBERG IN 1947 (1950)

[Victor Abend was a Polish doctor, born in 1901, who set up a practice in Krakow in 1931. His testimony, on April 11, 1947, was in response to questioning by prosecutor James M. McHaney.]

Q. Did there come a time when you were sent to a concentration camp?

A. Yes.

Q. When were you arrested?

A. In the year of 1943.

Q. Where?

A. At Tarnow.

Q. And what happened after you were arrested?

A. I was sent to a concentration camp in Schoebnik.

Q. How long did you stay there?

A. For 45 weeks.

Q. Then what happened to you?

A. Then I was transferred to Auschwitz.

Q. With how large a transport did you go to Auschwitz?

A. There were quite a few people.

Q. Well, was there a trainload?

A. Yes.

Q. Were you transported in freight cars?

A. Yes.

Q. How many prisoners were put into each car?

A. Quite a number.

Q. Well, were there as many as 75?

A. It depends on the size of the freight car.

Q. Was it very crowded?

A. It was very full. They were fully occupied.

Q. How long were you on the road?

A. Approximately 4 days and nights.

Q. Did you have anything to eat or drink during this journey?

A. No.

Q. Did the prisoners suffer much during this transporting?

A. Very much.

Q. And what happened after your arrival at Auschwitz?

A. In Auschwitz each car was unloaded separately.

Q. Then what did they do. Go ahead and describe what happened to you after you arrived in Auschwitz, what happened to you and the rest of the transport?

A. When our freight car was opened up at Auschwitz, several people within the car almost fell out unconscious, and part of them were driven out with whips and beatings. We then had to place ourselves before the camp physician. This camp physician asked us for our age and our profession. He then pointed with a finger, so and so (indicating). I went this way, to the left. After our car had been unloaded, other cars were also unloaded, and they were given the same procedure.

When all the freight cars had been unloaded, we were sent with SS guards who were heavily armed, and we were surrounded by them. We were without shoes, without pants, without gloves. Then we were sent into the camp under severe beatings. We were also hit with rifles and bayonets.

In the camp itself, we were sent into a stable where we spent all night, and where we had to stand up all night long.

The following day we went to be tattooed, again under severe beatings.

Q. Were you tattooed?

A. Yes. I have the number 160879. . . .

• • •

Q. Witness, what happened to the group that was sent to the right, after the transport arrived?

A. After a certain number had accumulated, these people were loaded on trucks without any guards, and accompanied only by a single SS man who was seated in the front of the truck they were led out.

Q. And do you know what happened to them?

A. Yes.

Q. What?

A. In the camp we were told that all the persons who had stood on the right side, and all the persons who had been loaded on trucks were sent directly to the crematorium.

Q. Do you mean they were gassed?

A. First they were gassed, and then they were sent into the crematorium.

• • •

Q. Do you remember in the year 1944 whether or not there was a large number of transports of Hungarian Jews to Auschwitz?

A. Yes. That was in April, the end of April and perhaps in early May 1944. That is when large transports of Hungarian Jews arrived.

Q. And what happened to those Hungarian Jews?

A. They also were selected in the selection procedure, and a certain number of people were again gassed and cremated.

Q. Were there so many people being gassed at this time that the normal facilities were not adequate?

A. Do you mean the facilities of the crematorium?

Q. Both the crematorium and the gas chamber.

A. Yes.

Q. Well, will you tell us how they gassed those who were unable to go into the normal gas chambers? How did they take care of that?

A. They were cremated at Pscezinki.

Q. Did they have a large barn there into which they crowded the people and then dropped the gas in through the chimney?

A. No. It was a small barn, and it was usually known under the name of the "white house."

Q. And will you describe that to us, what happened there?

A. The people were crowded into this barn, and after the whole barn was already filled up with people the door was closed, and the gas was thrown in through certain flaps.

Q. And were the people always killed by the gas?

A. Yes, in part, but part of them remained alive.

Q. What did they do with those?

A. Those who were still alive were thrown into the fire.

Q. And was this a way of cremating the bodies; that they dug big ditches close to this "white house" in which they built a fire and cremated the bodies?

A. Holes were made there, and wood was placed into these holes. Gas was poured on the wood and then the whole thing was inflamed.

Q. Now, Witness, do you know whether or not they took the clothes and valuables, trunks, similar items, from the inmates at Auschwitz when they arrived?

A. Yes. All our valuables were taken away from us and all our clothing, Our laundry was taken away from us also.

Q. Were there large quantities of clothing and shoes, valuables at Auschwitz which were taken away?

A. There was a very large number.

Q. Do you know what happened to that clothing and those valuables?

A. They were loaded and sent away.

Q. Loaded into what, freight cars?

A. Into freight cars.

Q. And was there a name around the camp by which these valuables were known, did the inmates have some expression they used with respect to the shipment of those clothing items?

A. Yes.

Q. What was that?

A. Well, it was usually said, "Here are the presents from Poland, for Pohl." (641–44)

(From the cross-examination of Dr. Victor Abend, by defense counsel Dr. Alfred Seidl:)

Q. Now you are living in Munich?

A. Yes.

Q. According to your testimony I have to assume that you were mistreated by the Germans during the war, and now I ask you: What are the reasons that prevent you now from going back to your Polish fatherland? After all, you are a Polish citizen, aren't you?

A. Because I do not want to.

Q. Well, I am asking you, why don't you want to go back?

A. Because I have lost everything I had in Poland. I lost my wife in Auschwitz, my child in Auschwitz; I have lost my apartment and furniture and all the property which I owned.

• • •

RE-EXAMINATION

PRESIDING JUDGE [ROBERT] TOMS: When you were arrested, what happened to your wife and children?

Witness Abend: On the second of October 1943, my wife and my child were sent away with a transport. Then, when I was at Auschwitz, I tried to obtain some information as to just what had happened to these transports. . . . Then I was told they were all sent to the gas chambers and cremated.

Q. Did you have two children?

A. Yes. One child is with me.

Q. Did you ever see your wife and your other child after you were separated from them?

A. I never saw them again. The last time I saw them was at the parade ground at Tarnow.

Q. You have no idea what became of them?

A. No, I only know that this transport, on the second or third of October 1943, left for Auschwitz; that all these people were immediately sent to the gas chambers without any previous selection.

Q. How were you able to save one child, the one who is with you now?

A. In the year 1942 when we were not as yet confined to the ghetto but when we were living in the Jewish part of town, then my maid took the child with her to a Polish village; and she kept it there. When I returned she had the child sent to me. It came to me in April 1946, to Munich. (645–46)

EXTRACTS FROM TESTIMONY OF PROSECUTION WITNESS JERZY BIELSKI

[Bielski was a half-Jewish medical student who was interned at Oranienburg, Sachsenhausen, and Auschwitz, at the last of which he worked in the sand pits. He was beaten and tortured for three months by the Gestapo, Hitler's secret police, losing twelve teeth (and another three at Auschwitz). His nose was broken, as were three ribs. He had suffered from typhus, and had become blind in his right eye. He was questioned on April 11 and 14, 1947.[38]]

[PROSECUTOR] MR. [JACK W.] ROBBINS: Was there a time in June 1943, when some prominent visitors came to Auschwitz?

WITNESS BIELSKI: Yes. That was in June 1943.

Q. And will you describe to the Tribunal the circumstances of that visit and the basis of your knowledge?

A. On this day, aside from the command of the electric and construction detachment, we inmates, a Kapo and one SS foreman, were sent from Auschwitz to Birkenau approximately at 7:30, and we arrived there and began some construction work. . . . We worked there and approximately around 10 o'clock in the morning in very good visibility, and the weather was very good, several cars drove out with SS officers, and they stopped at the hill. We already had heard from the day before that inspection of the camp was to take place by Obergruppenfuehrer Pohl, the Director of the Central Administration Agency of the Main Office. . . . They spent several minutes in the crematorium, and then they again went outside and they went to the gas chamber, and after a short time all of them went downstairs and entered the gas chamber. They remained there for approximately 45 minutes to 1 hour. After this time, they again came outside and then all of them were engaged in a discussion, and then first one car and then three trucks loaded with sick and exhausted prisoners came from the direction of Auschwitz. The cars came from the main road to the crematorium, and then approximately 30 people from the special assignment came and threw the patients and the sick people off the trucks. Then the trucks left and went back to Auschwitz and the prisoners from the special task groups all took the sick people who had been brought there into the gas chambers, carried them on stretchers, and they also carried them without stretchers. Ten minutes later an additional number of trucks arrived loaded with prisoners. There were approximately four or five, and in each truck there were approximately 25 to 50 people. Several of them were lying in the trucks and others were still able to stand. All of them were only dressed in a very short shirt. It was very short. They did not have anything else. And then the same story repeated itself. People were thrown off the trucks and they were carried into the gas chambers. Then two SS men appeared. They were lower, they were non-commissioned officers of the SS. Then came an ambulance with a red cross on it and which brought several tins. Already at that time, we knew that the tins were filled with cyklon gas.

This was not a secret, because approximately 100 meters from our camp at Auschwitz there was a so-called theater building where these tins of gas were stored. At that time we knew that these tins were filled with cyklon. The two SS men then walked over with these tins to a window of the gas chamber. The windows were above ground; the gas chamber was below the ground. The window worked from above. Therefore the windows could be opened and one could look at the prisoners inside, and it was also easy to throw in the tins of gas. The SS men stood by the windows, but they did not, as yet, throw the tins of gas inside, and then Pohl would come, escorted by five SS officers, and all the guests who had come from Berlin walked over to the window, and then he looked through the window for about 15 minutes. He looked below and watched the inmates who were inside the gas chamber. Then Pohl went back with his escort, from the gas chamber. (650–51)

[Bielksi testified that his work group was ordered away from the gas chamber for about half an hour.]

Then we came back and Pohl with all his officers were no longer at the gas chamber, only because they were still standing there. They were still standing where they were, on the road. And then we started to work and 10 minutes afterwards Pohl—and this time he was accompanied by Hoess—he and Hoess were the two first and then the others. Also, they came to the gas chambers, and Pohl and Hoess looked through the windows and then some of the others looked through the window, then they left the crematorium.

Q. Excuse me. This was about how long after the tins of gas had been thrown into the crematorium, that Pohl and his party returned?

A. Half an hour. We assumed that immediately after we left the tins were thrown inside, and we stayed in the other place a half an hour. After 10 minutes Pohl appeared once more. So the whole matter lasted 40 minutes. This was after the tins were thrown.

Q. Then were the bodies removed from the gas chamber to the crematorium?

A. Yes. As I looked again, they were all there, between the cars and the crematorium, and during that time about a hundred inmates from the special task groups came from the direction of the crematoriums one and two, and they together with the others who were already there opened the gas chamber and dragged the bodies out of these and brought them to the cemetery. They had a sort of small stretcher and they had also small carts with one wheel and two handles.

A French inmate of the German slave labor camp at Nordhausen, April 1945. This is the sort of image that shocked and horrified the world in the aftermath of World War II. How, people found themselves asking, could such evil happen? Reproduced from the collections of the Library of Congress (USZ62-120280)

Q. About how many truckloads of prisoners did you see taken from the gas chambers?

A. Altogether there were approximately nine to ten trucks in the first part, later approximately 13. I cannot state that exactly. Then a few additional ones arrived. I assume that altogether there were about 20 trucks. Then there was a second portion in the afternoon.

Q. Did Pohl and his party watch the same proceedings in the afternoon?

A. Yes. (652–53)

EXCERPT FROM RE-DIRECT EXAMINATION OF JERZY BIELSKI

[Bielski had just testified that trees and a fence were used to camouflage the crematorium and gas chamber.]

Later on, when we could no longer enter one could not see how the people were sent to the gas chambers. All we could hear were the screams and we could see the pile of smoke coming out of the chimney of the crematoriums, and we also used some sort of a camouflage—that was in 1944; that was when the Hungarian Jews arrived—we used a music camouflage. At the time the children were burned on big piles of wood. The crematoriums could not work at the time, and therefore, the people were just burned in open fields with those grills, and also children were burned among them. Children were crying helplessly and that is why camp administration ordered that an orchestra should be made by a hundred inmates and should play. They played very loud all the time. They played the Blue Danube or Rosamunde; so that even the people in the city of Auschwitz could not hear the screams. Without the orchestra they would have heard the screams of horror; they would have been horrible screams. The people two kilometers from there could even hear those screams, namely, that came from the transports of children. The children were separated from their parents, and then they were put to section III camp. Maybe the number of children was several thousand.

And then, on one special day they started burning them to death. The gas chambers at the time were out of order, at least one of them was out of order, namely, the one near the crematorium; it was destroyed by mutiny in a special commando in August 1944. The other three gas chambers were full of the adults and therefore the children were not gassed, but just burned alive.

When one of the SS people sort of had pity with the children, he took the child and beat the head against a stone first before putting it on the pile of fire and wood, so that the child lost consciousness. However, the regular way they did it was by just throwing the children onto the pile. (663)

Washington, DC: United States Government Printing Office, 1950.

TOPICS FOR WRITTEN OR ORAL EXPLORATION

1. Read about Hitler's rise to power and about Europe's strategy of "appeasement" before World War II. How does this situation parallel Jack's rise to power in the novel?

2. If, as Golding says, *Lord of the Flies* is about "why there is a Nazi system in one place" and how such a system can arise, what elements does he consider essential for nazism's success? What elements are represented by Jack, Ralph, Piggy, Simon, and the choirboys?

3. Are there world leaders today who resemble Jack? Are there other leaders from history who resemble him? Identify which ones and describe how they resemble Jack.

4. Golding once said that Piggy was supposed to be a naive scientist, unaware of the importance of human nature in the outcome of events. He said, "I would say Piggy ought to wear a white coat—one of these long white lab coats—and ramble round the island, probably writing papers about this, that, or t'other, and ending up at Los Alamos."[39] Why does Golding mention Los Alamos? Do you think this is an accurate assessment of Piggy?

5. Do you think a repressive dictatorship like Jack's, or Hitler's, could arise in our country? Why or why not?

6. Is there any way that Ralph and Piggy could have averted Jack's rise to power?

7. Britons of the 1940s and 1950s had plenty of cause to be pessimistic about the world. Would you consider yourself to be pessimistic or optimistic about the state of the world today? Make a list of reasons on both sides as you decide, and justify your answer.

8. Look at microfilm of newspapers and magazines from the United States, from any year between 1945 and 1954. How does the mood of the country differ from that in Britain?

9. Hold a "war crimes" trial, or write a transcript of one, for the characters in *Lord of the Flies*. Who should be indicted, and for what? Which boys could serve as witnesses?

NOTES

1. David Irving, *The Destruction of Dresden* (New York: Holt, Rinehart and Winston, 1963), 24–25.

2. Jack I. Biles, *Talk: Conversations with William Golding* (New York: Harcourt Brace Jovanovich, 1970), 51.

3. Ben Wicks, *No Time to Wave Goodbye* (New York: St. Martin's Press, 1988), 39–40.

4. T.E.B. Howarth, *Prospect and Reality: Great Britain, 1945–1955* (London: William Collins and Sons, 1985), 44.

5. Wicks, *No Time to Wave Goodbye*, 166–68.

6. David Irving, *The Destruction of Dresden* (New York: Holt, Rinehart and Winston, 1963), 75–76, 82–84, 95, 98–100.

7. Ibid., 113, 142–46

8. Ibid., 146–47, 153–54, 158, 162–63, 180–81.

9. Howarth, *Prospect and Reality*, 23.

10. Simon Raven, *The Old School* (London: Hamish Hamilton, 1986), 35.

11. C. S. Lewis, *The Lion, the Witch, and the Wardrobe* (1950; Reprint, New York: Collier, 1975), 1.

12. Wicks, *No Time to Wave Goodbye*, 76–97, 115–16, 121; Carlton Jackson, *Who Will Take Our Children?* (London: Methuen, 1985), 31.

13. Jackson, *Who Will Take Our Children?*, 1.

14. Wicks, *No Time to Wave Goodbye*, 34–36.

15. Jackson, *Who Will Take Our Children?*, 3–4.

16. Wicks, *No Time to Wave Goodbye*, 8.

17. Ibid., 31, 39.

18. Ibid., 32–33, 43.

19. Ibid., 43, 49–50.

20. Ibid., 34, 41.

21. Ibid., 48, 52.

22. Jackson, *Who Will Take Our Children?*, 17.

23. Ibid., 18–19; Wicks, *No Time to Wave Goodbye*, 52–61.

24. Jackson, *Who Will Take Our Children?*, 7.

25. Ibid., 19, 23, 33, 34; Wicks, *No Time to Wave Goodbye*, 97, 109, 113, 129

26. Jackson, *Who Will Take Our Children?*, 34.

27. Wicks, *No Time to Wave Goodbye*, 37.

28. Jackson, *Who Will Take Our Children?*, 26.

29. Ibid., 104–5, 108; Wicks, *No Time to Wave Goodbye*, 158.

30. Howarth, *Prospect and Reality*, 74.

31. Raven, *The Old School*, 43. "Choccies" is slang for "chocolates."

32. Howarth, *Prospect and Reality*, 167.

33. Ibid., 59.

34. Ibid., 20.

35. Christabel Bielenberg, *Christabel* ([originally published as *The Past Is Myself*, 1968], Reprint, New York: Penguin, 1989), 31.

36. Bernard Wasserstein. *Britain and the Jews of Europe 1939–1945* (Oxford: Clarendon Press, 1979), 28.

37. Ibid., 18–20.

38. *Trials of War Criminals Before the Nuernberg Military Tribunals Under Control Council Law No. 10*, Vol. 5 (Washington, DC: U.S. Government Printing Office, 1950), 407–12.

39. Biles, *Talk*, 14.

SUGGESTIONS FOR FURTHER READING

Bielenberg, Christabel. *Christabel.* (Originally published as *The Past Is Myself*, 1968.) Reprint. New York: Penguin, 1989.

Dawidowicz, Lucy S. *The War Against the Jews 1933–1945.* New York: Seth Press, 1986.

Gilbert, Martin. *The Holocaust: The Jewish Tragedy.* London: Collins, 1986.

Hachiya, Michihiko. *Hiroshima Diary.* Translated and edited by Warner Wells. Chapel Hill, NC: The University of North Carolina Press, 1955.

Hersey, John. *Hiroshima.* New York: Bantam Books, 1948.

Irving, David. *The Destruction of Dresden.* New York: Holt, Rinehart and Winston, 1963.

Shirer, William L. *The Rise and Fall of the Third Reich: A History of Nazi Germany.* New York: Simon and Schuster, 1960.

Wasserstein, Bernard. *Britain and the Jews of Europe 1939–1945.* Oxford: Clarendon Press, 1979.

Wicks, Ben. *No Time to Wave Goodbye.* New York: St. Martin's Press, 1988.

SUGGESTIONS FOR VIEWING

The Atomic Café (1982)
Battle of Britain, from the Frank Capra series *Why We Fight* (1943)
Hope and Glory (1987)
Mrs. Miniver (1942)
Schindler's List (1993)
This Happy Breed (1944)

Index

About the Author

KIRSTIN OLSEN has worked as book editor, high school English teacher, artist and author. Her published books include *Chronology of Women's History* (Greenwood 1994), *Remember the Ladies: A Woman's Book of Days*, and *Daily Life in 18th-Century England* (Greenwood 1999).

CPSIA information can be obtained
at www.ICGtesting.com
Printed in the USA
JSHW021521130421
13481JS00002BA/6